# Zero-Base Budgeting in Library Management:

## A Manual for Librarians

# Zero-Base Budgeting in Library Management:

## A Manual for Librarians

by Ching-chih Chen

A Neal-Schuman Professional Book

ORYX PRESS
1980

The rare Arabian Oryx, a desert antelope dating from Biblical times, is believed to be the prototype of the mythical unicorn. Nearing extinction two decades ago, the World Wildlife Fund found three of the animals in 1962 and sent them to the Phoenix Zoo as the nucleus of a breeding herd in captivity. Today the Oryx population is nearing 200 and herds have been returned to breeding grounds in Israel and Jordan.

Copyright © 1980 by
The Oryx Press
2214 North Central at Encanto
Phoenix, Arizona 85004

Published simultaneously in Canada

Printed and Bound in the United States of America

Distributed outside North America by
Mansell Publishing
3 Bloomsbury Place
London WC1A 2QA, England
ISBN 0-7201-0831-4

Library of Congress Cataloging in Publication Data

Chen, Ching-chih, 1937-
    Zero-base budgeting in library management.

    Includes bibliographical references and index.
    1. Library finance.   2. Zero-base budgeting.
I. Title.
Z683.C53        025.1'1        80-12055
ISBN 0-912700-18-1

*To my son*
*John*

# Contents

# Figures and Table in Part I

# Acknowledgements

Partial materials included in this book were covered in a few ZBB institutes directed by me, such as the Institute on Zero-Base Budgeting in Library Management at the School of Library Science, Simmons College, in the spring of 1978 and the American Society for Information Science Post-Conference Institute on Zero-Base Budgeting in New York on November 17, 1978. I am grateful to many faculty and participants of those institutes for their ideas, interactions, and stimulation. This book would not have gotten off the ground without the help of one of my former doctoral students, Andrea Hoffman, Assistant Director of the Teachers College Library, Columbia University. We worked on a preliminary simplified manual together, and I have benefited immensely from the materials which she has provided me and from her critical reading of the preliminary draft.

The book cannot be a helpful manual without the actual library ZBB materials given me by numerous enthusiastic colleagues. In particular, I am grateful to Mrs. A. M. Bystrom, Library Director of the Department of Fisheries and Environment of Canada; Mrs. Marcia Lowell, State Librarian of the State of Oregon; Ms. Diane C. Parker, Head of Reference of Lockwood Library of the State University of New York at Buffalo, N.Y.; Mr. John North, Library Director of the Ryerson Polytechnical Institute in Toronto, Ontario; Mr. John Sheridan, Head Librarian of the Transylvania University in Lexington, Kentucky; Ms. Ann Wolpert, Head Librarian of Arthur D. Little, Inc., Boston; and Ms. Olga Compton, Head Librarian of the Central Vermont Public Services Corporation.

Finally, but not the least, no book of mine can be completed without the collective support and encouragement of every memeber of my family, to whom all my books have been dedicated.

# Introduction

Zero-base budgeting (ZBB) is a planning and budgeting process which requires complete review and justification of an entire budget request. Old programs as well as new are scrutinized in three basic steps:

- Identification of *decision units,*
- Formulation of *decision packages,* and
- Ranking, consolidation, and resource allocation.

In other words, a manager identifies the organizational entities, known as *decision units,* that have identifiable managers and distinctive abilities. These units' activities are further divided into a series of *decision packages.* These packages are analyzed at various funding levels depending on the careful reappraisal of the unit's objectives, methods, and resources; and the costs of each package are substantiated. Finally, all decision packages are consolidated, if necessary, and then *ranked.* Depending on the available resources, cutoff funding lines can be fairly easily drawn. Thus, ZBB differs from the incremental budgeting systems traditionally used by most organizations. These processes place great emphasis on proposed increases, but give little scrutiny to old programs included in the current budget.

Given the components of ZBB, managers can use it for either planning and resource allocation, or evaluation and control. It also can be an effective communication device, since ZBB demands staff participation, from the bottom up, in going through the three major steps previously discussed.

ZBB has been greatly popularized since President Carter's presidential campaign and his order for its implementation in federal agencies on February 14, 1977. However, the concept of ZBB is certainly not new. It can be traced back to 1924 when E. Hilton Young advocated the complete justification of every item requested in a budget. Since then, ZBB has had its ups and downs in government and industry. The recent successful implementation of ZBB can be documented by Peter Pyhrr's positive experience with Texas Instruments, beginning in 1969. Because of this, ZBB has been considered by many to be the brainchild of Peter Pyhrr, who assisted Jimmy Carter in implementing ZBB in his administration in Georgia.

Like many budgeting systems, ZBB has its fervent admirers and harsh critics. Some have been suspicious of its prospects, denouncing it as a fraud,[1] and hostile to its implementation.[2] Others, such as Peter Pyhrr[3] and Logan M. Cheek,[4] have claimed that it is the most promising and exciting budgeting process, one which can cure almost all organizational ills. Most likely, the healthiest view is from the middle ground—ZBB is neither a fraud nor a panacea. Thus, it is this author's intent to provide a thorough and objective introduction to the ZBB process in Chapters Two through Five of Part I. Chapter Six is devoted to a discussion of the disadvantages and advantages, or problems and benefits, of the system. Further enumeration on the key factors in a successful ZBB is available in Chapter Seven, which relates ZBB's implementation to libraries. This author is neither an advocate nor a detractor of ZBB. Like Regina E. Herzlinger, this author believes that ZBB "can yield benefits if properly implemented, but . . . can be neutral or even pernicious in its effect if sloppily or thoughtlessly executed,"[5] as experienced by some federal government agencies. With this thorough discussion and the brief comparison with other available budgeting systems in Chapter One, library managers will have the information they need to decide whether ZBB can be a meaningful and suitable process for them in planning, budgeting, evaluation, and control.

Part II of this book provides seven actual ZBB preparations from diversified types of libraries—in a foreign federal agency, a state government, a large university, medium-sized and small colleges, and finally, large and small profit-making organizations and companies. Due to the substantial differences among these seven libraries in terms of library goals and objectives, type and scope of activity programs, size of the organization, amount of yearly budget, etc., the decision packages prepared by each library differ greatly in almost every respect. No value judgment is given by this author to the preparations of these decision packages; nonetheless, they can generate an enormous number of ideas by providing information for those library managers who are contemplating, developing, or implementing ZBB. These library ZBB examples should not be used as models.

Finally, to facilitate library managers' better understanding and/or implementation of ZBB, a glossary and an extensive bibliography are provided at the end of this book.

## NOTES

1. R. N. Anthony, ''Zero-Base Budgeting Is a Fraud,'' *Wall Street Journal* 189 (April 27, 1977): 26.

2. Regina E. Herzlinger, ''Zero-Base Budgeting in the Federal Government: A Case Study,'' *Sloan Management Review* (Winter 1979), pp. 3-14.

3. Peter A. Pyhrr, *Zero-Base Budgeting: A Practical Tool for Evaluating Expenses* (New York: Wiley, 1973).

4. Logan M. Cheek, *Zero-Base Budgeting Comes of Age: What It Is and What It Takes to Make It Work* (New York: AMACOM, 1977).

5. Herzlinger, ''Zero-Base Budgeting in the Federal Government.''

# Zero-Base Budgeting in Library Management:

## A Manual for Librarians

# PART I
# GENERAL DISCUSSION

# Chapter One
# Fundamentals of Budgeting

Budgeting is probably the most widely used type of financial management plan; it forecasts probable income, expenses, and benefit or profit that may be earned at the end of a specific period. A budget is generally described by both words and numbers. The words may identify sources of income or describe expenditures for certain items or functions, such as personnel, equipment, and supplies. The numbers represent the estimated amount of money for both income and expenses. Every organization has some economic limits; budgeting is a tool which may be used both in defining those limits and in enabling the organization to live within them.

A *budget,* then, may be defined as a "statement of the financial position of an independent entity for a specified future period of time based on planned expenditures during that period and proposals for funding them."[1] *Budgeting* is the systematic process through which budgets are created.

## USES FOR A BUDGET

The role of the budget is a major area of controversy, because the purposes and applications of a budget are numerous. The primary objectives of the budgeting process can be summarized as follows:

### The Budget as a Planning Tool

Basic to the function of budgeting are the elements of planning and controlling. Through budgeting, we are assured that necessary resources will be properly applied in order for specified goals and objectives to be realized. A budget, then, is a blueprint for the future or a plan of action expressed in monetary terms. The assumption underlying the preparation of a budget is that the organization know what its objectives are for at least the short-term future, which is generally defined as one year. Essentially, the budget expresses the thought of *we intend to* or *we shall.* If there are no established plans or objectives, then preparation of a meaningful budget is nearly impossible. The budgetary process is all too often reversed, and budgets are prepared before goals and objectives are determined.[2]

When a plan is established, management is in essence deciding what it wants to accomplish. Any accomplishments or results must have semiquantitative value or cost. In most cases this can be directly translated into dollar amounts. More simply, accomplishments, or programs, can generally be broken into tangible costs such as staff, materials, or facilities. If no limits are set and money is simply spent on these items, the organization may quickly discover that it is spending more funds on an activity than it is deemed to be worth. However, if costs and priorities are decided beforehand, the organization is in a position to make sounder judgments and decisions. If it is found that a desirable program cannot be afforded before the budget is finalized, management can alter its plans and objectives, change the program, or eliminate it altogether. Thus, broader options are available before a budget is prepared than after it is finalized. Budgets also form the basis for constructing models to show the interrelationships between the various parts of an organization's anticipated incomes, costs, and benefits. These models are essential for modern management planning and decision making.

### Using the Budget to Determine Causes of Action

An additional use of a budget is noted by Allen.[3] He explains that budgets enable management to make the most effective and efficient use of resources by providing a means, or structure, through which to determine alternative courses of action. Once a plan or an objective has been selected, the next step is to determine methods of achieving it. In many texts, the selected method is referred to as the *strategy*. When formulating alternative methods of action, one is reminded of the importance of a specifically stated objective.

A plan or goal should be broken down into specific objectives for different areas, with individual strategies for each. It is then that a manager can have confidence in his/her plans. A search for and selection of an effective strategy will ultimately offer a built-in review of not only future but present operations and programs.

## The Budget as a Control Agent

Contained in the budgeting function is a feedback system which enables management to control and direct activities of the organization. While the planning phase of the budgeting process expresses the intention of *we shall*, the control function is able to answer the question, *Did we?*[4] Managerial control is the counterpart of planning. Planning deals with *what* is to be done (goals and objectives) and *how* it is to be done (alternatives and strategies). The control element is basically a periodic

check or evaluation of the plan's progress and addresses the question, *Have we done it?*

Traditionally, bookkeepers have kept track of this activity by comparing columns of dollars and cents. However, the central function may also refer to the idea of binding managers or officials to their original goals and objectives. Appropriate techniques of observation and reporting are generally undertaken to insure that plans are being followed and that any deviations are properly analyzed and handled.[5] Budgets may be considered as control mechanisms for managerial performance, since in the preliminary stages they establish what it should cost to carry out a given activity. From a broader viewpoint, they can serve as a yardstick to measure both progress and accomplishments.

Basic to control is the definition of a standard of performance. How this standard is defined (quantitatively, qualitatively, or both) depends on what is meaningful in terms of the stated plan and the organization as a whole. Once a standard of performance has been defined, a measure of actual performance is made and then compared to the standard. If deviations are present, then corrective action (according to some criteria) should take place. This control process is graphically displayed in the following flow diagram:

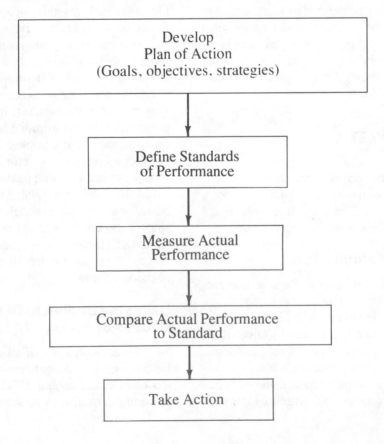

Some actions may be very easily measured and controlled numerically by comparing dollars budgeted with dollars actually committed or spent. For example,

| Account A | Budget | Actual | Difference | % Variance |
|-----------|--------|--------|------------|------------|
|  | $1,000 | $1,500 | (500) | -50% |

In account A $1,000 was allotted for a particular item or plan. A periodic progress report answering the question, *How are we doing in terms of the goal for the year?* compares actual performance ($1,500 spent) with the budget amount ($1,000) or plan. Before the budgetary period begins, management is wise to establish some standard by which to judge the flow of money spent. For example, some libraries may assume that half of their budgeted materials' funds should be spent by the time the fiscal year is half over. If the amounts reflected in account A are at that midpoint, then approximately $500 should have been spent. A comparison of the actual ($1,500) with the standard ($500) reveals a serious imbalance. While the midpoint standard is $500, the ultimate standard, of course, is $1,000—the full budgeted amount. At this point, some action must be taken to remedy the deviant situation. Such measures as transfer of funds from other accounts, cancelling of orders, or further fund raising may be undertaken to reconcile plan with performance.

It is commonly believed that, if a surplus of funds remains in an account at the end of a fiscal period, then a good situation exists. However, a surplus, like a deficit, may be an equally serious deviation. It suggests that the plan or goals and objectives have either not been followed or were ill-conceived in terms of financial realities. With these problems taken into consideration, control may simply be explained as "a disciplined effort to follow a plan or explain deviation from it."[6] Deviations may be foreknown or authorized in unusual or common-sense circumstances (i.e., due to large cost increases, changes in plan, etc.). The budget when used as a control agent may spotlight these deviations at an early enough time to allow remediation. Thus, the budget used in this sense may simply be viewed as a medium form of the old formula 'management by exception'.

### Using the Budget for Accountability

Accountability goes beyond the question, *Have we done it?* It is closely linked with planning and goes beyond the control of a specified quantity of resources (staff, dollars, space). It addresses such questions as *How well have we done it? Is it worth doing? Can we do better?* This requires one to make certain explicit commitments in terms of projected institutional, programmatic, or service objectives that are expressed in measurable terms.[7] If the product of the planning process is poor, fiscal accountability will be difficult, and the organization will suffer the potential loss of creditability with the funder.

The process of budgeting is a continuous year-round activity and a dynamic process of planning, controlling, and managing. Contrary to common practice, it is not and should not be a function which is performed once each year and then forgotten until the next period of preparation arises. Rather, its planning and control components are at the heart of the management process and should be ongoing. It may be considered synonymous with management inasmuch as it is an important tool to be used in achieving an organization's goals.

## WHO DOES THE BUDGETING?

The function of budgeting is often thought to reside solely in the hands of accountants or in the offices of budget officers and treasurers or top management. In reality, the process of budgeting must take place at all levels of management. While forecasting and major goal setting may take place at the highest levels of management, those at the operating level have the closest knowledge of particular functions. Each functional supervisor or manager should prepare his/her own budget which can then be submitted to higher management for review and approval. Upper management will have a broader picture and will then be able to judge the relative value of each proposal plan.

The budgeting process is also at the heart of the political process. In one sense the process of budgeting, which rests on the establishment of goals and plans, is in itself political. Gamesmanship is another aspect of politics which may take place in budgeting. For example, as budgets are passed from one level of management to another, successive pruning is commonly performed. In order to combat these cuts, lower-level managers will deliberately pad a budget request hoping to gain some leeway. This ends up being self-defeating, as higher management (former players of this same game) respond with even more vigorous trimming. Others believe personal friendships, persuasion, or *critical incidents* to be the real thrust of the budgeting process. It is difficult to deny that at times these tactics do assist budget decisions. In the end, most managers, knowing that *they* are accountable for their allocation decisions, will fund those activities or functions which reflect a realistic and thoughtful plan accompanied by established measures of performance or control.

## BUDGETARY CONTROL AND RESPONSIBILITY CENTERS

The process of budgeting is a management tool which can be used to track an organization's plans (or costs) and expenditures. An organization, such as a library, may be composed of functions and activities which are interrelated and whose objectives are impossible to describe in a single statement or plan. In this case, for the purposes of budgetary planning and control, it is helpful to decentralize or divide an organization into functions or *responsibility centers*. These centers break down the organization into smaller and more manageable pieces. Each center is headed by a supervisor or manager who has the authority to make decisions and is accountable for its operations. Among these operations are the managerial responsibilities of planning and control. "A responsibility center is a segment of a(n) organization to which a series of organizational . . . controls are applied to evaluate how effectively the manager of the unit is carrying out the responsibility delegated to him."[8]

A type of responsibility center generally associated with profit-making businesses but accepted by almost every type of organization is the *cost center*. The cost-center approach to organization assumes that each group (or center of function) is responsible for controlling the planned costs which are necessary to carry out its particular functions. With the cost-center approach, each cost center prepares its own budget at the beginning of the budgetary period. Once that budget has been reviewed and approved by top management, all incurred costs are accounted for by the cost center. Any deviations must either be explained or corrected by the responsible manager.

The cost center does provide management with a tool to keep track of costs as budgeted. Its shortcoming is that it does not, in itself, show the benefits which have been gained from spent funds. Thus, its approach is more or less like that of a line budget which is discussed in the following section.

## METHODS OF BUDGETING ANALYSIS

This is another major area of controversy. Some believe that only additions to the base or the current level of spending in the previous year's budget need to be analyzed and justified, while others maintain that the entire budget must be substantiated. There are also those who adopt a middle position somewhere between these two extremes.

## MANAGEMENT OF THE BUDGET PROCESS

Many management experts consider this the most controversial area of budgeting. Many budgeting systems are operated within a hierarchical structure. The top managers of the organization decide on the budget, what and where to spend in the budget, with little involvement or input from staff at lower levels of the organization. On the other hand, some organizations manage the budget process in a participatory manner with heavy involvement and input from staff on every echelon.

## TYPES OF BUDGETING IN LIBRARIES

Several distinct types of budgeting are used by libraries, and a combination of two or more types is not uncommon.[9] A library will often adopt the same budgeting method used by the parent organization—be it a school system, town, academic institution, business, etc. This also holds true for the budgeting cycle (i.e., calendar year or fiscal year).

Budgeting is usually carried out on a yearly basis. Many institutions, particularly academic, define their fiscal year as July 1 to June 30. Numerous public libraries, however, are now following the federal plan of budgeting according to the calendar year. Public institutions are often required to submit their proposed budgets two or even three years in advance; this can be particularly trying because it is often difficult to project needs and plan programs so far in advance.

Techniques of library budgeting fall into several groups, some simpler and some more analytic than others. However, the elements of planning and control should be contained in all approaches to budgeting. These aspects of management, however, are often more apparent and inherent in budgeting which relies on more analytic procedures. Below are brief descriptions of the major types of library budgeting techniques, ranging from simple to complex and analytic. Since the focus of this book is zero-base budgeting, the following brief descriptions of other types of budgeting are simply intended as points of reference.

## Line-Item Budgeting (Object of Expenditure Budgeting)

The most common type of budgeting is the traditional line-item budget, which is based entirely on *line-item* or *object* accounting. Thus, sometimes it is called

an *object of expenditure budget*. Essentially, expenditures are divided into broad categories or items, such as books, salaries, equipment, and supplies. In preparing this type of budget, an organization most often reviews how much was actually spent on each item or category during previous years. Amounts allocated for each item in the current year are listed, and then those figures plus additional costs for inflation and new programs form the basis for the projected budget for the following fiscal periods. A sample line-item budget is shown in Figure 1.1. This system, also known as *incremental budgeting*, focuses on increments to, or adding on top of, the current budget, accepting what is already in the budget.

## FIGURE 1.1   Line-Item Budget Summary Sheet

BUDGET REQUEST FORM 1
SUMMARY

Department or Program:     Hospital Library
Department Number:         01001
Fiscal Year:               1980-81

| Control Number | Expenditures | Actual Prior Year 1978-79 | Budget Current Year 1979-80 | Budget Request Next Year 1980-81 | Budget Approved Next Year 1980-81 |
|---|---|---|---|---|---|
| 001 | Salaries | 20,000 | 20,800 | 22,000 | |
| 004 | Staff Benefits | 4,000 | 4,160 | 4,400 | |
| 007 | Contracted Services | 350 | 350 | 375 | |
| 009 | Telephone Services | 400 | 425 | 450 | |
| 011 | Office Equipment | 500 | 500 | 400 | |
| 014 | Office Supplies | 500 | 550 | 600 | |
| 016 | Travel | 500 | 550 | 550 | |
| 018 | Collection | 20,000 | 20,500 | 23,000 | |
| | TOTAL | 46,250 | 47,835 | 51,775 | |

Thus, the approach is input oriented, focusing on dollars as inputs into the system. It illogically assumes that all of the previous year's spending and activities were essential and must be continued, and these activities and programs have higher priority over any new efforts. This concept is shown in Figure 1.2. On the other hand, the extreme opposite of line-item budgeting is zero-base budgeting, which does not take any existing activities and programs for granted nor recognize any historical base for continuing support of the previous year's activities.

There are a number of advantages to line-item budgeting. First, such a budget is relatively simple to prepare. The past year is used as a given base, and additional projected costs are simply added. Any increase in an item (books, salaries, etc.) can be easily recognized and understood by a funding authority. It is also simple to understand for the purpose of control and

is effective from that standpoint. For example, it is obvious that one should stop buying supplies, books, or whatever when the allocated amount is spent.

The disadvantage of a line-item approach is that it simply projects the current budget and does not contain a built-in mechanism for review of the necessity or effectiveness of past practices. Also, no direct relationship is drawn between input and expected output in terms of plans or services. As stated by Summers:

> The greatest flaw in the object of expenditure budget is the fact that while it is very effective in increasing accountability for dollars and cents, it cannot provide accountability for the performance of a governmental unit. The object of expenditure budget may well reveal how many pencils a given agency is acquiring and at what cost, but it cannot provide any indication of the appropriateness in terms of objectives of the uses to which the pencils will be put.[10]

**FIGURE 1.2  Traditional Budgeting Techniques (Stress on Past Expenditure Level)**

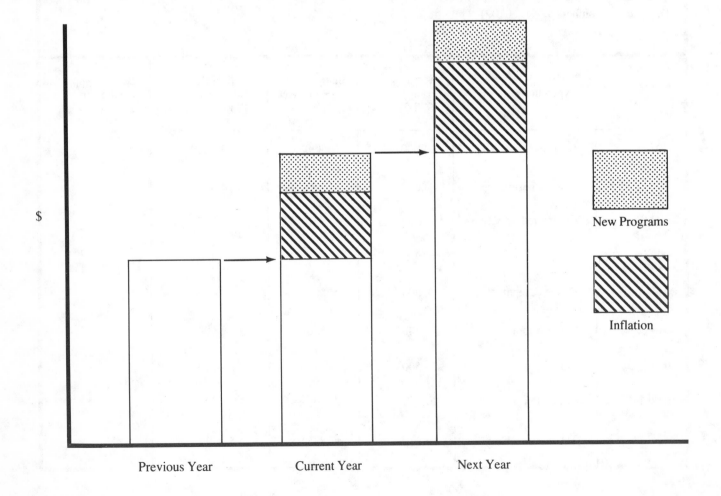

## Lump-Sum Budgeting

This budgeting system demands the least justification, because a given lump sum of money is allocated to the library as its budget for next year. It is the library's responsibility simply to spend it wisely. Although the actual categories of expenditure may very well be the same as those listed under a line-item budget, the lump-sum budget is more flexible in that there is no dollar limit on expenditure of any one category.

## Formula Budgeting

Formula budgeting tends to be unique to libraries and public agencies and is rarely seen in a business situation. Resources in formula budgeting are allocated according to some predetermined standards. For example, the number of students, faculty, graduate and undergraduate courses or library circulation are used in order to determine the *needed* amount of funds. Formula budgeting is generally adopted to insure objectivity in the distribution of funds. The formula approach is often used by large library systems for this reason; each library will then supposedly receive its fair share of resources.

Examples of the more popular types of formula budgets include the Clapp-Jordan[11] formula, originally intended to measure the adequacy of academic library collections; the Washington State formula[12] and the College Library Standards of the ACRL (Association of College and Research Libraries),[13] both providing formulas for library holding, staff, and facilities; and the new supplement to "Standards for College Libraries," which covers areas of collection, organization of materials, staff, delivery of service, facilities, administration and budget.[14] Figure 1.3 is the holding portion of the Standards (Formula A). Formula budgets have gained popularity because they are easy to prepare, require little justification, provide some sense of equality, and require few planning and budgeting skills to prepare. Most librarians find it difficult to resist a budgeting system with such apparent ease, economy, and simplicity of utilization. Furthermore, librarians find that such a budget seems more realistically defensible than one that is impressionistic and less amenable to a ready defense.

## FIGURE 1.3   Formula A*

The formula for calculating the number of relevant print volumes (or microform volume-equivalents) to which the library should provide prompt access is as follows (to be calculated cumulatively):

1. Basic Collection . . . . . . . . . . . . . . . . . . . . . . . . . . . . . . . . . . . . . . . . . . . . . . . . . . . . . . . . . . . 85,000 vols.
2. Allowance per FTE (full-time equivalent) Faculty Member . . . . . . . . . . . . . . . . . . . . . . . . . . 100 vols.
3. Allowance per FTE Student . . . . . . . . . . . . . . . . . . . . . . . . . . . . . . . . . . . . . . . . . . . . . . . . . . 15 vols.
4. Allowance per Undergraduate Major or Minor Field . . . . . . . . . . . . . . . . . . . . . . . . . . . . . . 350 vols.
5. Allowance per Master's Field, When No Higher Degree is Offered in the Field . . . . . . . . . . . . 6,000 vols.
6. Allowance per Master's Field, When a Higher Degree is Offered in the Field . . . . . . . . . . . . . . 3,000 vols.
7. Allowance per 6th-year Specialist Degree Field . . . . . . . . . . . . . . . . . . . . . . . . . . . . . . . . . . . 6,000 vols.
8. Allowance per Doctoral Field . . . . . . . . . . . . . . . . . . . . . . . . . . . . . . . . . . . . . . . . . . . . . . . . 25,000 vols.

A "volume" is defined as a physical unit of any printed, typewritten, handwritten, mimeographed, or processed work contained in one binding or portfolio, hardbound or paperbound, which has been cataloged, classified, and/or otherwise prepared for use. For purposes of this calculation microform holdings should be included by converting them to volume-equivalents. The number of volume-equivalents held in microform should be determined either by actual count or by an averaging formula which considers each reel of microform as one, and five pieces of any other microformat as one volume-equivalent.

Libraries which can provide promptly 100 percent as many volumes or volume-equivalents as are called for in this formula shall, in the matter of quantity, be graded A. From 80-99 percent shall be graded B; from 65-79 percent shall be graded C; and from 50-64 percent shall be graded D.

*From "Standards for College Libraries," *College and Research Library News* 9 (October 1975): 279.

Drawbacks to this form of budgeting are numerous. For example there is often little justification for the numbers which are part of the formula's set standards. There is also a possible[18] false relationship between the quantity and the quality of the outcome. Furthermore, this mechanical process offers little room for the use of professional judgment or for the consideration of unique programs or local environmental factors.

## Program Budgeting

Program budgeting emphasizes an organization's services and activities and allocates dollars according to the services provided in meeting the clientele's needs and organization's objectives. This budgeting system usually explores alternative ways of providing required services at different levels of funding and priority. A typical library program budget will be divided into several major programs; and, under each program, the budget will be further subdivided into categories, such as personnel, collection, and supply. For example, a library's information service program budget can be divided into budgets for serving the in-library users, the handicapped, the aging, etc. Each of these budgets is further itemized by staff, supplies, etc. Thus, it is easy for the manager to know the total budget for each service program, such as service to the aging; but it is not as easy to get a quick total of item expenditures, such as personnel for the total library program, since the total library personnel cost has to be pulled from budgets of all library programs.

## Performance Budgeting

Performance budgeting concerns itself mostly with the performance of activities and services. It is similar to program budgeting in format. However, it differs from program budgeting in emphasis. Program budgeting is activity and service oriented, while performance budgeting is efficiency oriented. Thus, the techniques of cost-benefit analysis are essential here. This approach emphasizes the amount of work to be done, the cost of doing this work, and the benefit received when the work is completed. Thus, the availability of a large amount of statistical data on activities and services is required, and quantitative measurement techniques are crucial. This budgeting system stresses accountability from the economic aspect, and thus it has been criticized for its underemphasis on the service aspect of the program.

## Planning-Programing Budgeting Systems (PPBS)

An innovation of the 1960s, PPBS was developed in the Department of Defense in order to increase efficiency and effectiveness in government and to provide a better rationale for the distribution of monetary resources. PPBS has several definitions. Essentially, PPBS combines the three elements of planning, programing, and budgeting into one integrated system:

- Broad goals and plans are developed and specifically stated.
- Short-term objectives are developed and specifically stated. These objectives are stated in a quantifiable or measurable manner, so that progress toward the organization's goals may be observed.
- Facts are gathered concerning who needs what and why.
- Priorities are established.
- Current programs are reviewed in terms of their necessity and effectiveness.
- In relation to proposed programs, alternatives are analyzed and the most beneficial programs are selected.
- Once programs are started, they are controlled or checked periodically to see if they are running on the right track.
- Evaluations of programs are made to see if they have fulfilled their stated objectives. Necessary alterations are then made on the basis of new information.

Thus, the basic elements of PPBS can be summarized as follows:

1. System concept and output orientation,
2. Identifiable and measurable outputs,
3. Stated objectives,
4. Consideration of alternative means to achieve objectives,
5. Activities grouped into program categories,
6. Measured progress toward objectives,
7. Analysis of benefits in relation to costs, and
8. Long-range planning.

Though the above process would seem to be an ideal application of the management theories of planning and control, the literature raises some questions as to its practicality in everyday application. Where PPBS has been tried, it is often reported that it has made little difference in overall management. Some reasons for the failure of PPBS are:

- Programs are often difficult to identify and evaluate.
- There is often too much concentration on ends without regard for means.

- Budgeting is often a political process to which more scientific approaches give way.
- PPBS requires a significant amount of centralization and coordination.

Although there are limitations, PPBS must still be respected for its more analytical approach, which should improve the decision-making process. The process of PPBS, or of any analytical budgeting system, provides a more comprehensive and effective information base from which a manager can make better decisions. The mechanics are quite simple in concept. It is their implementation which provides substantially more complex problems.

## NOTES

1. *Budgeting* (Alexandria, VA: United Way of America, Systems, Planning & Allocation Div., 1975), p. 4.

2. Malvern Gross, *Financial and Accounting Guide for Non-Profit Organizations,* 2d ed. (New York: Ronald Press, 1974), p. 293.

3. Louis A. Allen, *The Management Profession* (New York: McGraw-Hill, 1964), p. 147.

4. Allen Sweeny and John N. J. Wisner, *Budgeting Fundamentals for Non-Financial Executives* (New York: AMACOM, 1975), p. 88.

5. Reginald L. Jones and H. George Trentin, *Budgeting: Key to Planning and Control*, rev. ed. (New York: AMACOM, 1971), pp. 1-2.

6. James L. Pierce, "The Budget Comes of Age," *Harvard Business Review* (May/June, 1954).

7. Thomas J. Galvin, "Zero-Base Budgeting in Libraries and Information Centers," *Library Acquisitions: Practice and Theory* 2 (1978): 7-14.

8. Sweeny and Wisner, *Budgeting Fundamentals for Non-Financial Executives*, p. 16.

9. Kenneth Allen, *Current and Emerging Techniques in Budgeting in Academic Libraries* (Washington, DC: US Dept. of Health, Education and Welfare, Office of Education, 1972), ED 071-726.

10. F. William Summers, "A Change in Budgetary Thinking," *American Libraries* 2 (December 1971): 1176.

11. Verner W. Clapp and Robert J. Jordan, "Quantitative Criteria for Adequacy of Academic Library Collections," *College and Research Libraries* 26 (September 1965): 371-80.

12. University of Washington, Office of International Business Studies, "Model Budget Analysis System for Program 05 Libraries," mimeographed (Olympia, WA: University of Washington, 1970), pp. 1-6.

13. "Standards for College Libraries," *College and Research Library News* 9 (October 1975): 279.

14. "An Evaluative Checklist for Reviewing a College Library Program," *College and Research Libraries* 10 (November 1979): 305-16.

## REFERENCES

Burton, Robert E. "Formula Budgeting: An Example." *Special Libraries* 66 (February 1975).

Howard, Edward N. "Toward PPBS in the Public Library." *American Libraries* (April 1971).

Martin, Murray S. *Budgetary Control in Academic Libraries.* Greenwich, CT: JAI, 1978.

McAnally, Arthur M. "Budgets by Formula." *Library Quarterly* 33 (April 1963).

Stueart, Robert D. and Eastlick, John T. *Library Management.* Littleton, CO: Libraries Unlimited, 1977.

Young, Harold Chester. *Planning, Programing, Budgeting Systems in Academic Libraries.* Detroit, MI: Gale Research, 1976.

# Chapter Two
# What Is Zero-Base Budgeting?

## DEFINITION

Numerous definitions of zero-base budgeting (ZBB) can be found in literature. An informal definition can be given as: ZBB is a planning and budgeting process which requires justification of an entire budget request in detail without reference to what has happened in the past. This approach constructs a budget based on a fundamental reappraisal of purposes, methods, and resources, and it requires that all activities and operations be analyzed rigorously and identified properly in decision packages. Thus, techniques such as systems analysis are essential. These packages will then be evaluated by modern analytical methods and ranked in order of importance. A more formal definition can be given as: *It is a comprehensive, analytically structured process that enables management to make allocation decisions regarding limited resources*. Stonich and others[1] further clarify the terms used in this definition:

> *Comprehensive, analytically structured:* "A consistent framework within which all managers analyze their operations in terms of objectives, alternatives, performance measurements (both qualitative and quantitative) and incremental cost/benefit."[2] Cost-benefit analyses have to be made for several incremental levels of service and cost.
> *Allocation decisions:* Through prioritization or ranking process, the top management makes decisions in allocating resources by analyzing costs and benefits of each incremental level.

Zero-base budgeting differs from the various kinds of budgeting systems discussed in Chapter One. Essentially, it is an operational planning and budgeting process which involves constructing a budget without reference to what has happened in the past. The system subjects all activities and expenditures, not just requested increases, to scrutiny. It requires justification of everything that is done or will be done. Pyhrr stated that "the process requires each manager to justify his entire budget request in detail, and puts the burden of proof on him to justify why he should spend any money."[3] ZBB differs from other budgeting systems in that there is no automatic carry-over of funds with this approach. Everything begins at zero base[4] as shown in Figure 2.1. On the other hand, traditional budgeting techniques focus on the increment of past spending levels by extrapolating the past spending and allowing for inflation and increments for new services and activities, as shown in Figure 2.2.

In other words, zero-base budgeting encourages managers to identify priorities in their departments and to rank them according to the advantages which they yield. Managers are forced to answer the difficult questions: *Does the cost of this department exceed the benefits? Are there more effective ways of performing our operations? Are there higher priorities to be funded which would meet the organization's goals and objectives? What would happen if a certain service program were eliminated?* Instead of submitting annual budgets with the traditional suggested percent increases, managers must start each year from scratch, or at least from a minimal level of service, and present alternatives, based on approved objectives, to current methods of operation.

In order for a manager to justify resource requests, s/he must exercise creativity in identifying different alternatives to achieve the objectives of the department and to recommend the best alternative for funding. This process should result in delivering the same services for less cost or more or better services for the same cost.

In addition, this kind of budgeting will distinguish the basic or important activities from those which are more or less marginal in character. Spending levels can then be regulated, up or down, in accordance with resource availability.

**FIGURE 2.1 Zero-Base Budgeting**

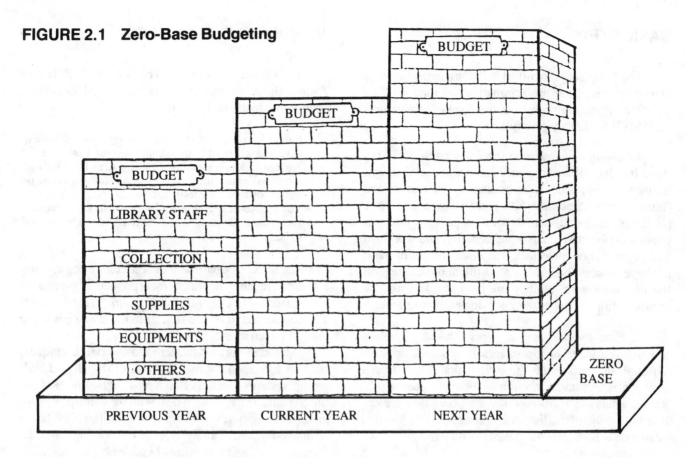

**FIGURE 2.2 Traditional Budgeting versus ZBB**

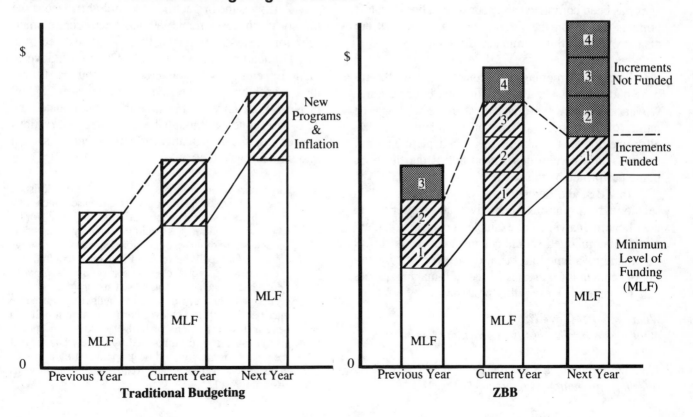

## BASIC STEPS

The basic steps involved in the implementation of zero-base budgeting are summarized as follows: (See Chapters Three through Five for detailed discussions and Part II for library examples.)

1. *Identify and develop decision packages*. This stage involves describing each activity and analyzing it into one or more decision packages. All current and future year expenditures are broken down into these packages. Included in each decision package are: unit goals and objectives, costs and benefits, and workload and performance measures. The development of these packages places the burden of justification squarely on the unit managers, as they are the ones who ask for appropriations to cover their activities and programs.

2. *Rank the decision packages*. This step involves the listing of decision packages in order of priority. Through this procedure the incremental level of each package is evaluated through cost-benefit and/or subjective analysis. Hard-core decision packages are entered at the top of the list, and more nebulously justified or marginal packages go toward the bottom.

3. *Allocate resources*. Once the ranking of packages has been completed and approved, a line or cutoff point is drawn on the list; all packages below it are disapproved and thus eliminated from funding.

Thus, as Brueningsen succinctly stated, "Zero-base budgeting is not a magic formula, but an attitude woven into a structured analytical process,"[5] and the nature of this process is functionally oriented. Generally, one does not think in terms of a department or of the staff in a certain department but of the functions being performed by this staff.

In ZBB, the budgeting process demands a rigid selection from various alternatives and subscribes to cost-benefit analysis. For example, a manager, in planning his/her budget, should not only consider the effect of expanding a function, but also the effect of eliminating or reducing it. A series of decision-making queries can be generated from this process:

*What would be saved?*
*What would be the results of providing lower-level service?*
*Can we maintain a tolerable level of effectiveness after the elimination or reduction?*

## WHERE HAS IT BEEN USED?

ZBB is not a new idea. As early as 1924, E. Hilton Young, British budget authority, advocated the rejustification of annual budget. He wrote:

> It must be a temptation to one drawing up an estimate to save himself trouble by taking last year's estimate for granted, adding something to any item for which an increased expenditure is foreseen. Nothing could be easier, or more wasteful and extravagant. It is in that way obsolete expenditure is enabled to make its appearance year after year, long after reason for it has ceased to be.[6]

In 1962, the US Department of Agriculture began using a budget technique which incorporated a ground-up reevaluation of departmental programs. This is generally considered to be the first formal use of ZBB in the federal government.

Although various modern managerial techniques, such as Management by Objectives (MBO), and budgeting systems, such as Planning-Programing Budgeting Systems (PPBS), also deal with the identification of goals and objectives, the setting of priorities, cost-benefit analysis, system analysis, problem solving, program management, and provision of viable alternatives, ZBB is intended to have more than these.

ZBB was the brainchild of Peter Pyhrr, who at the time of its conception in 1969 was a staff control manager for Texas Instruments. Pyhrr[7] was inspired by a Tax Foundation address on "The Control of Government Expenditures," delivered by Arthur F. Burns, then counsellor to the president, on December 2, 1969 in New York City. In his speech, Burns initiated the zero-base concept, though he expressed reservations concerning the practicality of implementing such a system. He stated that:

> Customarily, the officials in charge of an established program have to justify only the increase which they seek above last year's appropriation. In other words, what they are already spending is usually accepted as necessary, without examination. Substantial savings could undoubtedly be realized if it were required that every agency . . . make a case for its entire appropriation request each year, just as if its program or programs were entirely new. Such budgeting procedure may be difficult to achieve, partly because it will add heavily to the burdens of budget-making, and partly also because it will be resisted by those who fear that their pet programs would be jeopardized by a system that subjects every . . . activity to annual scrutiny of its costs and results.

Viewing the process of starting from scratch and justifying all expenditures to be valuable, Pyhrr applied this idea to industry, specifically Texas Instruments in Dallas, in revising and reducing the company's 1970 budget. The concept and evolution of ZBB at Texas Instruments began as far back as 1962 with the development of the company's objectives-strategies-tactics (OST)[8] system for evaluating research and development projects. To decide whether or not to proceed with a project, the company formed a description of the specific activity, the consequences of not going ahead with it, and estimated costs and benefits. This process eventually became the makeup of a *decision package*. Pyhrr began to popularize the idea of ZBB in an article which he wrote for *Harvard Business Review* in 1970,[9] which formally introduced the concept.

This article was read by Jimmy Carter, then the newly elected governor of Georgia. Carter was impressed with the concept and thought that the process could be applied to the preparation of the entire executive budget of his state government.

Pyhrr thus became a budget consultant to Carter and developed a complete budget recommendation for the State of Georgia's fiscal year 1972-1973. His experiences with the process were later incorporated into his book entitled *Zero-Base Budgeting: A Practical Management Tool for Evaluating Expenses*.[10] This is now considered the classic text on the subject.

Whether or not the ZBB implementation in Georgia was successful is still debatable. In spite of negative comments from some, Carter[11] claimed that by implementing ZBB, several major benefits for taxpayers resulted:

1. Computer systems, previously established in every major department, were centralized.

2. Forty-three print shops were merged into one.

3. One hundred Georgia patrollers assigned administrative duties were moved out to patrol the highways, and trained handicapped Georgians were hired for desk tasks.

4. Bookkeeper positions were eliminated by attrition, as they no longer served a useful purpose for the state.

Carter claimed that these savings resulted in a 50 percent reduction of administrative costs. He saw that the major benefits of ZBB were the reduction of duplication of efforts and the generation of more creative alternatives.

Pyhrr reported that "the first ZBB budget in Georgia faced a $57 million shortfall, and coped with it by cuts ranging from zero to 15 percent among the state's 65 agencies."[12] Suffice it to say that Carter believed in its worth, and further advocated and popularized it in his federal government. On February 14, 1977, President Carter asked each federal agency to develop its fiscal year 1979 budget using a ZBB system, in accordance with instructions to be issued by the Office of Management and Budget (OMB) headed by Burt Lance. The increasing interest in the *sunset* laws (see Glossary) has spurred even greater interest in ZBB.

In addition to the popularity promoted by the enthusiastic endorsement of President Carter, the recent increasing attraction of ZBB to government and industry can also be attributed to several other factors:

1. The term *zero base* has an appeal to the burdened taxpayer as it suggests the idea of starting from nothing and cutting governmental expenditures.

2. The impact of the recession of 1974-75 brought a number of local, state, and federal governments to fiscal crisis, as in the cases of New York City and State, and created a keen awareness among the people of limited government resources and of the need for assigning program priorities.

Currently it is estimated that over 500 organizations in North America have implemented ZBB with varying degrees of success. These include large business, banking, insurance, and many other types of organizations. Some of the commercial ones include Canadian Pacific, Federal Reserve Bank, International Harvester, Mead Corporation, New York Telephone, Texas Instruments, Westinghouse, and Xerox. It has been adopted by numerous US federal government departments and agencies. The system has also been popular with more than two dozen states and municipalities in the United States. In the foreign scene, ZBB has not been a stranger either, although the degree of acquaintance with this system varies greatly. For example, the Canadian federal government has implemented A-Base Review, essentially another version of ZBB, since the spring of 1977.[13]

The sudden push for ZBB caused by President Carter's enthusiasm and endorsement may not be healthy for the smooth implementation and adaptation of the budgeting system. The system requires a tremendous amount of paperwork and it is only successful and worthwhile when all staff members involved fully understand ZBB and work well together. Cooperation and communication among staff and advance and thorough training in the use of the system are essential. The executive order for the implementation of ZBB in the US federal system has created a necessity for federal agencies to produce ZBB requests even when their staffs are not well acquainted with the system. Thus, it is not difficult in private communications with federal employees to sense a strongly adverse feeling about ZBB among them, a number of whom are skeptical of the system because they never had an opportunity to understand it. Furthermore, the enormous political complexity of the federal government environment also makes it difficult to test the real potential of ZBB. It is not unlikely that the rankup of priorities of programs may be totally ignored when funding decisions are made by the top administrators, thus defeating the purpose of using ZBB. For example, it is very possible to find that, due to political reasons, a federal agency's program which is ranked No. 50 (No. 1 is most important) by agency administrators is funded instead of one which is ranked No. 5. In this type of situation, the adverse effect on staff who worked hard to push through the required budget paperwork is not difficult to imagine.

Since its implementation in the federal government in 1977, ZBB has yielded quite different results, not only among the agencies but within specific departments as well. An excellent case study of the experience of the Public Health Service was reported by Regina E. Herzlinger[14] recently. The experience has been mostly negative; however, the blame has been placed mainly on the misuse of the technique and the inappropriate application of such a system for the huge budget of a large political organization.

ZBB has been adopted under different names. The most prominent examples are the Canadian federal government's A-Base Review and Oregon State's Alternative Program Levels System (APLS).

## A-Base Review

In 1977, a few federal government departments in Canada, such as Environment Canada, voluntarily undertook the A-Base Review process to identify discretionary items and to determine what the department as a whole was doing. The fiscal year base was 1976-77, and the review involved five stages:

Stage 1: Senior managers identified the objectives and priorities of the department.
Stage 2: Responsibility managers described and justified the jobs undertaken and the resources used. These managers had to account for time, cost, output, and benefits provided.
Stage 3: Review task force analyzed the work program and produced a summary report.

Stage 4: Reallocation of resources for high priority programs by superiors.
Stage 5: Follow-up reviews.

Within Environment Canada, the Library Services Branch began the A-Base Review in early June 1977. For the readers' interest, additional information on its experience and some of the decision packages prepared are included in Part II, Example One. Since then, the Canadian federal government has provided its 50 plus departments and agencies with a detailed manual.[15]

## Alternative Program Levels System (APLS)

Senate Joint Resolution 23 of the Oregon Law 1977 states:

> The Governor is urged to submit as many 1979-81 state agency budget requests as may be feasible using the priority ranking and decision-making techniques associated with the concept of zero-based budgeting. The concept should be developed in consultation with the Legislative Fiscal Officer. By the completion of the budgeting and appropriation process for the 1983-85 biennium, all state agencies shall have been subjected to the concept of zero-based budgeting.

This state law provided the impetus for the Oregon state government to change its budgeting system. The Budget and Management Division of the Executive Department of Oregon assumed the responsibility for designing and implementing a system which is tailored to Oregon's unique needs, as recommended by the resolution. This system was named the Alternative Program Levels System (APLS) and a comprehensive manual of 103 pages was issued in March 1978.[16] The system has been adopted by numerous state agencies of Oregon, including the State Library, to prepare their 1979-81 biennial budget. Selected portions of the State Library of Oregon's APLS for 1979-81 are included in Part II, Example Two.

## HOW DOES ZBB WORK?

### ZBB Process—Overview

ZBB should not be considered a fixed procedure to be applied uniformly to all organizations. Instead, it is a general and flexible approach which can be adapted to all types of organizations with substantially dissimilar problems, needs, operations, activities, and service programs. ZBB has an essential planning component which assists each organization to establish plans and programs, to set goals and objectives, and to provide useful information for policy decisions. Thus, as Pyhrr indicated in his book, many managers have suggested that ZBB be renamed ''zero-base planning'' or ''zero-base planning and budgeting.''[17]

In ZBB, the whole planning and budgeting process has a relationship as shown in Figure 2.3. This is a dynamic, interactive process, and obviously the importance of planning should not be underestimated.

The foundation of ZBB is a four-step analytic process. These four basic elements are:

1. *Identification of decision units.* A *decision unit* is a grouping of proposed activities which can be identified as a *program*.[18] It is the lowest-level entity for which a budget is prepared. The unit may consist of only one distinct activity, or it may include several related activities.

Taylor noted that ''one important requirement is that each decision unit has an identifiable manager with the necessary authority to establish priorities and prepare budgets for all activities within the decision unit.''[19] Decision units are generally identified by the departmental head who can recognize discrete functions, activities, programs, and services within the department. The size of the organization is generally an influential factor in deciding the number of decision units of a department. It is generally the manager's responsibility to insure that the unit is ''large enough to provide flexibility and small enough to be manageable.''[20]

For example, a small library may decide that circulation is a single decision unit, while a large library may divide circulation operations into several decision units, such as check-in and check-out of library materials, reserve, overdue, etc.

2. *Analysis of decision units and formulation of decision packages.* ZBB goes through an analytic phase, during which the managers reexamine the objectives, activities, and operations of each decision unit. Basic questions such as the following are addressed:
- Is the decision unit necessary? Can it be eliminated? If so, what would be the consequences?
- How many ways can the decision unit's objectives be accomplished? Which is the most effective way?
- How can one improve the efficiency of the decision unit's operations? What different levels of services and costs are possible?

**FIGURE 2.3   Zero-Base Planning and Budgeting Process**

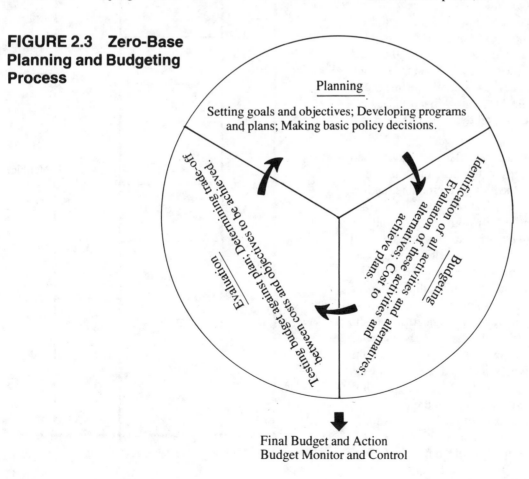

Planning
Setting goals and objectives; Developing programs and plans; Making basic policy decisions.

Identification
Budgeting
Evaluation of all activities and alternatives: Cost of these activities and alternatives; achieve plans.

Evaluation
Testing budget against plan; Determining trade-off between costs and objectives to be achieved.

Final Budget and Action
Budget Monitor and Control

Obviously, this process is a zero-base review of each of the decison units. Following this zero-base review, the decision-unit manager is required to segment the decision unit's activities into several alternate levels of services, or a series of *decision packages*. A reduced-budget level, which still achieves the most important objectives of the unit, is identified. In most cases, as noted by Taylor, "the first package contains those activities or portions of activities deemed highest priority,"[21] and the succeeding packages contain activities of next importance, and so on. Furthermore, the costs and benefits (or outputs) of each package are provided and documented for further review.

In other words, as pointed out by Singleton, "the manpower and other costs proposed to provide a given level of service may be examined for reasonableness. A given level of marginal cost may be compared to a given marginal increase in the quality or quantity of service."[22] Thus all activities are captured in decision packages. To each decision package, there are two types of alternatives to be considered: alternative ways of performing the same job and alternative levels of effort in performing the job.

3. *Priority ranking of all decision packages*. Following the above analytic process, all developed decision packages should be ranked in priority order by decision-unit managers and forwarded to the next higher level of managers for review. Decision-package priorities from multiple decision units will be integrated and merged into a single list of prioritized packages. Subject to detailed scrutiny, all decision packages are evaluated and ranked cost-beneficially.

4. *Allocation of resources*. The priority-ranked list of all decision packages in the entire organization is then reviewed in light of the projected probable funding sources available to the organization. Thus, it becomes the input for the allocation of resources. Generally, a new-year budget is limited and not sufficient to cover all the expected expenditures of the activities included in the entire list of decision packages, unless the organization chooses to seek an increase in funding. Starting from the top, the priority rankings determine those packages of activities which will be funded within the available resources and should, therefore, be included in the organization's formal budget request. On the other hand, those activities included in the decision packages which fall below the fundable line, as illustrated in Figure 2.4, are excluded from the next year's formal budget request, unless further funding is forthcoming. In Figure 2.4, the available funding level is five and the cumulative total of the fundable priority packages are packages one through four. Thus, all packages lower than priority four are left unfunded.

It seems necessary to stress that the successful application of ZBB depends greatly on the effective design of the budgeting procedures. To familiarize the readers with the basic elements described above, Chapters Three through Six are devoted in greater detail to these topics. During the whole process, two forms are basic and essential. They are the *decision-package* and *ranking-sheet* forms. Again, they will be treated in depth, together with sample forms, in Chapter Three. Actual library examples can be found in Part II.

## FIGURE 2.4   Funding Level and Ordered Decision Packages

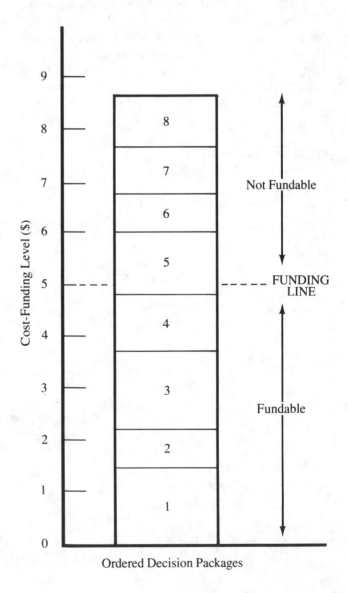

## WHAT IS DIFFERENT ABOUT ZBB?

Chapter One has already discussed some commonly used budgeting systems, such as the line-item budget and formula budget. In this section, we shall summarize the differences between ZBB and the traditional budgeting systems. They are:

1. ZBB exposes all ongoing activities to the same scrutiny, while traditional budgeting systems lend well to extrapolations of historical trends and to increments over the old budget. Under ZBB, all programs, whether new or old, compete for the limited resources.

2. ZBB is program oriented, by product or service, rather than function or accounting oriented by division or department, although a ZBB budget may indeed be divided by department or function.

3. ZBB determines minimum-service levels which usually are lower than the current levels of service, while the traditional budgeting systems take the current levels of service for granted as necessities.

4. ZBB examines alternative methods of service delivery and alternative ways of achieving organizational goals and objectives, which the traditional budgeting systems do not.

5. ZBB procedure exposes the inflators of budget and rewards the sponsors of carefully devised, well-documented, and result-oriented budget with well-prepared decision packages, while the traditional budgeting systems encourage the padding of budget requests for potential trimming. Although the padding of budget requests is also potentially possible for ZBB, the justification requirements make it less feasible.

6. ZBB applies *marginal analysis techniques* to provide decision makers with a priority-ordered set of budget choices, while the traditional budgeting systems do not.

7. ZBB is both an operating plan and a budget. From its analysis of decision packages, management gets both an operating plan and a budget, and the budget is a product of operating decisions. On the other hand, a traditional budget cannot be viewed as a planning tool.

8. ZBB can be used as a follow-up control mechanism. Under ZBB, the major result-oriented programs can be monitored, controlled, and checked to ensure that the planned objectives are achieved. This is not the case with traditional budgeting systems.

9. Finally, the burden of proof in ZBB requires that managers at all levels, particularly the subordinates, justify requests for funds as indicated on decision packages, while the burden of proof in conventional budgeting systems falls on the top manager.

## WHO CAN USE ZBB?

Theoretically, ZBB is a very flexible budgeting system which lends itself well to custom fitting. Since it is a planning, budgeting, and controlling tool, it can be used by any type of organization regardless of size, nature, and structure. Both profit and nonprofit, large and small, government and private, service or production organizations can benefit from ZBB activities, such as the following:

- Identification of organization's goals;
- Identification of organization's objectives in quantifiable terms;
- Exploration of spending alternatives;
- Justification of all planned expenditures;
- Ranking of activities and service programs.

Although there is no clear-cut formula to follow in identifying an organization's need for ZBB process, Stonich and others give some useful advice to the business world on who should use ZBB and who should avoid it.[23] They point out, in the following three categories, indications of a need for the ZBB process:

- *Financial*—Economical pressures, noncomparable income versus expenditures, unusual change of activity volumes, etc.
- *Management Process*—An organization's lack of ability to prioritize levels of service and cost or to develop performance measurements, etc.
- *General Management*—Current system is inefficient, poor communication, etc.

Stonich and others also point out the "red flag" situations in which ZBB may not be successful. These situations are:

1. The management is not interested in the process;

2. The organization is stable and the situation is well under control;

3. The organization is too small in size (for example, in a library situation a one-person operation can be considered too small).

With these suggestions in mind, libraries can evaluate their own situations and assess their need for the ZBB process. It seems likely that most libraries, regardless of size and type, will find that at least one of the three indications mentioned above exists in their library environments. Thus, a smaller library probably will avoid complications and adopt a less structured approach to the use of ZBB (e.g., use ZBB as a planning tool), while a larger library will likely require a much more formal preparation of the budgeting system.

Those organizations who have to prepare another kind of budget can benefit from ZBB by adopting its principles during their budgeting process, since, as stated earlier, ZBB is a management tool for both planning and accountability. It should be stressed that the prerequisites of ZBB are top management support and total staff involvement. Open, harmonious, and honest working environments are essential.

Budgeting is a political process. Heavy politics during the decision-making process can undermine the success of any budgeting system in a given organization. Certainly, ZBB cannot escape this. For example, if the top manager of an organization is going to fund a program—regardless of whether it is on the top or the bottom of the priority list—because of political reasons, then there is little need for the organization to waste time and effort to prepare a ZBB. In such a case, a simple line-item budget will serve the purpose.

## SUMMARY

ZBB is a flexible tool which can be applied to all types of organizations. However, as noted by Pyhrr, the "mechanical details of implementation (such as information and analysis required on each decision package, decision criteria used to evaluate and rank the packages, the level to which the packages are ranked, and so forth)"[24] have to be modified to suit the specific needs of each operation and organization.

In the following chapters, the discussion will be supplemented with actual library and nonlibrary examples in order to facilitate librarians' familiarization with this budgeting process and to enable them to develop and modify all the details of the ZBB process to fit their own needs.

## NOTES

1. Paul J. Stonich et al., *Zero-Base Planning and Budgeting: Improved Cost Control and Resource Allocation* (Homewood, IL: Dow-Jones-Irwin, 1977), p. 2.
2. Ibid.
3. Peter Pyhrr, *Zero-Base Budgeting: A Practical Tool for Evaluating Expenses* (New York: John Wiley, 1973), p. xi.
4. Theoretically, ZBB starts at zero base. However, in practice, it usually does not start at zero, but at some fraction of last year's expenditures. This fraction can be set at 75 percent or somewhat higher or lower depending on situations. For example, Pyhrr suggested that the minimum level be set at 50 to 70 percent. (*Zero-Base Budgeting*, p. 7).
5. Arthur A. Brueningsen, "SCAT—A Process of Alternatives," *Management Accounting* 58 (November 1976): 55-6.
6. A.E. Buck, *The Budget in Governments of Today* (New York: Macmillan, 1934), p. 172.
7. Pyhrr, *Zero-Base Budgeting*, p. 1.
8. At Texas Instruments, OST stands for: Define organization's major *objectives*, establish supporting *strategies*, and develop appropriate *tactics* to achieve objectives.
9. Peter Pyhrr, "Zero-Base Budgeting," *Harvard Business Review* 48 (November/December 1970): 111-21.
10. Pyhrr, *Zero-Base Budgeting*, p.1.
11. Jimmy E. Carter, "Jimmy Carter Tells Why He Will Use Zero-Base Budgeting," *Nation's Business* 65 (January 1977): 24-6.
12. *Wall Street Journal* (October 12, 1976): 26, col. 1.
13. Canada, Treasury Board, Planning Branch, *A-Base Expenditure Review: A Report on Recent Experience in the Federal Government* (Ottawa: Minister of Supply and Services, 1978).
14. Regina E. Herzlinger, "Zero-Base Budgeting in the Federal Government: A Case Study," *Sloan Management Review* (Winter 1979): pp. 3-14.
15. Canada, Treasury Board, Planning Branch, *A-Base Expenditure Review: A Report on Recent Experience in the Federal Government.*
16. Oregon, Executive Department, *1979-81 Biennial Budget Preparation Manual, vol. 2, Alternative Program Levels System (APLS)*, eds. Laurence R. Sprecher and Robert W. Smith (Budget and Management Division, Executive Department, State of Oregon, March 1978).
17. Pyhrr, *Zero-Base Budgeting*, p. 2.
18. David W. Singleton, Bruce A. Smith, and J.R. Cleaveland, "Zero-Base Budgeting in Wilmington, Delaware," *Governmental Finance* 5 (August 1976): 20-9.
19. Graeme M. Taylor, "Introduction to Zero-Base Budgeting," *Bureaucrat* 6 (March 1977): 33-5.
20. Walter D. Hill, *Implementing Zero-Base Budgeting—The Real World* (Oxford, OH: Planning Executives Institutes, 1977), p. 10.
21. Taylor, p. 33.
22. Singleton et al., p. 22.
23. Stonich et al., pp. 9-11.
24. Pyhrr, "Zero-Base Budgeting," pp. 111-21.

# Chapter Three
# Decision Packages

## DECISION UNITS IN LIBRARIES

The initial stage in the zero-base budgeting process is the identification and definition of *decision units*. A decision unit is usually an organizational entity or level that (1) has an identifiable manager and (2) consists of a group of discrete activities which can be meaningfully analyzed and influenced by management decisions. They are "the basic entities from which budgets are prepared."[1]

Determining these activities or organizational levels is one of the most crucial aspects of the ZBB process. Once the units have been determined, this step need not be repeated in future fiscal years unless programs are added, subtracted, or substantially modified. Of course, some decision-unit changes may be desirable from one budget cycle to another in order to improve the system. Basically, the decision units provide a relatively permanent structure for the zero-base system.

The next point of consideration is where decision units should be established. Each organization must determine for itself *what is meaningful,* and a key consideration in selecting appropriate decision units is the organization's responsibility structure. In many instances, the unit may correspond with traditional departmental budget units. Substantial activities within one of these departments could also be considered for separate analysis (see Part II, Example Three). Also, decision units may consist of special projects or programs (see Part II, Example One), substantial capital expenditures, or simply some line items from a traditionally organized budget. In small libraries, decision units may consist of two or more divisions and departments by functions and/or programs. In larger and more complex libraries, the units should probably be separated into numerous specific functions or operations. For example, a large technical services department may be divided into monograph acquisitions, serials acquisi-tions, monograph cataloging, and serials cataloging. A small or special library may want to define its decision units along the line items of personnel and materials. A library itself may also be considered a decision unit. Finally, special projects, such as a collection development or building program, may constitute a decision unit.

A number of important considerations must be made when selecting decision units. First, the units should be defined at the lowest organizational level possible. Equally important is to select decision units which carry the responsibility of budgetary decision making within the library. For example, consider an academic library system consisting of four divisional libraries. If the head librarian for each one of those libraries is responsible for resource allocation within his/her library, then each divisional library could be a logical decision unit. If, within each of those libraries, certain functions have identifiable managers or librarians, then each of those functions could be a unit (see Part II, Example Three). Finally, an additional alternative might be a head of technical services for all such operations in each of the four libraries. The technical services function would then be a logical decision unit. The key is to define the decision unit at the lowest possible level where responsibility for budget allocations may take place.

One should keep in mind that the use of an organization chart can be a valuable aid in determining appropriate decision units. Departments are a logical place to start since they were originally established to control similar functions. An interesting by-product of the zero-base process is that it encourages a systematic review of the organizational structure. In defining decision units, administration may become cognizant of such organizational problems as awkward reporting relationships, poor delegation of authority, improper staffing, and duplication of effort.

Other guidelines to consider when determining significant organizational levels for establishing decision units are:

## Size of the Organization Level

Though units may vary widely in personnel budget and amount of dollars, they should contain neither too few nor too many resources and should all be of approximately the same size in terms of personnel and dollars. If the units are of similar size, it is more feasible to make comparisons and cross-analyses. Similar requirements should be observed during the formulation of decision packages, because, in order to effect a productive and efficient ranking process, decision packages should be similar in size. One of the failures attributed to the National Institutes of Health's (NIH) ZBB experience is the size of the decision units, which hindered effective analysis. NIH, with a fiscal year 1978 budget request of $2.6 billion, was given 18 decision units, 11 of them corresponding to its member institutes.[2] Obviously, the unit is too big in terms of personnel and budget.

Accurate cost data can assist managers to determine the size of a decision unit. Generally, it should not be a cumbersome task to compile statistics on the appropriate expenditure items of an organization's cost centers (see Chapter One for a general discussion of cost centers). Many of these may be taken directly from the existing line-item budgets. However, there may have to be some accounting system changes made in order to more easily accommodate the ZBB system in future years.[3] Since size is one of the most important factors in the determination of decision units, an organization with a small staff will obviously contain fewer decision units than one with a large staff. Figure 3.1 illustrates various sizes of technical services staffs by function and indicates how they might be divided into decision units.

## FIGURE 3.1 Examples of Possible Technical Services Decision Units

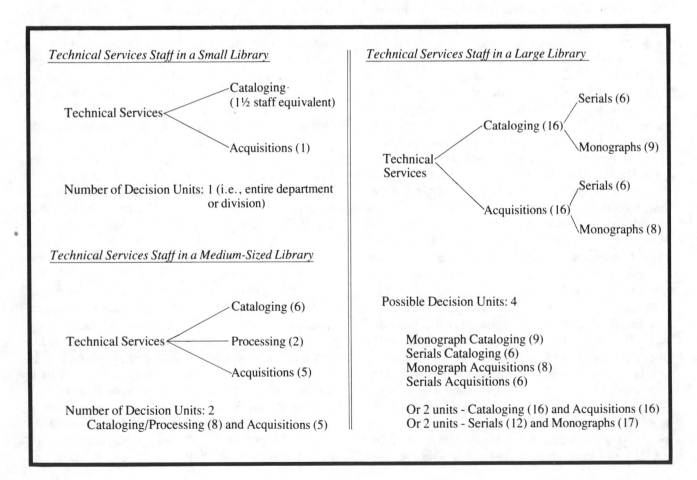

Which alternative division of decision units to adopt in this last grouping is a decision which must be aided by knowledge of reporting relationships and decision-making authority.

Decision units should be kept large enough in numbers of people so that a single decision package will not consist of a small fraction of a person, such as 0.2 full-time equivalent of staff. Pyhrr[4] indicates that such a package would not be meaningful as little money can be saved from eliminating a fraction of a full-time salary. Thus, decision units may be created at different managerial levels and may encompass a varied range of budgeted personnel and dollars. However, for the ease of appropriate analysis, decision units should be similar in size in terms of staff and dollars. They should also be structured in an organizational level high enough to enable the unit manager to have effective control over his/her budget.

## Decision-Making Ability

The possibility for managers to make decisions and develop alternatives should exist in every decision unit. This feature should be considered on two different levels. First, as previously mentioned, the responsible manager must have been delegated the authority to make the relevant budgetary and management decisions. If this has not been done, the ZBB effort will be little more than an academic exercise. Second, the possibility of realistic alternatives must exist in order for a decision unit to be viable. Such outside constraints as imposed standards (which may have a significant impact for school libraries), union regulations, and contracts may inhibit the proposal of alternatives and render that activity useless in decision making. More specifically, certain labor regulations may prohibit change or elimination of certain jobs. Other contracts, such as computer rental and depository agreements, could severely limit alternative courses of action. Breaking such contracts could cost more money than the benefits received from a supposedly more cost-effective course of action. Allocation of such resources as grant money may also be impinged upon by regulations.

## Time Constraints

Any organization is limited in the time which it can spend in preparing a budget. Large libraries with budget officers are more likely to have the time, staff, and expertise to install a more detailed version of ZBB than would small libraries employing only a limited library staff. Certain special business libraries are sometimes in

an advantageous position as they may more easily seek advice and direction from their parent company's financial staff, and thus are able to save some time in preparing their budgets. Publicly supported libraries whose states have adopted the zero-base budget system may be able to seek assistance from their state's budget staff in order to save time and effort. When Pyhrr was involved with the implementation of ZBB in Georgia, a staff of 12 budget experts was available to assist various agencies with the formulation of decision units and packages. In other words, most libraries should have some financial contacts, either in-house or extra-house, to which they can turn for assistance.

Either way, the library may be assured by the experts (Pyhrr and others)[5] that the first year of ZBB adoption will be more time-consuming and less rewarding than subsequent years. Librarians in particular may find ZBB difficult for the first year since most are not trained in strenuous financial analysis and planning. After a year or so of experience with the process, users will undoubtedly become more comfortable and practiced. This will mean both a shorter time commitment to the entire process, and the time to formulate decision units and packages at lower organizational levels.

## Summary

When libraries identify their appropriate decision units, it is necessary for them to take into account factors such as the following:

- Can existing cost centers (units) be appropriate decision units?
- Does the existing organizational structure define decision units?
- Are there special projects, activities, and programs which should be considered as decision units?

It is essential that a decision unit meet the following criteria:

- The decision unit's accomplishment can be accounted for by at least one individual or group of individuals.
- The decision unit's activities and functions can be reflected through quantifiable and measurable benefits.
- Both historical and projected data on the decision unit's fiscal and operational activities are available.
- The decision unit is neither too small to be insignificant nor too large to be cumbersome. It is at a level where policy decisions are significant to the organization.

Examples of possible library decision units follow. They by no means constitute an exhaustive list. Each library's decision unit will differ depending on its size in terms of dollars and personnel, organization, reporting relationships, job descriptions, etc.

**Examples of Possible Library Decision Units**

The Whole Library (if the library is very small)
Public Services
Technical Services
Cataloging (monograph and serial)
Acquisitions (monograph and serial)
Reference Services
Circulation Services
Collection Development
Interlibrary Loan
Administrative Services
Audiovisual Services

## FORMULATING DECISION PACKAGES IN LIBRARIES

Once a decision unit is identified, the manager divides the unit's activities into a series of *decision packages* which are analyzed at various funding levels. Decision packages are the meat of the analyses of a ZBB process; thus the development and formulation of decision packages are essential steps of the process. The components of decision packages are elaborated upon in the following discussion. (Actual examples can be found in Part II; see also the discussion on decision package forms in the following section.)

### Statement of Goals and Objectives

After the decision units have been identified, the basic concept of ZBB, i.e., breaking down activities into levels of effort, is applied. However, there are some preliminary activities which must take place before this process begins. First, a statement of goals and objectives for each decision unit should be made. If a manager is to carry out the goals of his/her department, s/he must fully understand the purposes and objectives of each decision unit formed. On a larger scale, managers should understand the basic goals of the entire library if they are to formulate their department or unit goals in keeping with those of the entire organization. This step may result in an additional by-product of the zero-base budget system, i.e., systematic review and communication of organizational goals. By stating the library's, department's, or decision unit's goals in general terms, a librarian may then establish an explicit or quantifiable set of objectives against which alternative means of operation may be evaluated.

The terms *goal* and *objective* are often used interchangeably. However, for the purposes at hand, a distinction is made between the two terms. A *goal* is a broad or general statement of desired and intended accomplishment. Its scope is broad and unspecific, and it is usually long-term in nature (two to five years). It may also describe the function which a department serves. For example, the goals of a reference department may be: "To provide quality information services to users." Note that broad terms, such as *quality information services*, do not offer any measurable conditions, which would be the role of an *objective* rather than a *goal*. The statement of goals simply allows a view of the forest instead of the trees.

While this exercise may not always be necessary in a small library, it does become more imperative for libraries whose parent institutions have adopted the ZBB system. For example, a college or university using ZBB might well find the statement of goals of considerable value. Those involved in the crucial ranking process will not necessarily be representatives of the library. Nonlibrarians, then, may not understand the purpose of a technical services department and would probably not appreciate the ramifications of the cataloging function. It is wise to formulate the statement of goals as clearly and concisely as possible for the layperson, avoiding the use of library jargon. An example of a clear goal statement for the cataloging function is: "To effectively and expediently provide author, title, and subject cards for the library's card catalog for each book and journal received by the library."

It is suggested that some statement of *strategy* be included to indicate how a unit plans to meet its goals.[6] Returning to the cataloging example, one library might suggest that the quality of the cataloging is of great importance, while a second library could stress expediency at the sacrifice of some other quality for the sake of shorter in-process time. Either tack will have some ramifications for the types and qualifications of personnel and services (e.g., computer-aided cataloging) involved in the function.

A statement of *objectives* is more precise than an expression of goal. In contrast to a goal statement, an objective is usually specific, contained within a short-term period, and quantitative in nature. It should also be realistic, verifiable, attainable, and contain an identifiable result. For example, a library's goal statement can be "to provide good information service to library users," while an objective statement can be "to extend library opening hours to Saturday afternoon (2-6 p.m.) in addition to the present weekday hours (9 a.m.-9 p.m.)." Objectives should be challenging and consistent with organizational goals, strategies, and policies.[7] These statements, he believes, are the key to the zero-base process, as they provide a reference point for budget justification and performance measures. Higher management might look to the statement of objectives as a guideline to evaluate the effectiveness of the person responsible for the activities described in the unit.

As with the determination of decision units, statements of objectives will vary from one situation to another. Though they are basically quantitative in nature, it is recognized that some qualitative factors must be taken into consideration. This point is particularly important for those functions, such as reference and collection development, which appear to defy a high degree of quantification. Another example of an appropriate statement of objectives for a college library's reference department might be: "To provide reference service by professional librarians at least 40 hours per week and to provide the incoming class of 200 freshmen basic bibliographic instruction within the first semester of the academic year." The above objective indicates measurable output (40 hours of reference service per week and bibliographic instruction to 200 freshmen) set within a time frame (the first semester of the year). The quality of service is also specified, that is, reference service provided by professional librarians rather than nonprofessional staff. This specific objective would be helpful in determining, for example, the number and type of reference librarians which are required to render the projected services during the next year.

Thus, the above discussion tells us that after decision units have been identified, managers begin their analyses by asking two questions:

1. *What is the purpose of their department or function?* (statement of goals)

2. *What activities are necesssary to fulfill this purpose?* (statement of objectives)

## Examination of Current Operations and Resources

The next question to ask during the zero-base process is: *How much money is necessary to carry out the stated goals and objectives?* At this point, it is helpful to summarize current expenditures. This step is simply a description of the way that the designated unit currently operates and of the resources which it requires. Per-

formance measures are developed to examine the strength and weakness of current operations. Again, a basic element of ZBB is the exploration of alternatives to present modes of operation. A description of the current services and resources required by the decision unit will allow for equivalent comparison of alternatives.

The manager need not make this a time-consuming step by describing his/her activities requirements in great detail. Itemizing the ordinary resource essentials, such as pens, pencils, and desks, is not necessary. Rather, the description should contain a list of the employees and those major resources which are unique to the operation. It may be helpful, particularly in more complex institutions, for resources to be described in terms of workload order. This would be particularly useful for a nonlibrarian reviewing a resource description of a technical services operation. Major special items, such as computer terminals, should also be included in the operation. A description of the resources in a decision package for reference services might be as follows:

One professional librarian for reference service and bibliographic instruction . . . . . . . . . . . . $12,000

One nonprofessional assistant for clerical duties . . . . . . . . . . . . . . . . . . . . . . . . . . . . . $8,000

Rental of one printer for online database searching . . . . . . . . . . . . . . . . . . . . . . . . . . . $3,000

Figure 3.2 is taken from the State of Delaware's Budget Form. It is a good example of one of the better, more elaborate ways of presenting the useful information on requested resources. By listing the percentage of the previous fiscal year under both fund and position categories, the reviewers of the budget can see clearly that although the total amount of the requested budget stays approximately the same as that of the previous year (98 percent), the number of positions requested actually suffers a 15 percent cut from that of the previous year.

## Identification of Alternatives

At this point managers should ask the question, *Is there a less costly and/or more effective way to achieve the specific objectives or to perform the functions of the decision units?* The uncomfortable question, *Is this function necessary?* should also be considered. Identifying and evaluating various alternatives against the present modes of operation will encourage the most

**FIGURE 3.2 Portion of the Budget Form Used by the State of Delaware**

| (16) Resources | | FY 79 Budget | This Level | Cumulative | % of FY 79 |
|---|---|---|---|---|---|
| $000.0 | General Funds | 303.5 | 297.6 | 297.6 | 98 |
| | Other Funds: | 150.4 | 150.4 | 150.4 | 100 |
| | | | | | |
| | | | | | |
| | Total Funds | 453.9 | 448.0 | 448.0 | 98 |
| Positions (FTE) | General Fund | 16.7 | 13.9 | 13.9 | 83 |
| | CETA | 2.1 | 2.1 | 2.1 | 100 |
| | Other: | | | | |
| | | | | | |
| | | | | | |
| | Total Positions | 18.8 | 16.0 | 16.0 | 85.1 |
| (17) Program Measures          N/A | | FY 79 Plan | This Level | Cumulative | % of FY 79 |
| | | | | | |
| | | | | | |
| | | | | | |
| | | | | | |
| | | | | | |
| | | | | | |
| | | | | | |
| | | | | | |
| | | | | | |

appropriate method to be implemented in the following year. This can be one of the most creative and difficult aspects of the zero-base process, for the underlying assumption is that having always done something a certain way in the past does not necessarily justify its continuance in the future. One might describe this as a *nothing-is-sacred* approach.

The term *alternative* is defined in our context as a different way of accomplishing a decision unit's goals and objectives. For example, if a library's circulation function consists of an overburdened manual system, an alternative could be the adoption of a computerized system.

There are numerous examples of types of alternatives reviewed in the zero-base literature (Stonich and others).[8] The following are representative of various modes:

- Adopting a machine system for manual effort;
- Centralizing certain functions;
- Decentralizing functions;
- Using an outside service for some functions;

- Performing services internally which are presently contracted outside;
- Transferring the functions to a different decision unit; and
- Eliminating the function.

To return to the circulation example, if a library has two circulation points, each staffed by a professional librarian and student assistants, some of the alternative ways of accomplishing the activity might be:

*Alternative A (Recommended Now)*
Combine the two circulation points into a centralized circulation service staffed by one professional, one nonprofessional, and fifteen student assistants. This plan will cost $4,000 less than the present operation without loss of user convenience and will accommodate present circulation demands.

*Alternative B*
Combine the two circulation points into a centralized service staffed by one professional, two nonprofessionals, and fifteen student assistants. One of the two nonprofessionals will be used to begin conversion from a manual to automated circulation system. After the

system is operable, services should be faster and create 60 percent less error. This alternative is not now recommended due to time and cost. However, further investigation is recommended during the upcoming year.

*Alternative C*
Retain present methods of operation. This strategy would continue to maintain the present level of service but is not cost-effective due to the nature of the tasks and high personnel costs.

Once all feasible alternatives have been investigated and reviewed, the manager of that decision unit should be able to select that alternative which would best meet the goals and objectives of both the decision unit and the library. As apparent in the above example, it is advised that each alternative be supported, especially if it is new and recommended, with a summary of the benefits, costs, and problems associated with it. A statement should be made explaining why an alternative was or was not selected, or how it partially or completely achieves the stated objectives. Due to limited time or other constraints, it may not be possible to capitalize on a desired alternative during the upcoming year. Even so, it should be listed, since a feasibility study could be initiated to encourage its acceptance in a future year. Alternative B in the above example is a case in point. At the hectic time of budget preparation, it would be unwise and almost impossible to quickly plan implementation of a complicated and expensive automated system without a substantial amount of preliminary study. However, if automation is part of a library's future plans, this may be a desirable time for the idea to receive some administrative and formal recognition.

In connection with the recommendation of a specific alternative, it is important to keep the budgeting aspect in mind. For example, to initiate online services in a library, there are numerous alternatives for budgeting including the following:

- Full cost subsidized by the library.
- Partial subsidy by the library and partial cost recovery by the users.
    Charge all users equally for all direct costs.
    Charge all direct costs to outside users only.
    Charge all direct costs to outside and nonprimary users only.
    Charge higher percent of all direct costs to nonprimary and outside users, and lower percent of all direct costs to primary users.
    Charge both direct and indirect costs to nonprimary and outside users, and only direct costs to primary users.
- Full cost paid by the users.

The focus of this activity is not just to think of different ways of doing a job, but to find ways of improving current practices. Improvement may be accomplished by finding less costly ways of doing things or by achieving more for the same number of dollars spent. This part of the zero-base process is the most creative and imaginative. One should not hesitate to suggest totally new approaches to a function. They may not only be good ideas in themselves, but may stimulate further thought and suggestions during the entire process. This is where input from the grass-roots level of the organization is so essential. The people who are actually performing the tasks may have a better notion of how to accomplish them than would higher management. Here is an opportunity for their suggestions to be heard.

The identification of alternatives was uniquely carried out by the Greece, N.Y. school system.[9] They altered the ZBB process by first identifying three different levels of service—business as usual, reduced minimum, and increment levels—for each decision package or function. The respective managers were then asked how each *level* could be provided in a different manner—an unconventional application of ZBB. Their plan for developing alternatives included meetings with each principal and his/her staff to develop ideas and meetings of various principles to consolidate their suggestions. All staff members, including the custodians, were encouraged to express their ideas. Any suggestions could be sent directly to the superintendent. This process resulted in the collection of approximately 1,000 different ideas from various people in the school system on how to save money and improve operations. Brueningson claims that the school system saved $1,000,000 through use of this modified ZBB process. One can imagine that communications may also have improved.

Cheek[10] has suggested that the process of formulating alternatives to present modes of operation need not and should not be limited to that time of year designated for budget preparation. Rather, he proposed that each involved staff member keep a personal, written file of ideas throughout the year. This practice may encourage managers and staff to think continually about how they could more effectively spend their budgeted funds. It is also likely that people forget about some innovative ideas which they have thought through in earlier months; a written file will preserve them until the next budget preparation. A collection of ideas of this type may provide a kind of *shopping list* for cost reduction or increased efficiency.

The selection of the best alternative, then, provides the basis for the decision package. All other alternatives, though documented, are discarded for the time being. In other words, once an alternative has been approved and accepted, it is then deemed the way in which the decision unit will operate during the next year.

## Workload and Performance Measures

The identification and quantification of meaningful workload and performance measures comprise an important step to achieve before the final incremental analysis can be conducted. If no measures are available, management will have no means by which to consider cost-benefit trade-offs. If these steps are completely ignored, one of the primary reasons for the implementation of zero-base budgeting will be lost. In other words, an organization must receive some identifiable benefits for spending its money, and *productivity in terms of cost* is certainly a key point. The workload and performance measures are an embodiment of these benefits. These measures, which may be either quantitative, qualitative, or both, should suggest not only how much but how well work is being done.

Obviously, some activities are more conducive to measurement than others, and developing appropriate measures for library services is a feat which has challenged the library world for some time. For example, among those activities which are the most difficult to judge and quantify are collection development and reference service. It is for programs such as these that the limitations of a budgeting approach such as zero-base must be recognized. It is not easy to show quantitatively why a librarian with ten years of experience and a subject master's degree would be more effective in a reference position than a new M.L.S. graduate, unless we conduct surveys and interviews of library users. We would, in most cases, assume that the experienced one would be better than the new professional in the field. It is, however, possible to provide some quantitative measurement in terms of library service as demonstrated in library literature. Chen's recent book[11] is a good example. To name a few types of measurements specifically, reference services can be measured in terms of the number of questions answered, the number of satisfied users who requested information, the speed of providing needed information (number of books, articles, etc.) provided. Technical services activities probably comprise the most manageable group of tasks to observe and measure since it is easy to count the number of books cataloged; the number of catalog cards typed, printed, and filed, etc. Yet, the measurability of the quality of cataloging is also an issue. It is safe to say that

there is no perfect way to measure and quantify library performance. Fortunately, what library managers need are not perfect measurements, but imperfect evaluations with usable data for decision-making purposes.

Although library literature is full of useful books and articles on performance measures, librarians should also keep in mind the diversity and number of helpful in-house manuals on the topic prepared by government agencies and nongovernment organizations. The following Draft Outline, or table of contents, is taken from a useful manual on the subject prepared for the Canadian federal libraries by Canada's Treasury Board in addition to its general *Manager's Guide to Performance Measurement*[12] and supplements, *Performance Measurement: A Guide to Successful Application*.[13]

*Draft Outline #2 (February 20, 1978)*
*Performance Measurement in Federal Libraries*

1.0  Introduction
    1.1  Purpose of publication
    1.2  Scope of publication

2.0  Performance Measurement Concept
    2.1  What it is—define the concept
        —define an indicator, measure, standard of performance
    2.2  What it is not—can not indicate validity of objectives
        —can not measure an individual's performance
        —is a gross not precise measure
    2.3  Why do it—dual objectives of performance measurement of accountability to senior management and for internal management

3.0  Performance Measurement in Federal Government
    3.1  Definition of treasury board concept
    3.2  Relationship to PPBS and MBO
    3.3  Implementation of performance measurement: historical perspective
    3.4  Current status of PMS
    3.5  Problems/Limitations of PMS
    3.6  Advantages/Uses of performance measurement
    3.7  Macro indicators of performance measurement
        3.7.1  Efficiency
        3.7.2  Service—Quality
                —Level
        3.7.3  Effectiveness
    3.8  Definition of PMS terms
        3.8.1  Output indicators
        3.8.2  Input indicators
        3.8.3  Weighting

3.8.4 Overhead
3.8.5 Reference or base year
3.8.6 Forecasting
3.8.7 Efficiency index
3.8.8 Unit cost
3.8.9 Aggregation
3.8.10 Changing indicators

4.0 Performance Measurement Development in Federal Government Libraries
    4.1 Development status: results of survey
    4.2 Major considerations
    (Redrafting of "OPMS Check List" from Treasury Board's *Operational Performance Measurement* [Vol. 2: Technical Manual], pp. 61-62 as it pertains to federal libraries)

5.0 (Former Sections 5-7 of January 8, 1978 Draft Outline) Redrafting postponed until meeting of March 17, 1978. It was agreed, however, that this section will include guideline indicators, measures, reporting mechanisms (data gathering and interpretation), PM used (i.e., program forecasts) branch and regional operations, implementation techniques, resources consumed, maintenance and review techniques.

6.0 Glossary of Terms
    —both library science and performance measurement terms used in this guideline

7.0 References
    —those relevant to Treasury Board's PM concept only

8.0 Supplementary Readings
    —selective and annotated bibliography of performance measurement and evaluation from the library literature. It was agreed that this would replace section 6.1 from the January 18, 1978 draft outline.

9.0 Sources of Information
    9.1 Working group on performance measurement
    9.2 Library documentation centre
    9.3 Federal libraries liaison office
    It was agreed that the information/aid contacts cited in the January 18, 1978 outline were subject to change over time. Therefore, it was generally felt that information on available PM related courses, federal library PM contacts, etc., should be reported in LIAISON to maintain currency.

Appendices
    A. Examples of Specific Federal Library PM Appiications
    B. Treasury Board Circular 1976-25 (on Performance measurement)
    C. Treasury Board Circular 1977-47 (on Program Evaluation)

Evaluation Form

For the readers' convenience, examples of feasible library quantitative work measurements are provided as follows.

*Cataloging:*
    number of volumes originally cataloged
    number of volumes routinely cataloged
    number of cards typed, produced, filed
    number of reclassifications
    time lapse between receipt of material and shelving

*Acquisitions:*
    number of orders processed
    number of materials received (unpacked, checked-in, etc.)
    number of invoices cleared

*Audiovisual Services:*
    number of equipment circulations
    number of equipment deliveries
    number of projectionist jobs completed
    number of formal workshops
    number of audiovisual production jobs completed (films, video, photography, transparency, etc.)

*Reference:*
    number of hours of public service per week
    number of one-step source questions answered
    number of two-step source questions answered
    number of directional questions answered
    number of telephone questions answered
    number of literature searches conducted

*Collection Development:*
    number of serial and monograph titles acquired
    number of circulations (in-house or extra-house)
    percentage of unfilled (or filled) demands

*Circulation:*
    number of circulations
    number of library opening hours

Qualitative work measurements can go into areas such as user satisfaction or supervisor's evaluation by utilizing different methodologies, such as personal interview, questionnaire survey, and direct observation. However, they are less frequently done.

In essence, all of the library services should be able to demonstrate some benefits or results. Essentially, outputs are measured against inputs stated in financial terms. This process generally measures output itself quantitatively and makes less of an attempt to judge the quality of the work performed. It does not attempt, for example, to measure how well librarians catalog or answer reference questions. This is an appraisal problem left to individual supervisors. Some inferences about quality can be made from designations such as professional and nonprofessional (i.e., we may assume that professional reference librarians are able to answer questions more effectively than nonprofessionals) and from measures such as percent of unfilled demands for materials and number of satisfied users.

Work measurement is a tool which must be developed and refined to meet any particular situation. The above list may simply serve as a proposed guideline to be altered for an individual library's services. Measures should be oriented toward output rather than activities, as their purpose is to reflect the results of the stated objectives for the decision unit. For example, the number of hours which a cataloger spends cataloging is not a performance measure; the number of books cataloged is such a measure.

These measures have a number of implications and uses both within and beyond the ZBB process. First, results procured and the money spent for them essentially reveal cost-accounting figures. As mentioned by Rider,[14] the figures may assist managers to reduce working costs by pointing out wastes and avoidable delays and to choose wisely between alternative methods of operation. This is one of the bases of zero-base budgeting.

Though not immediately apparent in the figures, the measurements may be helpful for functions such as scheduling. Schultz[15] offers a plan of reference service measurement by comparing the greatest degree of service that can be given at a particular time (i.e., number of questions adequately answered and aborted) with the combination of personnel (i.e., professional or nonprofessional) working at that time. Workload may then be met by scheduling appropriate personnel at the reference desk for the most cost-effective service. In other words, schedule more reference staff during the time periods when services are needed more.

As a final by-product example, Woodruff[16] mentions that work measures may be used both for justifying budget figures and developing standards of performance. For example, if most catalogers in a technical services division catalog 500 books per year, that figure might assist a manager in determining the needed personnel to handle the expected workload.

In conclusion, the specification of quantified workload and performance measures may aid a manager in assessing the potential benefits to be received, as well as indicating the after-the-fact effectiveness of the resource allocations.

## Preparation of an Incremental Budget for Levels of Services

Once an alternative method of operation has been accepted, decision-unit managers will develop an incremental budget for various levels of services for that alternative.

The decision-unit manager starts the incremental analysis by determining from zero base which are the most essential services or programs provided by his/her unit. Those activities of the highest priority will be first in the minimum-budget or funding level. In most cases, the first-level services will require lower expenditure than what is currently provided, thus they are often referred to as the *reduced-level budget* or *minimum-level budget*.

### The Reduced-Level Budget

The basic principles of ZBB are that an organization's budget should justify, in great detail and in priority order, every dollar proposed for expenditure; and that an organization's *top priority* objectives can be achieved with a reduced-level budget. While ZBB is threatening to many because of the false and literal interpretation of zero base as starting each budget from zero, the reality is that ZBB does not start at the lowest level from zero. It requires, however, that each decision-unit manager assess the current activities and services within the unit from zero base until the appropriate priorities are set in terms of the unit's objectives. This enables the decision-unit manager to wisely determine an appropriate reduced-level budget, which can carry on the unit's *most important* activities and accomplish the unit's most essential objectives. Frequently, the decision-unit managers will see what barebone services can be provided with, for example, 75 percent of the current budget (of course, the actual percentage varies from one organization to the other.) In the case of the State of Oregon, for example, its *1979-81 Biennial Budget Preparation Manual* suggests that the total of all reduced-level budgets may not exceed 85 percent of the agency's adjusted budget, which excludes capital improvement, capital construction, debt service, and nonlimited expenditures.[17] Thus, in most cases, the first level offers services of a narrower range and/or reduced quality and quantity.

### The Nonreduced First-Level Budget

In some extreme cases, it is possible to have a first-level budget which is higher than the current one and which proposes better and more extensive services. For example, if government's legislative mandate requires the creation and/or expansion of a new program, then obviously the current level of operation is not only inadequate but also unacceptable. In this case, the first level budget for next year's operation can be 50 percent higher than the current one, or at least the same as the current budget, and the further incremental level can be 200 percent or 300 percent higher.

Once the first level of service (Level I) is determined and its required budget is set, it is reasonably easy to develop successive incremental or improved levels of services and costs. Level II would be more costly than Level I, but offers additional services (of second priority) than those bare-bone ones (of highest priority) in Level I. Similarly, Level III will cost more than Level II, but will offer even more services than Level II. Figure 3.3 shows the decision-package increment structure. These packages are called *increment packages* because they reflect different levels of effort which may be expended on a specific function. The first-level package, or *base package*, establishes a minimum level of services and activities. Incremental packages identify better service and higher activity and cost levels. Once the most viable package is selected for funding, all others of the same decision unit are discarded. For example, Figure 3.3 is a graphic representation of decision-unit increment structure of the reference department of a given large academic library. There are three decision units of the department—ILL, manual reference services, and online reference services. For each of the three decision units, there are four incremental packages, each of which costs the department a given amount of money. All programs and services included in the first-level budget (I—1, M-1, and O-1) are considered to be most essential and basic, while all activities and services included in the highest-level budgets (I-4, M-4, and O-4) are considered to be most extensive and, therefore, most expensive. Once one of the four decision packages in each decision unit (say I-2, M-3, and O-1) is selected for funding, all other decision packages will not be considered for funding.

**FIGURE 3.3   Decision-Unit Increment Structure of a Reference Department in an Academic Library**

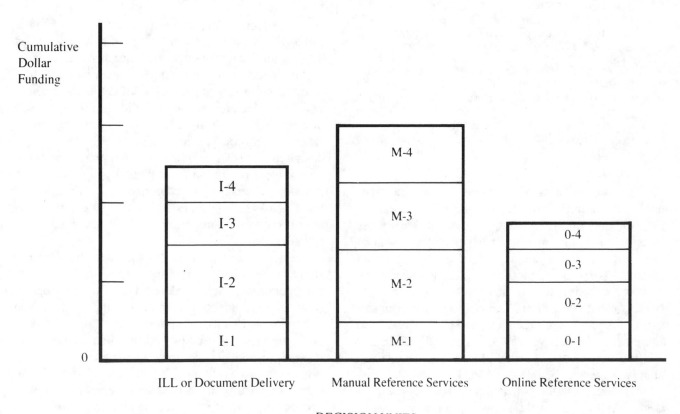

An actual incremental decision package is given in the following:

Library X's planning department currently consists of four planners. The library manager believes that the minimum requirements for planning can be achieved with a reduction of one planner. In this case, s/he can identify the first-level, or base-level, and incremental packages for his/her recommendations as follows:

*Base Package:* Reduce one staff from the current operation, and retain the other three planners. The minimum operating requirements are to coordinate the newly instituted services and programs and to plan scheduling. Due to the reduction of one planner, operations related to long-range planning, library collections inventory control, quality control, library marketing research, and system modification have to be curtailed. Budget for this level of operation is $40,000.00.

*Incremental I Package:* Add one planner to the minimum three planners required at the base level (or current staff size). As a result of this increment, planning can be made two years in advance instead of one, collection inventory reports can be issued every month rather than quarterly, system modification for four departments instead of two can be accommodated, and monthly library marketing surveys on new services can be conducted. The increase of budget for this level of operation over the base-level budget ($40,000.00) is $13,000.00. Thus the total budget is $53,000.00.

*Incremental Package II:* Add another planner in addition to Incremental I staff. This new staff will introduce new types of planning work such as forecasting and prediction of users' needs. The new allocation requires an additional $15,000.00 and thus brings the total budget request for this level of operation to $68,000.00.

The descriptions of the three decision packages above are simple summaries. Naturally, the library decision-unit managers need to spell out clearly the benefits (in dollar terms) gained to offset the additional price tags. In this example, a total of three decision packages are prepared for the decision unit—the library planning department. The first base-level package can be designated as *P 1 of 3* (Planning Department number one of the total three packages), and Incremental I and Incremental II packages can be designated *P 2 of 3* and *P 3 of 3* accordingly. Further library incremental decision packages can be found in Part II.

Having described in detail the development of decision packages, we can sum up the guidelines as follows:

- Each decision package should represent a single and clear-cut decision unit.

- Each decision package should include specific objectives and the expected cost to accomplish them.

- A decision package emphasizes program proposed. thus all costs related to the proposed program should be clearly identified.

- A decision package should not be prepared for a single item of expenditure only, such as the staff position, supply, or equipment.

- A decision package should assess various alternatives of achieving the program objectives and should identify the most viable one.

- A decision package should stress the potential program impact or benefit. In the case of a newly proposed program, estimated benefit should be clearly stated.

## DECISION PACKAGE FORMS

The decision package is a request for allocation of funds budgeted to support a specific recommended level of services, activities, and programs. It is essential that the decision package represent the manager's best effort to provide all necessary justification information which can enable his/her superiors to easily reach budgetary decisions and to assign priority. The importance of decision package forms is evident. A well-designed form can facilitate the ZBB process and provide a clear but to-the-point picture of the process to decision makers. On the other hand, a poorly designed form can create unnecessary work for the staff and confusion to decision makers at a high level of the organization.

Each organization has its own unique background, source of income, expenditure items, and budgetary considerations. Each must design its own forms to meet its planning, budgeting, and controlling needs. Seven examples in Part II show clearly that the formats of decision packages used by various libraries differ substantially in details, yet they all have the same barebone elements as shown in Figure 3.4. Figure 3.5 provides for additional supplementary elements of a decision-package form. Additional sample forms can be found in Part II.

**FIGURE 3.4 "Bare-Bone" Elements of a Decision-Package Form**

| PROGRAM NAME: | RANK: |
| --- | --- |
| | LEVEL ___ OF ___ |

| BUDGET UNIT: | PREPARED BY: | DATE: |
| --- | --- | --- |

GOALS AND OBJECTIONS:

FEASIBILITY ASSESSMENT:

BENEFITS:

| COSTS: | STAFFING: |
| --- | --- |

ALTERNATIVE WAYS AND LEVELS OF ACHIEVING THE OBJECTIVES:

    Ways                           Levels

CONSEQUENCE OF NOT APPROVING THE PACKAGE:

| APPROVED BY: | DATE OF APPROVAL: |
| --- | --- |

**FIGURE 3.5   Decision–Package Summary Form**

| 1) Decision Unit Name | 2) Department | 3) Unit Manager | 4) Date | Increment |
|---|---|---|---|---|
| | | | | of |

| 5) Goals | 6) Objectives |
|---|---|
| | |

7) Current operations and required resources.

| 8) List alternatives which would accomplish objective(s) and reason for using or not using in 19___. | 10) Workload and performance measures |
|---|---|

| 9) Brief description of increments and services provided* | | Incremental | | | | Cumulative | | | | | | | | | |
|---|---|---|---|---|---|---|---|---|---|---|---|---|---|---|---|
| | | Prof. | Non-Prof. | Wk. Study | Other Exp. | Empl. FTE | (a) % | Total Exp. | (a) % | | | | | | |
| | _of_ | | | | | | | | | | | | | | |
| | _of_ | | | | | | | | | | | | | | |
| | _of_ | | | | | | | | | | | | | | |
| | _of_ | | | | | | | | | | | | | | |

| 11a) Resources required and services performed | 19___ Plan | | | | | | | | |
|---|---|---|---|---|---|---|---|---|---|
| | | Increment | | | | Cumulative | | | |
| | b) Increment resources required | Prof. | Non-Prof. | Wk. Study | Other Exp. | Empl. FTE | (c) % | Total Exp. | (c) % |
| | | | | | | | | | |
| | c) Decision unit resources used this year | | | | | | | | |

12) Changes in service between existing and planned operations through this increment.

13) What would be the consequences of not funding this increment?

|  | | 19___ Plan | |
|---|---|---|---|
| 14) Planned workload and performance measures. | 19 ___ | Increment | Cumulative |
| | | | |
| | | | |
| | | | |
| | | | |

(a) This year's budgeted amount    *Indicate current level

## NOTES

1. Graeme M. Taylor, "Introduction to Zero-Base Budgeting," *Bureaucrat* 6 (March 1977), 33-5.

2. Regina E. Herzlinger, "Zero-Base Budgeting in the Federal Government: A Case Study," *Sloan Management Review* (Winter 1979), pp. 3-14.

3. Taylor, "Introduction to Zero-Base Budgeting."

4. Peter Pyhrr, *Zero-Base Budgeting: A Practical Management Tool for Evaluating Expenses* (New York: John Wiley, 1973), p. 49.

5. Ibid.

6. Walter D. Hill, *Implementing Zero-Base Budgeting—The Real World* (Oxford, OH: Planning Executives Institutes, 1977), p. 8.

7. Ibid.

8. Paul J. Stonich, "Zero-Base Planning—A Management Tool," *Managerial Planning* 25 (July/August 1976): 1-4.

9. Arthur A. Brueningson, "SCAT—A Process of Alternatives," *Management Accounting* 58 (November 1976): 55-6.

10. Logan M. Cheek, *Zero-Base Budgeting Comes of Age* (New York: AMACOM, 1977).

11. For more discussion, see Ching-chih Chen, ed., *Quantitative Measurements and Dynamic Library Service* (Phoenix, AZ: Oryx, 1978).

12. Canada, Treasury Board, *A Manager's Guide to Performance Measurement* (Hull, Ontario: DSS Publishing Center, October 1976).

13. Canada, Treasury Board, "Performance Measurement: A Guide to Successful Application," 1978. Mimeographed. (Supplement to *A Manager's Guide to Performance Measurement.*)

14. Fremont Rider, "Library Cost Accounting," *Library Quarterly* 6 (October 1936): 331-81.

15. J.S. Schultz, "Program Budgeting and Work Measurement for Law Libraries," *Law Library Journal* 63 (August 1970): 353-62.

16. Elaine Lindholm Woodruff, "Work Measurement Applied to Libraries," *Special Libraries* 48 (April 1957): 139-44.

17. Oregon, Executive Department, *1979-81 Biennial Budget Preparation Manual, vol. 2, Alternative Program Levels System (APLS)*. (Budget and Management Division, State of Oregon, March 1978), p. 6.

# Chapter Four
# The Ranking Process and Resource Allocation

Once the decision packages have been completed, management is ready to start the review process by ranking all decision packages in terms of descending order of importance, benefits to the organization, and/or effectiveness. To facilitate this process, many managers find that keeping a running account of the cumulative totals of decision packages is helpful. The line-item summary form, shown in Figure 4.1, can be used for this purpose. The ranking sheet in Figure 4.2 shows that a running account of the cumulative total of money or other required resources (such as personnel) can be kept to indicate the sum of each package and its preceding package(s), which are judged to be of higher priority. Theoretically, once a budget amount is set by the management, the packages down to the spending level can be accepted. Thus, as stated by Pyhrr, "The ranking process provides management with a technique to allocate its limited resources by making management concentrate on the questions: *How much should we spend? and Where should we spend it?*"[1]

The process enables the management to concentrate its limited resources on those functions, activities, and programs which are of greatest significance and benefit to the organization. On the other hand, the process assists the managers to delete their support of those functions and activities which have lost their significance through obsolescence, inefficiency, or change of policy and objectives. This is one of the major advantages of ZBB compared with traditional budgeting systems, under which an organization's functions and activities—regardless of their significance—will continue to survive due to the automatic carry-over from one year to the next.

## THE RANKING PROCEDURE

The ranking process should start with the basic decision-unit manager, or at the cost-center level, where the decision packages are developed and formulated. This enables the decision-unit manager to evaluate the relative significance of his/her own functions and activities by ranking the developed decision packages accordingly. In essence, the decision-unit manager is accountable for his/her proposed activities in terms of accomplishments.

Reviews on the next level up the ladder can either follow or cross organization lines, depending on organization and/or program structure. However, in most cases the ranking process will follow organization lines, going upward through one or more middle consolidation levels before it will reach the top or final consolidated level. The number of middle levels which the process has to go through depends mainly on the size and complexity of the organization.

Figure 4.3 exhibits the various consolidation levels in an organizational structure. This means that at the lowest decision-unit level (D), each of the nine decision-unit managers must evaluate, assess, and prioritize anywhere from two to four decision packages related to his/her own programs and activities. The nine ranking lists of $D_1$ to $D_9$ will be presented to four lower-level middle-managers (C), each of whom, with the assistance of decision managers under them, will rank between six and eight decision packages submitted to them from two or three decision units. Then, accordingly, the two upper-level middle-managers (B) must rank and consolidate thirteen and fifteen packages submitted to each of them from two subordinate middle-managers. Finally, the chief administrator of the organization (A) must rank the total of 28 decision packages involving two major departments or programs ($B_1$ and $B_2$). Practically, in large organizations, the decision packages are consolidated before being ranked in order to minimize the paper flow.

Figure 4.4 is a much simplified graphic presentation of an organizational structure which fits most

**FIGURE 4.1    Line-Item Summary Form**

| 1) Decision Unit Name | 2) Department | | 3) Manager | | 4) Date | |
|---|---|---|---|---|---|---|
| 5) Account Number | 6) Account Name | 7) Levels | | | | | 8) Total all levels |
| | | 1 | 2 | 3 | 4 | 5 | |
| | | | | | | | |

**Figure 4.2    Ranking Sheet**

| | | | Increment | | | | | | Cumulative | | | | | | | |
|---|---|---|---|---|---|---|---|---|---|---|---|---|---|---|---|---|
| Rank | Decision Unit Name | Inc. No. | Prof. | Non-Prof. | Wk. Study | Empl. FTE | Exp. | Prof. | Non-Prof | Wk. Study | Empl. FTE | % Curr. Budget | Exp. | % Curr. Budget | Notes |
| | | _of_ | | | | | | | | | | | | | |
| | | _of_ | | | | | | | | | | | | | |
| | | _of_ | | | | | | | | | | | | | |
| | | _of_ | | | | | | | | | | | | | |
| | | _of_ | | | | | | | | | | | | | |
| | | _of_ | | | | | | | | | | | | | |
| | | _of_ | | | | | | | | | | | | | |
| | | _of_ | | | | | | | | | | | | | |
| | | _of_ | | | | | | | | | | | | | |
| | | _of_ | | | | | | | | | | | | | |
| | | _of_ | | | | | | | | | | | | | |
| | | _of_ | | | | | | | | | | | | | |
| | | _of_ | | | | | | | | | | | | | |
| | | _of_ | | | | | | | | | | | | | |

**FIGURE 4.3    Various Consolidation Levels in an Organizational Structure (Number of Decision Packages)**

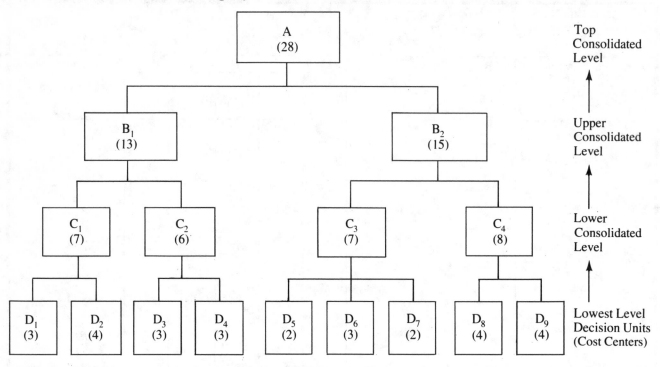

**FIGURE 4.4    An Organizational Structure of a Medium-Sized Library**

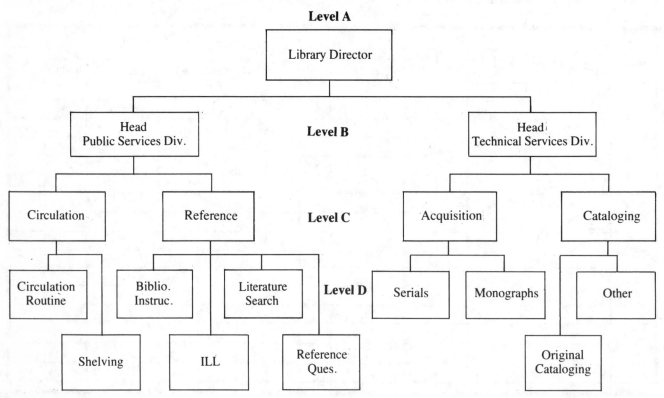

medium-sized libraries. Comparing the structures of the two figures, one can easily translate the consolidated ranking process of Figure 4.3 into library situations as structured in Figure 4.4.

## PROBLEMS WITH THE RANKING PROCESS

In a larger and more complex organization, such as a large university, company, or city government, the consolidating levels are numerous, and the structure is complicated. The total number of decision packages accumulated at the top level A can be several hundreds. Thus, several difficulties with the ranking process become serious:

1. The large volume of decision packages creates a very difficult task for top management, which simply cannot afford the enormous amount of time and effort required to complete the review and rank process.

2. Top- and high-level middle-managers are generally not familiar with lower-level activities and programs; thus, they feel both reluctant and unconfident to rank them.

3. Managers are reluctant to judge the relative importance of numerous dissimilar activities.

To offset some of the difficulties expressed above, various suggestions and recommendations have been offered by ZBB experts:

1. To reduce the number of decision packages to be evaluated and ranked by successively higher levels of management, a cutoff expense line should be established at each organizational level beginning with the highest consolidation and descending to the lower levels. These cutoffs should be set before consolidation of any level starts. Pyhrr suggested that the best way to set the first cutoff is for the top manager to estimate the expenditures which will likely be approved at the top level and "then set the cutoff far enough below this expected expense figure to allow the desired trading-off between the decisions whose packages are being ranked."[2] The lower consolidation levels will set lower cutoffs. Figure 4.5 shows how this cutoff expense process works in the decision-package ranking process.

2. To practice the above ranking and reviewing exercise is to concentrate the managers' attention on those decision packages which are not of the highest priority and are not necessarily considered as requirements from legal and operational points of view. Thus, a considerable amount of time and effort can be saved. Furthermore, this exercise stresses the importance of

## FIGURE 4.5 Cutoff Expense Process

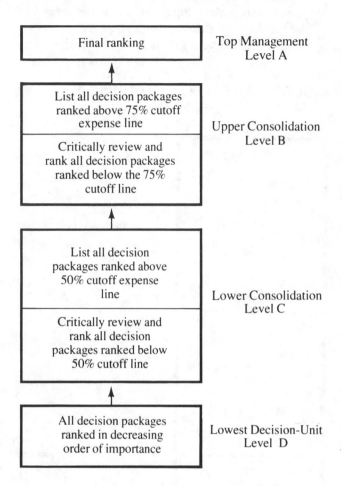

ranking among levels of expenditure but not necessarily within the same level of expenditure.

For example, 20 decision packages are ranked in decreasing order of importance from No. 1 (most important) to No. 20 (least important), as shown in Figure 4.6 in four levels of funding possibilities. Then the ranking order between decision package No. 4 and No. 5 is not really important. What is important is that decision package No. 5 is definitely more important than decision package No. 10 and that decision package No. 18 is indeed one of the least significant packages. In other words, do not waste time and effort over *priorities* and decimal accuracy. Instead, keep the programs' strategic objectives in mind.

3. To partially deal with the difficulties regarding managers' familiarity with lower-level activities and programs and their unwillingness to assign ranking order to dissimilar activities, ZBB experts have suggested various mechanisms. These include ranking by a committee chaired by the level manager but consisting of

subordinate-unit manager members. As these subordinate-unit managers developed the initial packages and voting mechanism, the committee can avoid excessive political maneuvering among decision makers.

**FIGURE 4.6    Four Levels of Funding Possibilities**

| Ranked Decision Packages | |
|---|---|
| 1 | |
| 2 | |
| 3 | *Top Priority* |
| 4 | Must be funded |
| 5 | |
| — — — — — — — | |
| 6 | |
| 7 | |
| 8 | *2nd Priority* |
| 9 | Most likely to be funded |
| 10 | |
| — — — — — — — | |
| 11 | |
| 12 | |
| 13 | *3rd Priority* |
| 14 | Can be delayed in funding |
| 15 | |
| — — — — — — — | |
| 16 | |
| 17 | |
| 18 | *Lowest Priority* |
| 19 | Most likely will not be funded this coming year |
| 20 | |

Ranked
Decision
Packages

## RANKING APPROACHES

Ranking is probably the most sensitive and political part of ZBB. Thus, it is essential to each ranking process to know who makes the ranking decisions and how these decisions are made. If these two areas can be addressed clearly, the ranking process has most likely been well planned and, thus, will most likely be successful.

Ranking decisions can be made by either individual managers or by various forms of management committees. In a complex situation, the committee approach is advisable and is more likely to yield success in terms of staff acceptance of the final ranking (in this case, the managers are jointly accountable for the budget decision).

How the ranking decisions are made is a more complex question and refers to the criteria and methods used by managers to rank the decision packages. Decision packages are judged in various ways by using different approaches and criteria. The following are a few of the most commonly used ones:

### Single-Standard Approach

This approach is the simplest and the most suitable for dealing with a single program or several similar programs. This method reviews all decision packages against a single criterion, which can be effectiveness, dollar savings, cost-benefit ratio, growth, etc. Once the single criterion is selected by the managers, all decision packages are evaluated and ranked in decreasing order of priority by using the chosen standard. This approach cannot justify support of those activities which are not cost-beneficial, cost-effective, etc., but only legally mandated programs which do not show immediate beneficial returns to the organization. For example, *use* is deemed by the administration as the only important criterion to judge the importance of library services and programs; only decision packages which generate high use will be ranked with high priority. In a library situation, this may be a rather dangerous approach, particularly with those new and service-oriented information programs.

### Voting Approach

The voting approach can be used by either individual managers or committees. It is a more sophisticated method than the single standard one. Each decision package is assessed on a voting scale such as the one shown in Figure 4.7.

## FIGURE 4.7 Voting Scale for Determining Priority

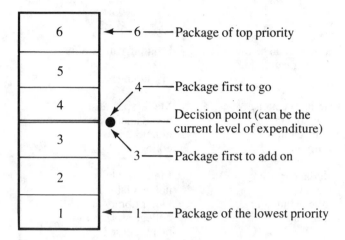

Then point counts of all packages are reviewed; major differences, if any, are resolved; and a consensus ranking list is made up for the next management level. The voting approach offers various possibilities. If the managers' subjective criteria are used, the results of the voting can be biased and political. However, if careful and strenuous criteria are used, the approach can be simple yet helpful.

## Major-Category Approach

This approach essentially consists of three steps: defining the major categories which influence the organization's budgetary decisions; grouping the decision packages into these major categories; within each category, ranking the decision packages either by individual managers or by committee.

The number of major categories varies from one organization to another. They could be:

- Programs which are legally mandatory or contractually required, such as the medical regional libraries' document delivery operations;
- Programs and activities which can generate greater income than expenditure, such as the supply of periodical photocopy requests in some libraries; and
- Programs and activities which can break even at the end of first-year operation.

With these categories, the decision packages can be better organized for reviewing and ranking purposes; thus, this approach is helpful when the number of decision packages is large and the organization structure is complex.

## Multiple-Standard Approach

This can be considered the most sophisticated approach among the four. First, all decision packages are grouped in major categories as outlined in the major-category approach. Then the decision packages are further sorted and ranked by various issue criteria related to an organization's needs and economic feasibilities. With the combination of these multiple standards, decision packages are grouped and ranked.

Some of the issue criteria can be assessed from the following angles:

- Contractual,
- Technical,
- Operational,
- Economic.

For example, the Medical Library Act requires the National Library of Medicine to establish a National Biomedical Communication Network (NBCN). Among the many activities of the NBCN, document delivery is legally required. The technical and operational feasibilities of providing document delivery service are high; however, the economic feasibility is from medium to low, since it will cost the NBCN a considerable amount of money.

To further illustrate this approach, an example of criteria for ranking a college library media program from the technical, operational, and economic points of view is provided in Table 4.1.

In establishing criteria to use for ranking decision packages, library managers should attempt to establish quantifiable criteria whenever possible, otherwise they will leave room for political shovelling which can be damaging to the process. For example, in the case of the federal government's Public Health Service (PHS), the agency managers used the following six criteria:

1. health impact,
2. potential effectiveness,
3. sensitivity,
4. negative impact,
5. conformity with health strategy, and
6. appropriateness of the federal role.

Only one of these six addressed the budgetary concern with effectiveness and efficiency. Thus, there is much room for subjective political judgment or rating rather than an analytical approach.

**TABLE 4.1  Sample Criteria for Ranking a College Library Media Program**

|  | High | Medium | Low |
|---|---|---|---|
| Technical | Program can be run easily | Program can be run after some training | Program can be run after a great deal of training |
|  | Media specialist on library staff now | Media specialist available in college but not in library | Media specialist not available in either library or college |
|  | Media hardware available in library | Media hardware available in college but not in library | Media hardware not available in either library or college and has to be purchased |
| Operational | Media program can be accommodated within the current library organizational structure | Media program can be accommodated within the library with some organizational modification | Media program can not be implemented without substantial change of library organizational structure |
| Economic | Cost-benefit ratio is 1:2 for the first two years | Cost-benefit ratio is 1:1.5 for first two years | Cost-benefit ratio is 1:1 for the first two years |

## RANKING FORMS

Decision-package forms are essential in the development of decision packages. So are the various kinds of ranking forms used by managers for the ranking process. A good ranking form can fulfill several functions, such as those shown in Figures 4.2, 4.8, and 4.9.

1. Prioritize the decision packages.

2. Provide summary information of dollars and staff required for each package activity in both the current and the requested years.

3. Furnish accumulated expenditure of packages.

Figure 4.8 is a completed ranking form, which can also be graphically elaborated as in Figure 4.9. Since the base-level decision packages are the minimum requirements, they are naturally included at the top of the priority ranking list. Note that ranks No. 1 to No. 6 of both figures are all base-level decision packages (*1 of 3* or *strong* justification). In other words, the ranking

sheet lists decision packages by priority with *bone* (equals *strong* justification) at the top, *muscle* (equals *medium* justification) in the middle, and *fat* (equals *weak* justification) at the bottom. Further versions of the ranking forms can be found in Part II.

There are numerous ways to facilitate the ranking exercise and process before the final ranking list of decision packages is formulated. For example, Logan Cheek suggests the use of decision cards on each of which the summary information of a decision package is provided. Figure 4.10 shows the front and the back of a decision card proposed by Cheek.[3] The front of the card provides space for summary information on objectives, approach, alternatives, and consequences of disapproval of a decision package at a given level, while the back of the card provides space for summary accounting. Since these essential data are handily displayed, presumably they will aid the managers during their ranking process. Furthermore, the convenient size of the decision cards, normally about four inches by six inches, makes them easy to switch back and forth during the ranking process. If you take the 18 decision packages listed in Figures 4.8 and 4.9 as examples, you will find that there are 18 decision cards with three each for the six decision units — Administration, Reference, Circulation, Cataloging, Acquisition-Monograph, and Acquisition-Serial. After having completed all the summary information for each decision package on the card, the library managers will rank the 18 decision packages by placing the respective cards in order of priority. Figure 4.11 demonstrates the following steps in the ranking process.

1. Start with the most important decision package by using its decision card as the first one.

2. Place the next important decision card immediately behind the first card, and allow the top margin of the second card to show up.

3. Continue the same process for the next important decision cards until all the cards are ranked.

4. Decide whether the final ranking is satisfactory, as shown in Figure 4.11.

5. If yes, collapse the cards and prepare the final ranking list of decision packages; if not, switch the cards to the desired order of ranking before finalizing the ranking list.

## FIGURE 4.8    A TYPICAL ZBB RANKING SHEET

| | ZERO-BASE BUDGET REQUEST DECISION PACKAGE RANKING | | | | | | |
|---|---|---|---|---|---|---|---|
| Library _____  Department _____ | | | | | | | |
| Rank | Decision Package Name | Justification | FY 1978/79 Budgeted by Program | | FY 1979/80 Requested by Package | | Cumulative Requested | |
| | | | Fund | Positions | Fund | Positions | Fund | Positions |
| 1. | Administration (1 of 3) | Strong | 38,000 | 2.5 | 40,000 | 2.5 | 40,000 | 2.5 |
| 2. | Reference (1 of 3) | Strong | 54,000 | 3.5 | 60,000 | 3.5 | 100,000 | 6.0 |
| 3. | Circulation (1 of 3) | Strong | 12,000 | 1.2 | 15,000 | 1.3 | 115,000 | 7.3 |
| 4. | Acquisition-Serial (1 of 3) | Strong | 10,000 | 1.0 | 10,000 | 1.0 | 125,000 | 8.3 |
| 5. | Cataloging (1 of 3) | Strong | 50,000 | 4.0 | 60,000 | 5.0 | 185,000 | 13.3 |
| 6. | Acquisition-Monograph (1 of 3) | Strong | 10,000 | 1.0 | 10,000 | 1.0 | 195,000 | 14.3 |
| 7. | Reference (2 of 3) | Medium | | | 20,000 | 1.5 | 215,000 | 15.8 |
| 8. | Circulation (2 of 3) | Medium | | | 10,000 | 1.0 | 225,000 | 16.8 |
| 9. | Administration (2 of 3) | Medium | | | 10,000 | 1.0 | 235,000 | 17.8 |
| 10. | Cataloging (2 of 3) | Medium | | | 20,000 | 2.0 | 255,000 | 19.8 |
| 11. | Acquisition-Serial (2 of 3) | Medium | | | 5,000 | 0.5 | 260,000 | 20.3 |
| 12. | Reference (3 of 3) | Weak | | | 20,000 | 1.7 | 280,000 | 22.0 |
| 13. | Circulation (3 of 3) | Weak | | | 5,000 | 0.5 | 285,000 | 22.5 |
| 14. | Administration (3 of 3) | Weak | | | 10,000 | 1.0 | 295,000 | 23.5 |
| 15. | Acquisition-Monograph (2 of 3) | Medium | | | 5,000 | 0.5 | 300,000 | 24.0 |
| 16. | Cataloging (3 of 3) | Weak | | | 20,000 | 2.0 | 320,000 | 26.0 |
| 17. | Acquisition-Monograph (3 of 3) | Weak | | | 5,000 | 0.5 | 325,000 | 26.5 |
| 18. | Acquisition-Serial (3 of 3) | Weak | | | 5,000 | 0.5 | 330,000 | 27.0 |
| | DEPARTMENT TOTALS | | 174,000 | 13.2 | 330,000 | 27.0 | 330,000 | 27.0 |
| Approved by _____ | | | | | Date of Request _____ | | | |

## FIGURE 4.9 The Decision-Package Ranking Process

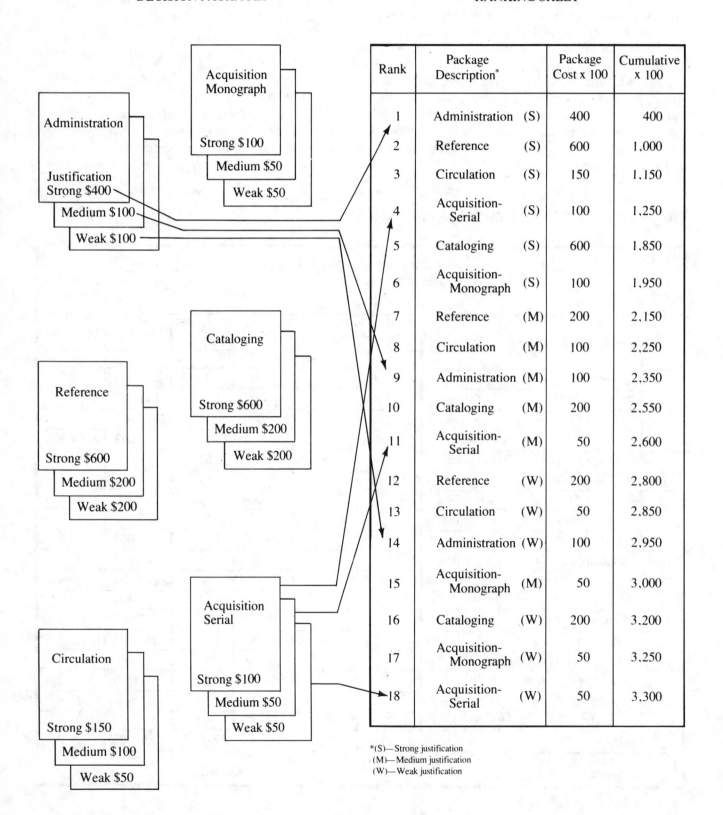

DECISION PACKAGES                    RANKING SHEET

| Rank | Package Description* | | Package Cost x 100 | Cumulative x 100 |
|------|---------------------|---|------|-------|
| 1 | Administration | (S) | 400 | 400 |
| 2 | Reference | (S) | 600 | 1,000 |
| 3 | Circulation | (S) | 150 | 1,150 |
| 4 | Acquisition-Serial | (S) | 100 | 1,250 |
| 5 | Cataloging | (S) | 600 | 1,850 |
| 6 | Acquisition-Monograph | (S) | 100 | 1,950 |
| 7 | Reference | (M) | 200 | 2,150 |
| 8 | Circulation | (M) | 100 | 2,250 |
| 9 | Administration | (M) | 100 | 2,350 |
| 10 | Cataloging | (M) | 200 | 2,550 |
| 11 | Acquisition-Serial | (M) | 50 | 2,600 |
| 12 | Reference | (W) | 200 | 2,800 |
| 13 | Circulation | (W) | 50 | 2,850 |
| 14 | Administration | (W) | 100 | 2,950 |
| 15 | Acquisition-Monograph | (M) | 50 | 3,000 |
| 16 | Cataloging | (W) | 200 | 3,200 |
| 17 | Acquisition-Monograph | (W) | 50 | 3,250 |
| 18 | Acquisition-Serial | (W) | 50 | 3,300 |

*(S)—Strong justification
(M)—Medium justification
(W)—Weak justification

Acquisition Monograph
Strong $100
Medium $50
Weak $50

Administration
Justification Strong $400
Medium $100
Weak $100

Cataloging
Strong $600
Medium $200
Weak $200

Reference
Strong $600
Medium $200
Weak $200

Acquisition Serial
Strong $100
Medium $50
Weak $50

Circulation
Strong $150
Medium $100
Weak $50

**FIGURE 4.10 A Sample Decision Card***

| RANK | PROGRAM NO./Name | SPONSOR | LEVEL | | PLAN YEAR RESOURCES | |
|---|---|---|---|---|---|---|
| | 2: Secretarial support | Admin. Services | 2 of 4 | ☐ Legal | 7 People | $126.00 Dollars |
| | | | | ☐ Policy | | |

**OBJECTIVE: What are you trying to do?**

Provide secretarial support for 35 department managers on basis of 1:5 support ratio. That is, seven incremental secretaries to level 1 of 4.

**APPROACH: How are you proposing to do it?**

Add back seven secretaries to level 1 of 4 decision card using present conventional equipment.

**ALTERNATIVES: How else might you do it?**

See decision matrix for secretarial services. Although more cost-effective, other alternatives cannot be pursued until next July.

**CONSEQUENCES OF DISAPPROVAL:**

Not cost-effective to have managers type and file.

### ACCOUNTING DETAIL

| General Ledger Number | Description | Dollars | |
|---|---|---|---|
| | | 1978 | 1979 |
| A-0001 | Exempt Labor | 0 | 0 |
| A-0002 | Non-exempt Labor | $70K | $73.5 |
| B-0001 | Office Supplies | $28K | $29.4 |
| B-0002 | Copying | $7K | $7.4 |
| B-0003 | Contract Services | $7K | $7.4 |
| B-0004 | Telephone and Telex | $14K | $14.4 |

*Courtesy of Mr. Logan M. Cheek

## RESOURCE ALLOCATION

Once a consolidated ranking list is developed on the ranking sheet with the cumulative column showing the funds required, as shown in both Figures 4.8 and 4.9, and the organization's budget cutoff line(s) is(are) set, the manager can easily decide on the programs to be approved for next year's funding, as shown in Figure 4.12. In other words, as illustrated in Figure 4.12, if Library X approves a final budget of $240,000.00, then the first nine of the eighteen decision packages (from ADMINISTRATION-Strong to ADMINISTRATION-Medium) will be approved for funding. If the library has a final budget of $280,000.00, then, in addition to the first nine decision packages, three others (CATA-LOGING-Medium, ACQUISITION-SERIAL-Medium and REFERENCE-Weak) will also be supported.

## FIGURE 4.11 The Ranking of Decision Cards

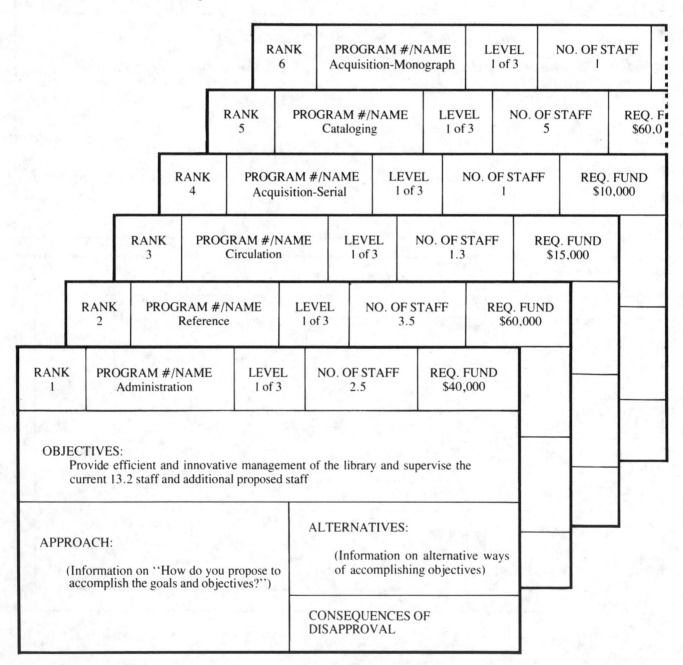

## FIGURE 4.12 Ranked Decision-Unit Increments

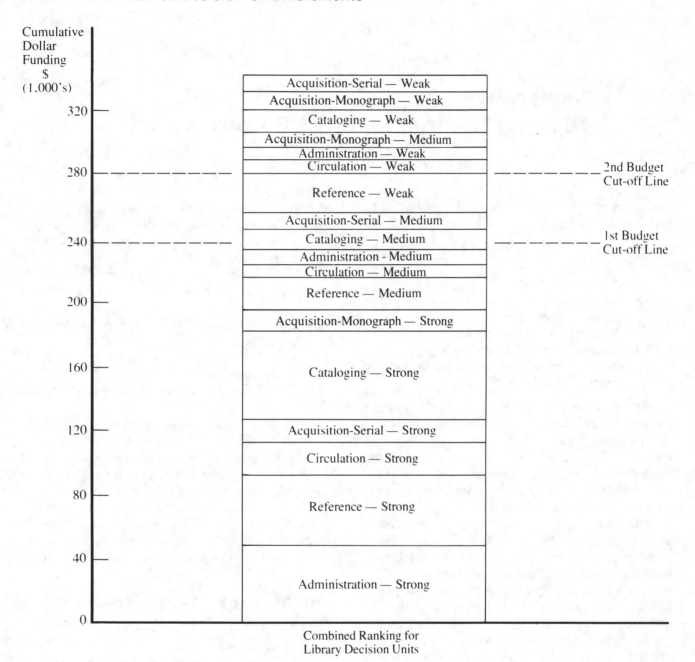

NOTES

1. Peter A. Pyhrr, "Zero-Base Budgeting," *Harvard Business Review* 48 (November/December 1970): 111-21.
2. Ibid.
3. Logan M. Cheek, "Xerox Learning Systems—Zero Base Budgeting Decision Card Exercise," 1977. Mimeographed.

# Chapter Five
# Follow-up Controls to the ZBB Process

Management involvement in the ZBB process can be summarized in six steps:

1. Planning and assessing organizational goals and objectives,
2. Identifying decision units,
3. Conducting decision-unit analysis and preparing decision packages,
4. Ranking decision packages,
5. Preparing final budget, and
6. Ongoing evaluation of results and performance control and auditing.

The first five steps have been discussed in previous chapters; this chapter is devoted to the discussion of step six. The budget control and audit essentially seek to find out whether the managers have delivered with the funded budget what they promised in the budget request. Auditing is not a new concept at all. In fact, various kinds of auditing are related to our daily activities. For example, a bank audit is a kind of financial audit to check whether one's bank account deposits, withdrawals, and balances have been accurately kept as reported. The kind of control and audit in the ZBB process is related to operational efficiency and effectiveness in terms of the jobs performed or benefits delivered. Since budgeting is not a one-time exercise but an ongoing process, one can look upon performance auditing and control as a check for the past year's spending and a preparation for the next year's new budget request.

## WHAT IS PERFORMANCE EVALUATION?

Performance evaluation is a management process which insures proper conduct and efficient delivery of services. It requires accountability for the utilization of an organization's resources. In conducting a performance evaluation, a manager seeks to do the following:

1. To verify the merits of the objectives of the program,
2. To determine the viability of the alternatives,
3. To determine the practicality of the approach taken,
4. To make sure that the program is cost-beneficial,
5. To provide necessary quantitative measures of performance, and
6. To assure that the proposed benefits are realistically delivered.

The evaluation assesses and reviews on the bases of services delivered and benefits provided. It reassesses the program objectives and audits the program performance in terms of effectiveness and efficiency measures. The process is conducted on a periodic cycle, usually at the end of a budgetary period. Frequently, intermediate performance evaluation is also conducted to prevent unhealthy spending of the budget and to insure that the program is heading in the right direction.

## WHERE SHOULD THE PERFORMANCE AUDIT START?

As ZBB starts from the basic decision units, so should the performance audit. In other words, each decision unit can be considered a performance unit. If the unit managers have conducted their ZBB process well by preparing excellent decision packages, they should find their follow-up budget control processes easy and constructive. As stated in earlier chapters, each decision package must clearly identify the goals and objectives of the program, determine all possible alternatives for achieving these objectives, select the most viable alternatives, provide performance measures for workloads, indicate potential benefits of the program if supported at the designated level, etc. If this information is clearly provided, particularly in measurable terms, the performance audit can simply seek to verify the viability of the program objectives, to assure that the selected alternative was the most cost-beneficial and realistic one, and to ascertain that the promised benefits were delivered in the way originally expected.

## WHO SHOULD BE INVOLVED IN PERFORMANCE CONTROL AND EVALUATION?

Theoretically, this should be the business of every program staff and manager, from bottom to top management. However, the size of an organization may dictate the makeup of the auditing team and the way the evaluation and control process is conducted. In a small organization, the auditing process may involve every manager in a rather cordial and informal way. On the other hand, in a large governmental or profit-making organization, the audit and control process can be formal and require a great deal of paperwork and reports, and most likely separate budget auditing staffs will work with unit and middle managers.

## HOW DOES THE PERFORMANCE AUDIT WORK?

ZBB provides two types of data for management review. They are the financial cost data and the workload and performance measurements.[1] Thus, the decision-unit managers are held responsible for both costs and performance through measurement and control. The audit process can start as soon as the detailed budget is prepared; and the financial and performance reviews can be taken at any desirable interval of time, whether monthly, quarterly, or semiannually.

The process can vary greatly in terms of complexity and work. In library situations, a relatively simple but effective audit can serve the purpose well. For the reader's convenience, a simple version of preparation instructions on performance evaluation in the State of Georgia is presented in Figure 5.1, and Georgia's performance evaluation data form is shown in Figure 5.2.

All performance control and audit processes involve some basic steps. Cheek and Austin outline them as follows:[2]

1. Preparing the audit requirements,
2. Establishing responsibilities,
3. Setting up a phased schedule,
4. Structuring the methodology and performance measures,
5. Conducting review,
6. Providing preliminary feedback, and
7. Presenting the final report.

We shall elaborate upon these major steps in the following:

1. *Plan the audit requirements well in advance.* Although the auditing process actually starts after the approval of the budget, plans and considerations should start from the very beginning of the ZBB process to ensure that the decision packages contain all the necessary information for both budgetary decision and control. A preplanned form, such as that of Figure 5.3, can be helpful.

2. *Assign auditing responsibilities.* In essence, the question, *Who should be responsible for what aspect of the control process?* should be answered. Although performance audit is every staff's responsibility, it is advisable to divide the auditing responsibilities in order to maximize staff effort.

3. *Set up an implementation schedule.* The timing of the follow-up audits should be scheduled as soon as the proposed budget is approved. Certain key packages should be selected for review, and the auditing schedule in the following year should indicate when the selected packages are to be audited. Generally, an organization does not have the time and staff to audit all packages, and a selection of five to ten percent of the total is quite sufficient. The number of packages audited would depend on the size of an organization. As to the evaluation schedule, Stonich and others[3] suggest the following:

- Monthly financial review of each decision unit and ranking unit. It is cost-based by comparing budget to actual expenditure.
- Quarterly output review of each decision unit and ranking unit. Various performance measures are used.
- Quarterly or periodical planning and budgeting revision for the decision units. Revisions should be made based on performance to date and environmental factors.

4. *Set up control mechanisms and performance evaluation criteria.* The evaluation mechanisms and methodologies employed by managers can vary greatly. Since each organization's objectives, programs, and activities are unique, each should set up its own evalua-

**FIGURE 5.1 State of Georgia Performance Evaluation Procedure**

PREPARATION AND SUBMISSION INSTRUCTIONS

FOR

FISCAL YEAR 1977 ANNUAL OPERATION BUDGET

PART II-PERFORMANCE EVALUATION

I.  INTENT AND PURPOSE—PART II

Performance Evaluation is the result of Governor Busbee's commitment to require accountability for the utilization of Georgia's fiscal resources in the delivery of services by State Government. Simply stated, Performance Evaluation is an attempt to establish an information system within State Government to assist the Agencies and the Governor in management and decision making. Performance Evaluation is application of the concept of ''Management by Objectives'' to State Government.

II.  GENERAL INFORMATION—PART II

The Performance Evaluation process will be conducted on an annual cycle and will involve the following steps:

A.  Identification of programs.

B.  Establishment of 'major' and 'limited' objectives for those programs.

C.  Identification of the effectiveness and efficiency measures as indicators of the degree to which limited objectives are being met.

D.  Quarterly reporting on the performance of each program in terms of effectiveness and efficiency measures.

E.  Annual evaluation of program performance, and reassessment of objectives and measures.

This approach to budget development and execution is relatively new to State Government. The first step was taken last year when Agencies were asked to submit objectives and effectivenes and efficiency measures for each program. That information will now be refined and used for quarterly program reporting during FY 1977. In addition, the development of FY 1978 budget requests will be initiated using the same concept. Specific instructions for the submission of FY 1978 budget requests will be published in mid-May.

III.  EXPLANATION OF TERMS—PART II

The following terms will be used in the Performance Evaluation process for work related to both FY 1977 and FY 1978:

Activity:                  An Activity is a major category by which funds are appropriated by the General Assembly.

Program:                   A Program is a major function below the Activity level for which there exists a purpose and objective(s) and where State cost data can be reported in total.

Program Purpose:           A clear and concise statement of why the Program or Activity is being conducted. The Program Purpose should help answer the question of whether the Program should exist.

**FIGURE 5.1 (Continued)**

| | |
|---|---|
| Major Objective(s): | The ultimate but realistic outcome expected from the Program expressed in measurable terms, assuming unlimited resources. To achieve a Major Objective, more than one budget year is generally required. (The Major Objective is not a statement of workload.) |
| Limited Objective(s): | The interim outcome expected, using the same measurable terms as used for the Major Objective, established in light of budget constraints in a given fiscal year. For example, given a level of appropriation, what results are expected from the Program during the applicable fiscal year. |
| Program Effectiveness Measure(s): | (Objective Accountability): Key indicators of the degree to which the Program achieves the Limited Objective. |
| Workload Efficiency Measure(s): | (Resource Accountability): Key indicators of the degree to which the Program economically manages the workload associated with meeting the Limited Objective. The measure usually will be expressed in terms of cost per unit of workload or output. |
| (Note) | Effectiveness and Efficiency Measure(s) should provide a method of monitoring the success of the Program in meeting its Limited Objective(s) in the given fiscal year. |

IV. FISCAL YEAR 1977—PART II

Prior to the beginning of FY 1977, State Agencies are requested to establish major objectives for each program, which will be used to establish the direction of future program efforts.

In addition, each Agency is requested to develop limited objectives for each program which are applicable only to the upcoming fiscal year. These limited objectives should be based on the actual amount appropriated for each program. Key effectiveness and efficiency measures also should be submitted as indicators of the extent to which each limited objective is being achieved.

The Office of Planning and Budget Form 10 is provided for use in submitting this information. These forms are due to this Office by June 1 (see sample). Particular attention should be paid to the Explanation of Terms included in these instructions to insure that the information developed is consistent with other programs and Agencies. Members of the Office of Planning and Budget (OPB) Divisions also are available to assist you in developing this information.

Following their submission, the major objectives, limited objectives and corresponding effectiveness and efficiency measures for FY 1977 will be reviewed by OPB and discussed with the agencies if there are any questions. They will be used during the upcoming fiscal year for quarterly reporting of program information in addition to fiscal information. Forms for quarterly program reporting will be issued at a later date.

**FIGURE 5.2   State of Georgia Performance Evaluation Data Form**

OPB ● Budget ● 10
FY 1977

ANNUAL OPERATING BUDGET
PERFORMANCE EVALUATION DATA

| Natural Resources | Environmental Protection | Water Quality |
|---|---|---|
| Department | Activity | Program (Function) |

1. Program Purpose:  To provide for the prevention and control of water pollution as provided by State and federal laws, rules and regulations in order to protect the health and safety of the public.

2. Major Objective(s):  To achieve zero-discharge of pollutants into the State's waters by the year 1985 as mandated by the 1972 Amendments to the Water Pollution Control Act.

3. Limited Objective(s)  (F Y 1977):  To place all sources of pollution on a schedule to achieve the major objective. To achieve Tertiary Treatment in 22% of the wastewater treatment facilities in the State. To achieve Secondary Treatment in 48%. To achieve "drinkable water" in 90% (18,000 miles) of the State's 20,000 miles of rivers.

4. Evaluation Measures:

|   | Actual FY 75 | Actual FY 76 | Expected FY 77 |
|---|---|---|---|
| A. Program Effectiveness Measures |   |   |   |
| 1. % sources on schedule for compliance | 40% | 72% | 100% |
| 2. % facilities with tertiary treatment | 9% | 16% | 22% |
| 3. % facilities with secondary treatment | 35% | 42% | 48% |
| 4. # miles of rivers in compliance with w/q standards | 16,000 | 16,500 | 18,000 |
| B. Workload Efficiency Measures |   |   |   |
| 1. Average cost of conversion from primary to secondary treatment | $2.5 mil | $2.1 mil | $1.8 mil |
| 2. Average cost per water sample taken and analyzed | $3.20 | $3.14 | $2.96 |
| 3. # samples taken per field technician | 480 | 480 | 480 |

**FIGURE 5.3  A Sample Performance Audit Plan**

| ORGANIZATION NAME | DEPARTMENT |
|---|---|
| PACKAGE NO./NAME | RANK |

INSTRUCTIONS:  At the end of each year's ZBB cycle, all approved packages will be subjected to performance review. As outlined in Library manual, Section_____, certain packages will be chosen for audit. Please complete this form for your package and return to the Library Director's Office.

POTENTIAL AREAS FOR AUDIT: (To be completed by unit head)

CHECK APPROPRIATE ONE:

| Reviewer | Time | Comment |
|---|---|---|
| Unit head_____ | Annual_____ | |
| Dept. head_____ | Semi-annual_____ | |
| Budget officer_____ | Quarterly_____ | |
| Assist. Direc._____ | Monthly_____ | |
| | Program completion date____ | |

COMPLETED BY:                               DATE:

tion criteria. In determining the type of measures or criteria they need, managers should consider carefully the nature of their program and the environment in which their programs and organizations operate, the use and application they will make of the criteria for their management purposes, the significance of the various aspects or components of the program, the susceptibility to managerial control, and other relevant factors.[4]

Figures 5.1 and 5.2 provide us with some simple but useful information on performance evaluation criteria. The Canadian government's guide to successful application of performance measurement has a helpful section on the uses and types of indicators required by managers. This section says:

> In selecting performance indicators, managers will be guided by their needs. Before choosing any indicator, they should consider the uses and application that will be made of it, and what the effect the choice will have on their focus. If it is not clear what information a particular indicator will be providing and how it might be used, then it is not worthwhile to proceed with the establishment of that indicator. One major obstacle to successful application of performance measurement has been the development of measures to meet the perceived program forecast needs of the. . . .
>
> Generally, managers will require indicators that will help them make decisions, better manage their programs, and answer the following types of questions:
>
> (a) To what extent are the intended results of the program being achieved?
> (b) To what extent are the various goods and services produced contributing to the achievement of the intended results?
> (c) Are the results being achieved as inexpensively as possible? Is the public getting value for their money? Is the program providing an adequate level of service at minimum cost?
> (d) Is the cost per unit of output (where this can be determined) of the program increasing, constant or decreasing, and why?
> (e) Do the goods and services conform to specifications? Is the quality of goods and services produced improving, constant or falling, and why?
> (f) How sensitive is the program to the needs of the public it serves? Is it adequately responding to these needs in terms of quality, timeliness, scope, and manner of delivery of its services?
>
> In addition to indicators that provide the means of answering the above questions, managers may require other indicators for control and planning purposes, such as:
>
> (a) Planned and actual resource allocation, utilization and percentage distribution by major activities, projects, tasks, overhead, etc.; for management control of resources.
> (b) Comparative performances of different locations or organizational components; for identifying causes of changes and differences in their performance and ultimately achieving performance improvement.
> (c) Comparative unit costs of the organization's goods and services and those of similar organizations in the private sector or other levels of government; for 'make or buy' decisions and performance improvement.
> (d) Cost ratios, e.g., overhead ratios; for monitoring and controlling resources devoted to administrative support functions or operations producing intangible goods and services, etc.
> (e) Factors which give rise to, or increase/decrease the amount of work; for planning and resourcing.
> (f) Factors considered in the assessment and selection of projects in the context of departmental priorities, objectives and available resources.
> (g) Project milestones and planned resources, actual target accomplishment, and slippages, etc.; for project management and control.
> (h) Project results compared against initial expectations; for making either 'further expenditure' or 'close down' decisions, and to complete fundamental project management accountability responsibilities.
> (i) Impact or contribution (positive and negative) of identifiable external factors to the accomplishment of a program objective.
> (j) Effects or impact of the program which are not intended or desired; the type of indicators mentioned here and in (i) will be useful for policy formulation or modification.
> (k) Other factors unique to programs as required by the manager.[5]

5. *Conduct the audit and review.* When the process is going on, emphasis should be placed on the essential components of the decision packages under review. For example, pick the programs which utilized a large portion of the organization's resources, and check on the items which seemed to be most costly. Similar tactics to those used by IRS auditors in auditing income tax returns can be adopted. However, it is essential to stress the importance of establishing a cordial and friendly rapport between the auditor and the decision-unit managers and staff. The success of the performance audit will rest partially on how much the decision-unit manager has confidence in the budget controller (or auditor) and how much s/he is willing to share pertinent information with him/her. In other words, if the auditor creates a role as the income tax auditor ('try to get you' image), it is likely that the whole review process can be unproductive and frustrating.

6. *Sum up findings.* Discuss the preliminary findings with decision-unit managers, solicit further discussion and modification, and prepare a report on findings and recommendations.

## SUMMARY

The performance audit is an essential part of the whole ZBB process. Library managers should keep in mind the factors which contribute to the success of the performance audit, as pointed out by Cheek and Austin:[6]

- Do not audit every decision package—be selective!
- Do not audit every element of a chosen package.
- Establish cordial and helpful relationships with staff members.
- Maximize opportunities for self-audit.
- Clearly delegate authority from the top.
- Give positive management support.
- Establish and plan the audit schedule early.
- Give clear guidelines and instructions.

## NOTES

1. Paul J. Stonich et al., *Zero-Base Planning and Budgeting: Improved Cost Control and Resource Allocation* (Homewood, IL:Dow-Jones-Irwin, 1977), p.30.
2. Logan M. Cheek and Allan Austin, *ZBB Handbook* (New York: AMACOM, 1980), ch. 5. Forthcoming. Supplied by the courtesy of Logan M. Cheek.
3. Stonich et al., *Zero-Base Planning and Budgeting*, p. 30.
4. Canada, Treasury Board, ''Performance Measurement: A Guide to Successful Application,'' 1978, pp. 11-2. Mimeographed. (Supplement to *A Manager's Guide to Performance Measurement*.)
5. Ibid., pp. 13-7.
6. Cheek and Austin, *ZBB Handbook*.

## REFERENCE

Cheek, Logan M. and Austin, Allan. *ZBB Handbook*. New York: AMA, 1980. Forthcoming.

# Chapter Six
# The Disadvantages and Advantages of ZBB

It is difficult to categorize clearly the disadvantages and advantages of ZBB. Some disadvantages or problems to a certain portion of the staff in the beginning of a budgeting planning process can be considered by the managers at the higher levels as potential benefits in the administrative process, and vice versa. Thus, readers are advised to evaluate critically all the items listed under *problems* and *benefits*. Conceivably, many of the problems listed can be easily overcome, and benefits could be potentially generated by some of the requirements considered problems.

## PROBLEMS

1. *ZBB is threatening.* ZBB is a relatively new budgeting system which had not been popularly accepted by organizations until President Carter's introduction of the system to government agencies. Generally, people are reluctant to accept new things and resistant to change. Furthermore, the very name of the budgeting system—*zero base*—is threatening to a large number of managers, particularly to those who are not familiar with the basic concept of ZBB. They cannot accept the idea that their organization has to start with a budget from zero base. It is important to stress again that ZBB *does not* necessarily propose a budget from zero base.

2. *ZBB is time-consuming.* ZBB is a complicated process. As outlined in Chapters Two through Five, it requires a great deal of staff time and effort, particularly in the beginning stages. Managers at all levels need to understand the system thoroughly; then they need to have thorough and efficient communication among themselves, and between them and their staff, through frequent staff meetings at all levels.

A great deal of time needs to be spent by all concerned during the ZBB process (see Chapters Three through Five); and a great deal of paperwork is required to prepare decision packages and their justifications. Naturally, the size of an organization is an important factor in determining the amount of time needed to complete a thorough ZBB process. It is not surprising to hear that library managers had to spend several months preparing a ZBB. It is probably a consolation that the amount of time and effort required for ZBB preparation generally decreases over time. After the first year the investment of time required decreases sharply and then flattens after a couple of years.

Time can be a big problem to many organizations, particularly when they are short staffed. However, if the management is interested in ZBB and is determined to go through a ZBB process, allowance must be made for this consideration.

3. *ZBB requires more paperwork.* As described in Chapter Three, various decision packages and appropriate justifications have to be prepared by decision-unit managers. These decision-unit managers are involved in the analysis and evaluation of activities and recommend operating improvements and budget allocations. Thus, an enormous amount of paperwork is required for this initial preparation and processing, so that the higher level manager can have sufficient information to make rational decisions on allocating resources intelligently to high-priority activities. This can potentially be a problem to many organizations when staff time is limited.

4. *ZBB requires a concerned management.* The ZBB process requires a total involvement of all managers at different levels. The total commitment of the management is the key to the successful implementation of a ZBB process. Generally, it is easier to locate support for a new system from staff and managers at the middle- and lower-management levels than at the

higher levels, because these managers are more eager to test new methods. In the case of ZBB, the process has also been supported by the top-level management who introduced its implementation to the organization. For example, President Carter was involved with the process when he was Governor of Georgia, and as President he has mandated that federal government agencies adopt the ZBB process. In this case, the successful implementation of this system in the federal government will depend greatly on whether the staff and managers at the lower echelon of the federal governmental structure are equally interested in and committed to the process. However, it is worth noting the relative importance of top-level support. These top-level administrators have the authority to make appropriate allowances for staff time and other factors affecting the implementation of ZBB. Because ZBB requires this kind of concerned management, it often becomes a difficult process to implement.

5. *ZBB requires well-conceived communication.* To present ZBB planning, the communication in the organization should be well conceived both vertically and horizontally. A series of meetings with decision-unit managers and the chief executive have to be arranged. All these are healthy processes badly needed in any organization; they have great potential to enhance staff morale and promote organizational dynamics. Nevertheless, communication has long been a problem in any organization. A situation generally cannot be changed overnight, and communication, above all, is a very slow process. Thus, ZBB becomes both a problem and a challenge to managers. Theoretically, concerned management and well-conceived communication among staff should be listed under 'advantages' rather than 'disadvantages'. However, most organizations find that these are highly desirable but difficult to obtain. Thus, they become factors which contribute to the failure of implementing ZBB.

6. *ZBB requires extensive training in its techniques.* Since ZBB is relatively new and most managers are not familiar with the process, it is imperative that they be well trained in the process. Besides the top executive's introduction, briefing, and group training sessions, individual training is highly recommended for managers at all levels and particularly for decision-unit managers. Each person's thinking process and working habits are different and could profit from individualized training, which offers a less threatening and individually paced alternative to group instruction. The instructor should be objective and, in most cases, an instructor from outside the manager's organization is less threat-

ening to the managers because no self-interest is involved. But, this approach is both time-consuming and costly.

7. *ZBB poses a psychological threat.* ZBB requires a new mode of operation and is a new alternative to existing budgeting systems. It poses a serious psychological threat, particularly to those managers who are not very secure in their positions. They are afraid that the new mode of operation may reflect that their prior performance was not efficient.

8. *ZBB requires work measures and evaluation data as well as analysis.* All of these requirements can be potentially difficult for those managers who are not familiar with scientific management. Many organizations have plenty of statistical data, but find it mostly unusable and/or incomplete. Furthermore, some of the work is more qualitative in nature than other work and, thus, it is difficult to measure quantitatively. In the very beginning of a ZBB process, many problems exist in this area. However, in the long run, this requirement is not only healthy, but essential, and is viewed by many as a potential benefit of the ZBB.

9. *ZBB's reviewing of decision packages presents a problem.* Decision packages are prepared by decision-unit managers, and then reviewed by general managers who set priorities and allocate limited funds and resources. This reviewing has frequently been difficult, because many high-level administrators may not have sufficient knowledge of ZBB or of the details of its operation within a particular department. This problem is closely related to the training problem mentioned earlier. A more serious problem is that top management is frequently not knowledgeable about specific tasks or needs of departments with which they are not directly working. Therefore, they may not be knowledgeable enough to appropriately coordinate activities across various departments. For example, a collection development package to spend X amount to purchase 10,000 books may be ranked highly, whereas a decision package from the cataloging department to catalog these 10,000 books may be ranked lowly and thus not funded.

10. *ZBB forces decisions and its prioritizing process is a political nightmare.* ZBB forces managers at all levels to evaluate their existing operations; prioritize alternatives in terms of levels of support; and make hard decisions on budgetary and resource allocations supporting both old and new operations, services, and programs. Theoretically speaking, if every manager were objective, unselfish, and willing to give up a certain area of responsibility in order to maximize the

efficiency of the total organization, there would be no problem. However, human nature does not work in this way. Most likely, each decision-unit manager will try to hold on to everything s/he has and, thus, evaluating *priority* or *required* packages can become a political nightmare.

## BENEFITS

Despite the problems discussed above, ZBB offers substantial benefits, such as the following:

1. *ZBB combines planning, budgeting, proposals, and operational decision making into one process.* Every stage of the process is essential and cannot be isolated or dropped. It is more than a means of control in budgeting. It is also a planning instrument, and the establishment of a financial planning phase is prior to budget preparation.

2. *ZBB gets more people to identify with the organization.* As more people in the organization are involved in the planning and budgetary functions of the organization, more identify with the organization. It makes "managers of all levels more knowledgeable about the role of their function within the overall organization and more cognizant of the basic interrelationship within the structure."[1] As Carter stated, it broadly expands "management participation and training in the planning, budgeting, and decision-making process."[2]

3. *ZBB improves communication within an organization.* It can be an invaluable "communication tool that improves decision-making and fosters innovation throughout the organization."[4] The process can be used to communicate ideas and legitimate needs from the lower echelon upward to the high-level management.

4. *ZBB examines all programs and activities, old and new.* It provides a method of making organization-wide reviews of programs and priorities more realistic.[4] It forces managers to analyze their departments, to rank their functions, and to establish priorities, thus providing a healthy and rational mechanism for managers to intellectually make changes in the budget. The process forces managers "to identify the inefficient or obsolete functions within their areas of responsibility"[5] for elimination without jeopardizing essential operations and activities.

5. *ZBB identifies every discretionary cost in an organization.* All expenditures are critically evaluated. Then, all operations in an organization are evaluated in great detail in terms of their cost-effectiveness and cost-benefits. Thus, the process forces managers to consider alternative methods of operation and leads to more efficient procedures. It also provides a system to trade off between long-term and short-term needs, as well as a follow-up tool on cost and performance during the year.[6]

6. *ZBB focuses the management process on analysis and decision making.* It provides answers to managerial questions related to what, why, and how issues.[7] In order to do this, the process generates a wealth of critical and analytical information and justification to aid top managers in making decisions.

7. *ZBB identifies similar functions among different departments for comparison and evaluation.* Thus, it enables managers to reduce duplication of effort among different units.

8. *ZBB is cost centered (more so than PBBS).* By establishing and justifying priorities for current and new programs, ZBB provides a sound basis for cost reductions and additions as determined by the new fiscal budget and by appropriate justifications. As long as it can be justified, it is possible to have a budget increase. During a period of extreme budgetary shortage, it enables the achievement of dramatic cost reduction without hurting any high-priority activities and programs.

9. *ZBB is a helpful tool for participative management.* It is a good training device to educate newer employees concerning the goals, objectives, operations, and functions of an organization. ZBB provides employers more opportunities to participate and to involve themselves in the budgeting process at the activity level. On the whole, it increases analysis and encourages better and more efficient internal communication; thus, it improves the quality of management.

10. *ZBB is flexible.* It is a tool that can be applied selectively. It does not have to be applied throughout the entire organization, or even throughout all of the service departments. The managers can select those areas of highest concern in which to implement ZBB. "Likewise, it can be limited to the time, money, and people who are available to install, monitor, and operate it."[8]

## USERS' EVALUATION OF ZBB

The above-mentioned concerns and benefits of the ZBB process seem to have been clearly shared by users of ZBB. Of the questionnaire survey conducted of the

1,000 Fortune companies, 113 responded. Of these respondents, 54 organizations used ZBB and 59 did not. Of those who used the process, only 9 percent of the decision-unit managers felt that ZBB was of no value to them; about 5 percent were undecided; and 86 percent, the overwhelming majority, acknowledged the value of ZBB. As reported by Stonich et al.,[9] the expressed users' concerns about the process and the advantages of the approach can be categorized as follows:

*Concerns*
- Top management commitment is vital.
- Process is time-consuming.
- Cost-cutting feature should not be overplayed.
- Effective staff work is needed.
- Process is not panacea.
- Process must be carefully planned and developed.

*Advantages*
- Costs can be cut.
- Resources can be reallocated.
- Contingency planning can be made (see Glossary).
- Alternative method of operation can be implemented.
- Employees learn about the organization.
- Thought is stimulated.
- Communication is increased.

These users' evaluations of ZBB provide some very interesting insights into the system. Consistently, the majority of the decision-unit managers ranked the following as the most essential benefits derived from the process:

- Identification of activities and cost,
- More explicit and careful planning by unit managers,
- Clarification of goals and objectives, and
- More informed decision making.

Interestingly, justification for additional funding came next after the above four.

It is also interesting to note that despite the problems previously discussed, one quarter of the respondents, according to Stonich et al.,[10] expressed no difficulty with the process. Similar survey results were reported in another recent study of the American Management Association.[11] While 6 percent of the respondents felt that ZBB was of little value to them, about 94 percent of them agreed that the process achieved its purpose (25 percent *extremely well*, 43 percent *very well*, and 26 percent *fairly well*). The purposes for using ZBB were responded as follows:

| | |
|---|---|
| Better resource allocation | 30% |
| Improved decision making | 25% |
| Better management planning | 20% |
| Cost and staff reduction | 12% |
| Other | 13% |
| | 100% |

This latest survey brings to light a most encouraging fact: ZBB has come to be valued primarily as an excellent management tool rather than a cost reduction technique. Cost reduction is only a distant objective for implementing ZBB. Appropriately, ZBB is a tool which can help answer the questions, *What is the reason for our organization's being? Why we are there and what it is we are supporting?* ZBB also provides a forum in which employees' contributions to their organizations' objectives can be rationalized, understood, accepted or rejected, or modified.

Of all the users' evaluations of ZBB, the most negative and damaging responses have come from federal government agencies. Although a few did feel ZBB to be helpful and some were neutral, others condemned it as a fruitless drain on resources and some were literally hostile, such as several administrators from the National Institutes of Health (NIH).[12] Yet, according to Herzlinger, who evaluated the NIH's implementation of ZBB through an extensive series of interviews, ZBB is a process which can yield substantial benefits if properly implemented. The failure at the federal government agency is mainly due to technical and managerial problems. Some of these problems are: the size of the federal organization, the size of decision units, the imposition of uniform guidelines on funding levels of the decision units in creating decision packages, the ranking process in a political environment, the impossible timetable to be followed, the limitation of work force for ZBB, the lack of adequate training, and absence of motivation for cooperation among federal government staff.

## SUMMARY

Keeping in mind the discussions on the concerns and benefits of ZBB, it is encouraging to note the analyses of some of the most recent implementations have given high marks to areas that originally were considered by managers as by-products of the process.

If the technical and managerial problems discussed are appropriately addressed and avoided, ZBB can be a useful management planning tool in libraries. It can also be a much-welcomed process of alternatives for library administrators, an effective resource allocation tool, and a tool for learning more about one's library.

## NOTES

1. James F. McGinnis, "Pluses and Minuses of Zero-Base Budgeting," *Administrative Management* 37 (September 1976): 22-3.

2. Jimmy E. Carter, "Jimmy Carter Tells Why He Will Use Zero-Base Budgeting," *Nations Business* 65 (January 1977): 24-6.

3. Logan M. Cheek, "Zero-Base Budgeting in the Federal Government: A Performance Audit of the First Year," Summary of talk to Federal ADP User's Group, Washington, DC, October 20, 1977, p. 4.

4. James D. Suver and Ray L. Brown, "Where Does Zero-Base Budgeting Work?" *Harvard Business Review* 55 (November-December 1977): 76-84.

5. McGinnis, "Pluses and Minuses of Zero-Base Budgeting."

6. Carter, "Why He Will Use Zero-Base Budgeting."

7. Ibid.

8. Suver and Brown, "Where Does Zero-Base Budgeting Work?" p. 82.

9. Paul J. Stonich et al., *Zero-Base Planning and Budgeting: Improved Cost Control and Resource Allocation* (Homewood, IL: Dow-Jones-Irwin, 1977), pp. 12-6, 93-4.

10. Stonich et al., *Zero-Base Planning and Budgeting*, pp. 15-6.

11. L. Allan Austin, *Zero-Base Budgeting: Organizational Impact and Effects* (New York: AMACOM, 1977), p. 15.

12. Regina E. Herzlinger, "Zero-Base Budgeting in the Federal Government: A Case Study," *Sloan Management* (Winter 1979), pp. 3-14.

# Chapter Seven
# Managing ZBB and Its Implications for Library Managers

John Carroll, a former consultant of Arthur D. Little, Inc. (ADL), in his talk on "Zero-Base Budgeting Case Study in a Non-Library Setting"[1] at a ZBB institute at Simmons College, described in great detail the process of applying ZBB in a high technology engineering environment. Although not all the examples and steps are applicable to library situations, the principles of Arthur D. Little's approach should be of interest to library managers.

Figure 7.1 is an overview of a system presented by Carroll. It starts with corporate strategy, and goes to business unit strategy to budgeting planning and finally to accounting and control. Carroll stated that the principles of ADL's approach are as follows:

1. *Develop corporate strategy*. Strategy is defined as the macro perception, or perception in a general and broad sense, of a corporation's organizational behavior. Thus, corporate strategy deals with factors such as entity, growth/renewal, financial, managerial systems, and external relationships.

2. *Plan around business units*. A corporation is built up of numerous building blocks, known as business units. In order to understand a corporation's behavior, it is essential to understand the behavior of each business unit through the use of a technique called *profiling*. Profiling will identify the strategic business units that are independent with regard to price, quality, customers, conditions, and divestment. It will study the environment of the business unit through situation analysis on growth factors, competitors, barriers to entry, and critical success factors. It will also present a unit's characteristics by studying its constraints in relation to its maturity/competitive position, as shown in Figure 7.2.

3. *Invest in strategies*. Strategic development will involve the classification of each action or program by its requirements, probable consequences, and risk; the study of its natural period of strategy execution, as shown in Figure 7.3; and the exploration of strategic options, as illustrated in Figure 7.4.

4. *Manage and deploy resources to achieve strategic objectives*. One uses what Carroll called *implementation analysis* to identify each program and resource by function, resource requirements, and milestones.

5. *Judge managerial performance against strategy*. Develop selected indicators to measure strategic performance, as shown in Figure 7.5.

6. *Order interfunctional commitments against strategies at all levels*. An organization is an interrelated set of functions; thus, one has to thread all the way through the organization to ensure that the commitments against strategies exist at all related levels.

7. *Improve communications both vertically and laterally*.

In summarizing ADL's ZBB approach, Carroll clearly pointed out the following:

- Budget can only be described in terms of business actions, i.e, strategy.
- Business actions can only be postulated by recognition of constraints, i.e., maturity/competitive position.
- Spending supports strategic action,
    No spending/no action
    No action/no spending.
- Functional spending programs must be synchronized.
- Level of effort and spending are determined by what has to be accomplished and how difficult that task is.

Thus, the budget decision is made and coordinated in relation to corporate strategy.

## FIGURE 7.1 Overview of System

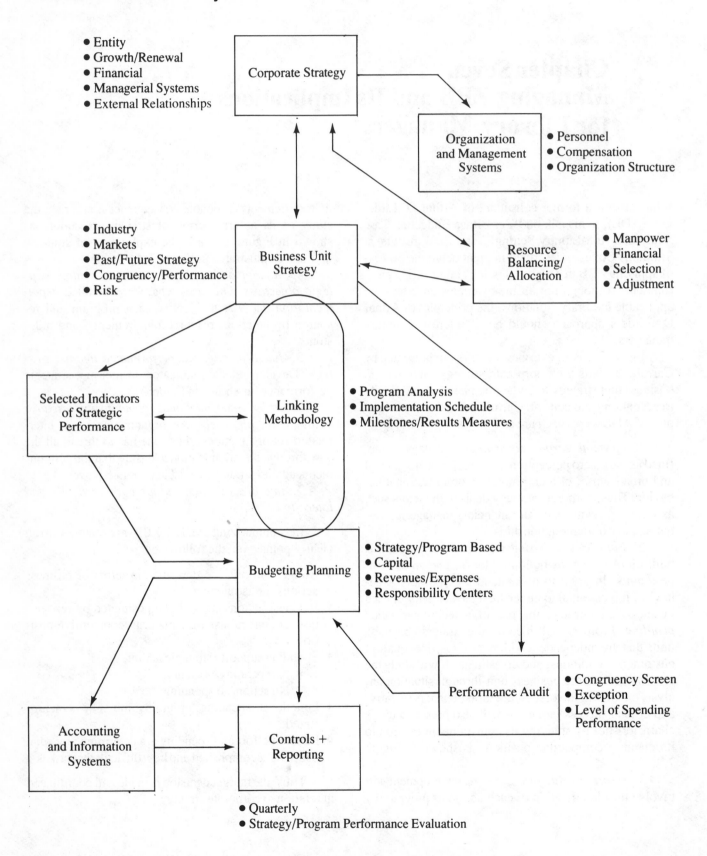

- Entity
- Growth/Renewal
- Financial
- Managerial Systems
- External Relationships

Corporate Strategy

Organization and Management Systems
- Personnel
- Compensation
- Organization Structure

- Industry
- Markets
- Past/Future Strategy
- Congruency/Performance
- Risk

Business Unit Strategy

Resource Balancing/ Allocation
- Manpower
- Financial
- Selection
- Adjustment

Selected Indicators of Strategic Performance

Linking Methodology

- Program Analysis
- Implementation Schedule
- Milestones/Results Measures

Budgeting Planning
- Strategy/Program Based
- Capital
- Revenues/Expenses
- Responsibility Centers

Performance Audit
- Congruency Screen
- Exception
- Level of Spending Performance

Accounting and Information Systems

Controls + Reporting

- Quarterly
- Strategy/Program Performance Evaluation

**FIGURE 7.2 Present Unit Character**

UNIT _____

ASSETS _____
SALES _____
PROFITS _____

PCT. OF CORPORATE ASSETS _____
PCT. OF CORPORATE SALES _____
PCT. OF CORPORATE PROFITS _____

|  | EMBRYONIC | GROWTH | MATURE | AGING |
|---|---|---|---|---|
| Dominant |  |  |  |  |
| Strong |  |  |  |  |
| Favorable |  |  |  |  |
| Tenable |  |  |  |  |
| Weak |  |  |  |  |

● No Change        ◄─────── Change in Maturity or Competitive Position
∧ Increase Sales
∨ Decrease Sales

10/25/76

Arthur D. Little, Inc.

**FIGURE 7.3 Natural Period of Strategy Execution  (of Business Units of a Corporation)**

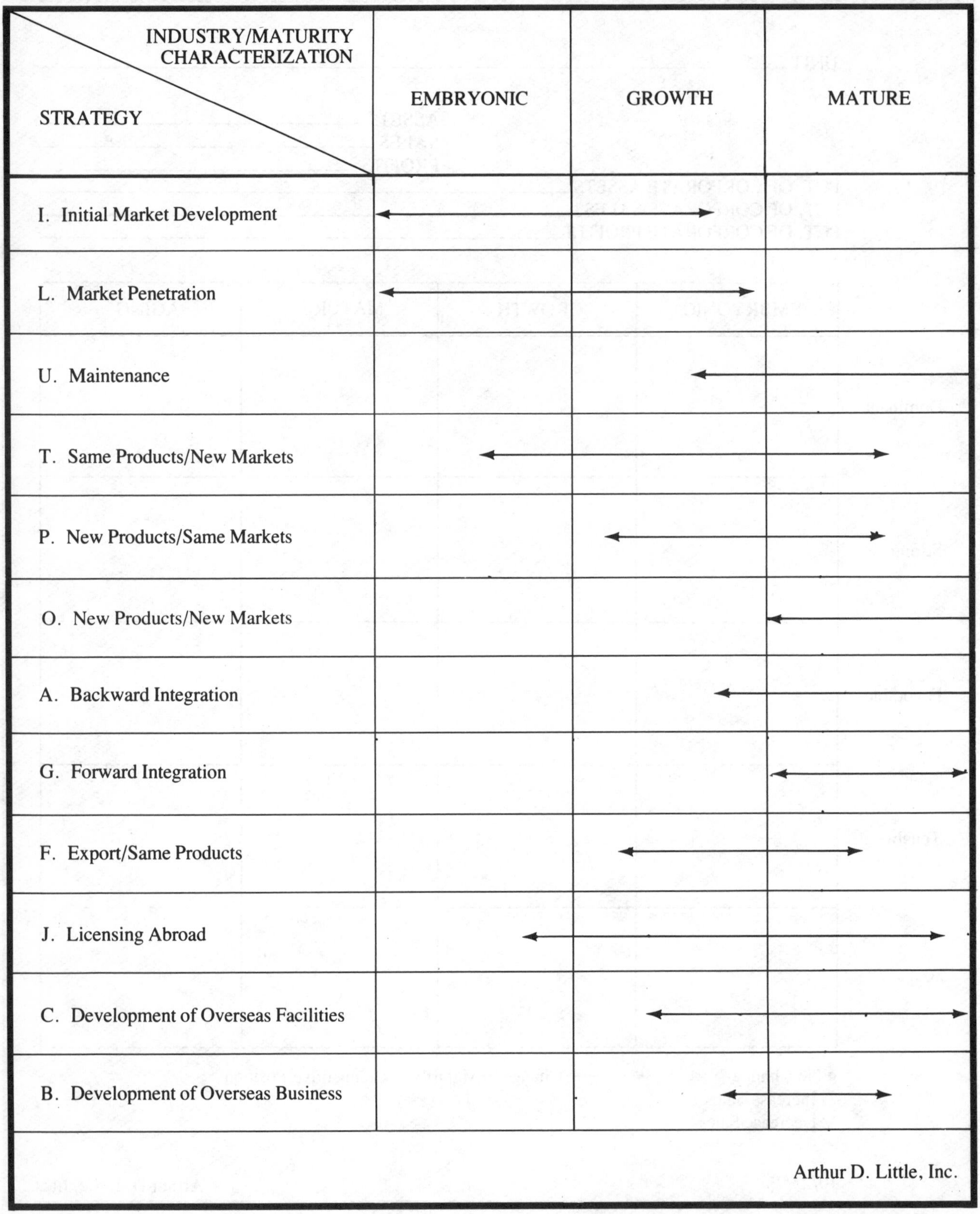

| INDUSTRY/MATURITY CHARACTERIZATION  /  STRATEGY | EMBRYONIC | GROWTH | MATURE |
|---|---|---|---|
| I.  Initial Market Development | ←———————— | ————————→ | |
| L.  Market Penetration | ←——————————— | ——————————→ | |
| U.  Maintenance | | ←——————— | |
| T.  Same Products/New Markets | ←——— | ——————————————— | ——————→ |
| P.  New Products/Same Markets | | ←——————— | ——————→ |
| O.  New Products/New Markets | | | ←——————— |
| A.  Backward Integration | | ←——— | |
| G.  Forward Integration | | | ←————————→ |
| F.  Export/Same Products | | ←——————— | ——————→ |
| J.  Licensing Abroad | | ←——————— | ———————————→ |
| C.  Development of Overseas Facilities | | ←——————— | ———————————→ |
| B.  Development of Overseas Business | | ←——————— | ——————→ |

Arthur D. Little, Inc.

**FIGURE 7.4 Strategic Options**

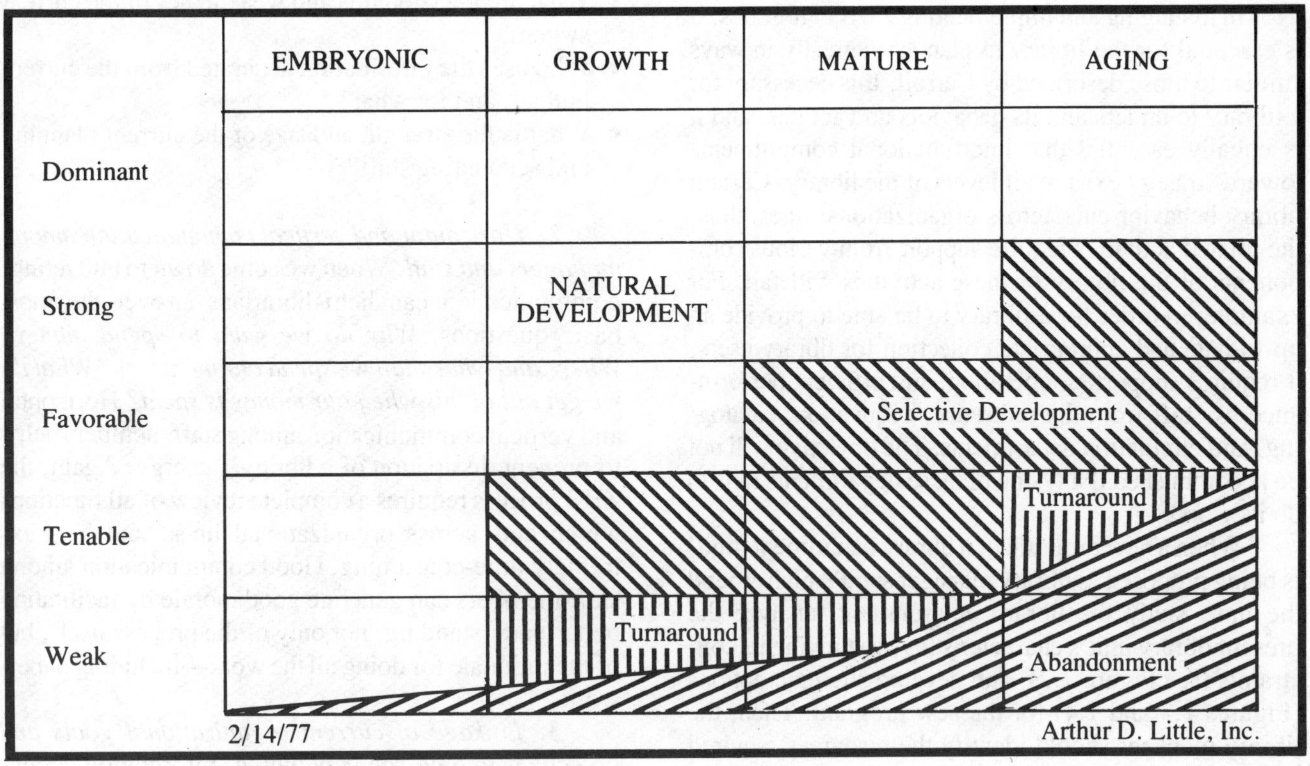

| | EMBRYONIC | GROWTH | MATURE | AGING |
|---|---|---|---|---|
| Dominant | | | | |
| Strong | | NATURAL DEVELOPMENT | | |
| Favorable | | | Selective Development | |
| Tenable | | Turnaround | | Turnaround |
| Weak | | Turnaround | | Abandonment |

2/14/77 — Arthur D. Little, Inc.

**FIGURE 7.5 Selected Indicators of Strategic Performance**

| STRATEGIES \ MEASURES | 1. Sales Volume ($) | 2. Sales Volume (Units) | 3. Market Share % | 4. Sales of Product New Since ___ | 5. New Product Development Expenditure as % Sales | 6. Days Slippage New Product Program | 7. Number of Customers | 8. Number Customers Added Since ___ | 9. Sales to Customers Who Were New Since ___ | 10. Number Companies Using Product | 11. Sales and Marketing |
|---|---|---|---|---|---|---|---|---|---|---|---|
| I. Initial Market Development | | | | | | | | | | | |
| L. Market Penetration | | | | | | | | | | | |
| U. Same Products/Same Market | | | | | | | | | | | |
| T. Same Products/New Markets | | | | | | | | | | | |
| P. New Products/Same Market | | | | | | | | | | | |
| O. New Products/New Markets | | | | | | | | | | | |

## LIBRARY STRATEGY PLAN

In managing and implementing ZBB in libraries, it is essential for the library to plan strategically in ways similar to those described by Carroll. It is necessary for a library to understand its behaviors and actions, and it is equally essential that interfunctional commitments toward strategy exist at all levels of the library. Certain library behavior cuts across organizational lines; thus, the related activities require support from various components of the library or these activities will fail. For example, in order for a library to be able to provide an up-to-date and appropriate collection for library users, it requires support, cooperation, and efficient performance by staff from the reference, acquisition, cataloging, and circulation departments. The objective will not be accomplished if any one of these departments fails to do its work.

When a new program of a library department (unit) is being proposed, a library manager should plan around the unit, study the library environment, analyze the present library unit's characteristics by studying its constraints (see Figure 7.2), and develop strategic options (Figures 7.3 and 7.4) for the new program. Then, the library manager should identify the resources required to achieve strategic objectives and make sure that appropriate interfunctional commitments exist at all related levels of the library.

## KEY FACTORS FOR SUCCESSFUL ZBB

Numerous factors are essential to the library's successful implementation of ZBB. They include the following major ones:

1. *Thorough knowledge of the organization.* As stated earlier in this chapter, a thorough knowledge of the organization is essential to develop an organizational strategy. Similarly, the library managers must carefully weigh questions such as the following:

- What are the characteristics of the library?
- What are the library's objectives? Who uses the library's services?
- What are the well-conceived programs and activities of the library?
- Who supports the library and for what?
- What is the library organizational structure, specifically in terms of profit centers and cost centers?

- What are the existing accounting structure and budget process?
- What are the strengths and weaknesses of the current system?
- Who uses the information generated from the current budget, and for what?
- What is the strength and size of the current planning and accounting staff?

2. *Horizontal and vertical communication among managers and staff.* When we come down to budgeting, communication can help librarians answer the most basic questions, *Why do we want to spend money? Where and what shall we spend our money on? What do we get out of this when our money is spent?* Horizontal and vertical communication among staff members helps to prevent dissipation of a library's energy. Again, the ZBB process requires a complete review of all functions which cuts across organizational lines, and it is extremely time-consuming. Good communication among staff members can generate good morale by facilitating better understanding, not only of the process itself, but of the rationale for doing all the work—including paperwork.

3. *Linkage of current organizational goals and objectives to long-range planning.* Information obtained from the thorough self-examination of the library, such as the identification of goals and objectives and inventory of current activities, will provide a sound basis for long-range library planning. In fact, this is one of the major benefits of ZBB.

4. *Definite need to implement ZBB.* Given the limitations and potential benefits of the ZBB process as discussed in Chapter Six, a library's need to adopt ZBB over other budgeting systems has to be compelling. This need can be determined by numerous factors, such as a potential budget cut or the demand for strenuous accountability. Whatever the cause, the need must be shared by all managers. For example, when the need for implementing ZBB is clear at the top-management level but is not shared at the subordinate levels, the success of ZBB implementation will be jeopardized. This is the case in some current government situations.

5. *Systematic and well-developed procedures.* ZBB should be designed to meet the specific needs and characteristics of a library. Although the basic steps are relatively simple, as discussed in Chapters Two through Five, the procedures can vary greatly depending on the complexity of the library's organizational structure. This is evident from the seven library examples presented in Part II. Nevertheless, these procedures should

be systematic, be stated as clearly as possible, and should consider questions such as the following:

- Should the ZBB process be accepted on a trial basis in the first year?

- Should ZBB be introduced to a small part of the organization first, or should it be implemented across the board?

- What should be the implementing guidelines, schedule, format, and instructions?

- What are the decision units in a department or division? What are the guidelines in terms of number of staff, budget, amount, etc.?

- What types of analyses should be emphasized?

- What forms should be used to prepare the decision packages and to facilitate their ranking?

- Do the forms include all items needed for budgetary consideration of the organization?

- How should the process be conducted? Who should be involved?

- What is the appropriate role of a computer?

- What kinds of data are necessary for various performance evaluations?

From the above illustrative questions, it is clear that a simple, straightforward ZBB manual which is tailored to the library's needs and structure will be extremely helpful, particularly when sample packages and illustrations are provided. Several sample manuals for different types of libraries can be found in Examples Two, Four, and Seven of Part II.

During the phase of designing procedures to meet the organization's needs, a ZBB expert's services can be potentially useful. A consultant's experience and knowledge of the process can save the organization a substantial amount of time and effort. In library situations, a consultant's knowledge of library operations and services is an important determining factor in assessing his/her services.

6. *Extensive training opportunities.* ZBB can be very confusing in the beginning to those managers who have had little knowledge of or exposure to the process. Thus, initial training of all managers, particularly decision-unit managers, is imperative. This training can be provided through different formats, such as short-term, intensive courses or workshops. Adequate follow-up training and assistance should be provided

whenever necessary by the organization's budget officer and supervisors so that the ZBB process can be implemented consistently and smoothly. Accurate, concise, and easy-to-follow manuals can also help. ZBB is a process which involves managers on every level. Thus, all managers should be familiar with the process.

7. *Strong management involvement and commitment.* Most ZBB experts have advocated the importance of senior management commitment, particularly in profit-making organizations where top managers are too busy to concern themselves with the budgeting process. However, middle- and lower-level (basic unit) managers' endorsement, support, and close involvement are equally important. The latter is particularly needed in the federal government, since the endorsement of President Carter has made ZBB the budgetary system for many federal departments and agencies and many state and local government agencies, as well. In these cases, the top manager's commitment is clear, but the middle- and lower-level managers are sometimes skeptical of the process.

8. *Adequate time allocation to implement ZBB.* ZBB is a time-consuming process, particularly in the first year. The size and complexity of an organization are key factors which determine the amount of time needed to design and implement ZBB in a given environment. It is not unusual to hear that unit managers spend one man-year or more to implement ZBB. Thus, it is imperative that an adequate amount of time and staff be allocated to insure that the procedures are systematically and carefully planned, key issues and problems are thoroughly analyzed, sufficient amounts of data for various analysis purposes are collected, etc. The time required for ZBB can vary greatly depending on an organization's size, budget, and scope of activity.

To ensure the smooth planning and implementation of ZBB during the entire budgeting process, library managers may find preplanned calendars of events, such as those in Example Four of Part II, helpful.

9. *Human factor considerations.* ZBB, as alluded to in previous chapters, is sometimes threatening. It is generally true that there is a natural resistance to something new. Thus, one must find innovative ways to *sell* the new approach if one believes in it. In selling ZBB, one should be honest in pointing out that it is no panacea for all previous budgeting and planning ills. It unquestionably has limitations, but its benefits can outweigh its problems. It is important to make the library managers comfortable with the process and excited about its potentials.

## SUMMARY

Keeping these factors in mind, ZBB experts have also suggested setting up a task force to administer and implement the process. The task force should be made up of both operating and financial managers of an organization, and it should report to the chief executive officer (who has the direct authority given by the head of the organization) on all matters related to the ZBB process.

Librarians should keep in mind that in most cases they probably do not have the privilege to select a budget system for their library. They have to adopt whatever system is used by the parent organization. Thus, if the parent organization implements ZBB, most likely it will also be used in the library. In this case, library managers are well advised to keep in mind all the factors influencing the successful implementation of ZBB as discussed above. They can make up, if they wish, a long list of do's and don't's in order to assure the smooth start of ZBB. I hope that these librarians will know how to 'make a virtue of necessity'. To further facilitate their preparation for the process, extensive illustrative decision packages actually prepared by managers of various types of libraries — large and small, academic, special, state and federal government, etc. — are included in Part II. While no judgment is given on the quality of these decision packages, they are presented for the following purposes:

- To provide actual examples,
- To demonstrate the mechanics of the ZBB process,
- To show the variety of formats used in preparing ZBB, and
- To stimulate ideas in designing new forms.

We have cautioned the reader about the need to design ZBB procedures for an organization's own needs. Every library, with its unique needs, requirements, and programs should develop its own ZBB procedures.

A few final words seem appropriate for those library managers whose parent organizations are not adopting ZBB. As pointed out in this book, ZBB can be used as a planning tool; thus, library managers can use this tool to strengthen their planning and preparation for any budgeting system with increased and improved justification, accountability, and productivity. A manager should learn to build upon the strength of other systems. In almost all environments, and particularly in a tight economic situation, the library is likely to be a low-priority item in the minds of administrators. Thus, library managers should welcome any approach which can help them to demonstrate more convincingly the value, importance, and promise of libraries and library services.

Library literature is full of criticisms made by both library and nonlibrary professionals regarding libraries' loss of sight of their purposes and functions, inability to identify and evaluate alternatives, insensitivity to cost-beneficial considerations, unwillingness to account for their performance, reluctance to prioritize their programs and functions, and many others. The economic reality is such that either the library managers will wake up from the ideological illusions, such as 'the library is a must for everyone', and run their libraries like any other organizational entity which is struggling for survival, or they will suffer the financial defeats which are properly due them. A process such as ZBB can, therefore, be a useful tool.

## NOTES

1. John Carroll, ''Zero-Base Budgeting Case Study in a Non-Library Setting'' (Paper presented at the Institute on Zero-Base Budgeting in Library Management, School of Library Science, Simmons College, March 31-April 1, 1978).
2. Ibid.

# PART II
# LIBRARY ZBB EXAMPLES

# Example One
# Department of Fisheries and Environment of Canada Library, Ottawa, Canada

## Background Information

The Canadian Federal Government is composed of about 50 departments, of which the Department of Fisheries and Environment is one. The Department is made up of five programs:

> Administration
> Fisheries and Marine
> Environmental Management
> Atmospheric Environment
> Environmental Protection

The Department is highly decentralized and two-thirds of departmental staff is located in the regions. The library service reflects the overall departmental organization. Most of the research libraries are attached to institutes and laboratories with a library headquarters coordinating the activities of the network.

The Departmental Library in Headquarters is in the Administration Program and services all headquarters' staff directly and regional users indirectly. More than 50 regional libraries across Canada report to the Director of the research activity in the region and have functional direction from the Departmental Library.

## Librarian's Comment on ZBB Experience

The A-Base Review of Canadian Federal Governmental departments first started late in the spring of 1977 with the voluntary participation of the Department of Fisheries and Environment. The review of the library began in early June 1977 with a three-week time frame in which to gather data, document the library's work program, and make a presentation to the Director General responsible for library operations. Mrs. A. M. Bystrom, Director of Library Services, indicated that the main difficulty was to develop an approach to appropriately present the library operations to the task force and senior management of the Department. She chose not to adopt the traditional approach by dividing the library operations into acquisitions, cataloging, circulation, reference, etc. Instead, she presented four isolated jobs:"

Job 1 Provision of library services to users in the National Capital Area.

Job 2 Provision of "backup" services to libraries in regions.

Job 3 Coordination and network function (includes systems).

Job 4 Purchasing materials for nonlibrary retention (i.e., office use).

Mrs. Bystrom reported that the review process provided her with a unique opportunity to understand and to document her library operations better and from a different perspective.

## Sample Forms Used by Fisheries and Environment, Canada

Material on Zero A-Base Review
Department of the Environment, Canada

DEPARTMENT_____FISCAL 19___ BUDGET

<u>BUDGET PACKAGE INDEX</u>

Branch/Directorate/Service_____ Date_____

|  | Number of Pages | Page Number |
|---|---|---|

<u>Form Description</u>

1. Statement of mission, role or mandate

2. Statement of fiscal 19___ objectives

3. Organization chart

4. Management job description

5. Cross impact analysis

6. Decision package

7. Decision package ranking

8. Expenditure summary

9. Expenditure explanation

10. Monthly expenditure

11. Salary schedule

12. Capital expenditure schedule

13. Expenditure comment



This budget package
was prepared by:    _____


Title:    _____

DEPARTMENT_____FISCAL 19__ BUDGET                    1

STATEMENT OF MISSION, ROLE OR MANDATE

Branch/Directorate/Service_____Date_____

DEPARTMENT_____FISCAL 19__ BUDGET     2

STATEMENT OF FISCAL 19   OBJECTIVES

Branch/Directorate/Service_____Date_____

3

DEPARTMENT_____FISCAL 19__ BUDGET

ORGANIZATION CHART

Branch/Directorate/Service_____Date_____

DEPARTMENT_____ 4

## MANAGEMENT JOB DESCRIPTION

| Branch | Directorate | Service |
|---|---|---|

| Job Title: | Posts Supervised: |
|---|---|
| Reports To: | |

Basic Functions:

Major Duties:

DEPARTMENT_____FISCAL 19__ BUDGET    5a

CROSS IMPACT ADVICE (TO SUPPLIERS)

*

TO:         Branch:

            Manager:

            Location:

FROM:       Branch:

            Manager:

            Location:

In the preparation of our fiscal 19__ budget, we have identified your organization as a supplier of services to us in that year.  A brief description of the services we expect to receive is presented below.  Please advise if these data are not correct.

DEPARTMENT_____FISCAL 19__ BUDGET

<u>CROSS IMPACT ADVICE (TO RECEIVERS)</u>

TO:          Branch:

             Manager:

             Location:

FROM:        Branch:

             Manager:

             Location:

In the preparation of our fiscal 19__ budget, we have
identified your organization as a receiver of our services
in that year.  A brief description of the services we
intend to provide is presented below.  Please advise if
these data are not correct.

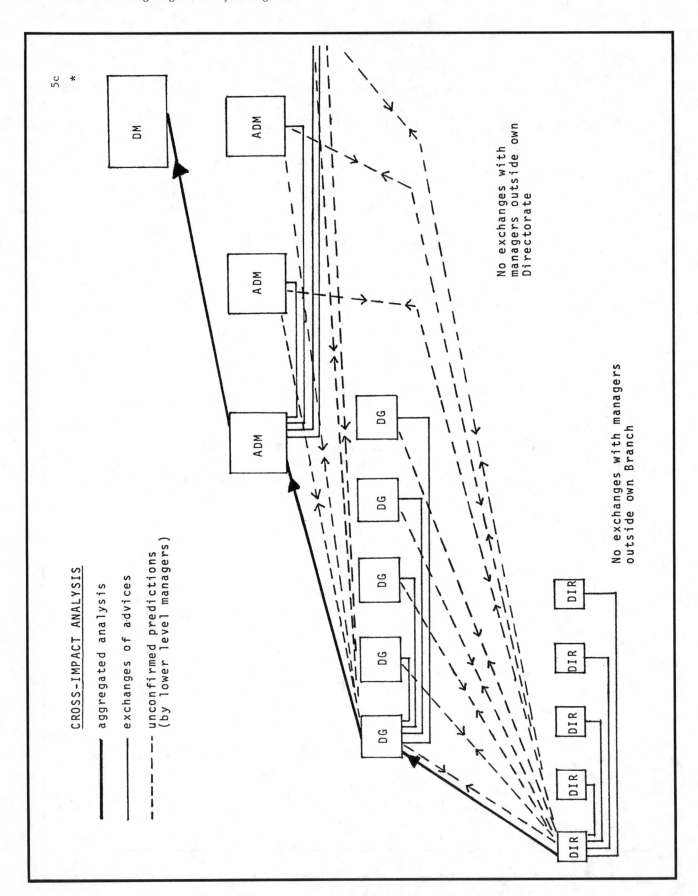

DEPARTMENT_____FISCAL 19__ BUDGET          5d

CROSS IMPACT ANALYSIS

Branch/Directorate/Service_____Date_____

| Activities | | | | | | | | | | | | | | | | |
|---|---|---|---|---|---|---|---|---|---|---|---|---|---|---|---|---|
| Receivers | | | | | | | | | | | | | | | | |
| | | | | | | | | | | | | | | | | |
| | | | | | | | | | | | | | | | | |
| | | | | | | | | | | | | | | | | |
| | | | | | | | | | | | | | | | | |
| | | | | | | | | | | | | | | | | |
| | | | | | | | | | | | | | | | | |
| | | | | | | | | | | | | | | | | |
| | | | | | | | | | | | | | | | | |
| | | | | | | | | | | | | | | | | |
| | | | | | | | | | | | | | | | | |
| | | | | | | | | | | | | | | | | |
| | | | | | | | | | | | | | | | | |
| | | | | | | | | | | | | | | | | |
| | | | | | | | | | | | | | | | | |
| | | | | | | | | | | | | | | | | |
| | | | | | | | | | | | | | | | | |
| | | | | | | | | | | | | | | | | |
| | | | | | | | | | | | | | | | | |
| | | | | | | | | | | | | | | | | |

DEPARTMENT_____FISCAL 19__ BUDGET        6a

DECISION PACKAGE

Branch/Directorate/Service_____Date_____

| Package Name: | _____of_____ |
| --- | --- |
| | organization |

Statement of Purpose:

| Fiscal 19__  Personnel Breakdown($000) | 1st Qtr | 2nd Qtr | 3rd Qtr | 4th Qtr | 19__ Budget | 19__ Budget |
| --- | --- | --- | --- | --- | --- | --- |
| Personnel (MY) Salaries | | | | | | |
| Total Expenses | | | | | | |

| Fiscal 19__  O&M Breakdown ($000) | 1st Qtr | 2nd Qtr | 3rd Qtr | 4th Qtr | 19__ Budget | 19__ Budget |
| --- | --- | --- | --- | --- | --- | --- |
| Travel Other Trans. and Communication Professional and Special Services Repairs and Upkeep Materiel and Supplies | | | | | | |
| Total Expenses | | | | | | |

| Fiscal 19__  Capital Breakdown ($000) | 1st Qtr | 2nd Qtr | 3rd Qtr | 4th Qtr | 19__ Budget | 19__ Budget |
| --- | --- | --- | --- | --- | --- | --- |
| | | | | | | |
| Total Capital Expenditure | | | | | | |

DEPARTMENT_____FISCAL 19__ BUDGET

6b

DECISION PACKAGE

Branch/Directorate/Service_____Date_____

Benefits:

Receivers:

Consequences of Not Approving Package:

Consequences of Approving 1/3 of Package Expenditure:

Consequences of Approving 2/3 of Package Expenditure:

Alternatives Considered:

DEPARTMENT_____FISCAL 19__ BUDGET

DECISION PACKAGE RANKING

Branch/Directorate/Service_____ Date_____

| R A N K | Package Name | 19__ | | | 19__ | | |
|---|---|---|---|---|---|---|---|
| | | MYs | Expense Budget ($000) | Cap. Expend. Budget ($000) | MYs | Expense Budget ($000) | Cap. Expend Budget ($000) |
| | | | | | | | |
| | TOTAL | | | | | | |

DEPARTMENT_____FISCAL 19___ BUDGET    8

EXPENDITURE SUMMARY

Activity_____Date_____

| | 19__ Budget ($000) | 19__ Budget ($000) | Change ($000) |
|---|---|---|---|
| _____ Personnel _____ | | | |
| Personnel (MY) Salaries | | | |
| Total Expenses | | | |
| _____ O&M _____ | | | |
| Travel Other Trans. and Communication Professional & Special Services Repairs and Upkeep Materiel and Supplies | | | |
| Total Expenses | | | |
| _____ Capital _____ | | | |
| Total Capital Expenditure | | | |

9a

DEPARTMENT_____FISCAL 19__ BUDGET

EXPENDITURE EXPLANATION

Branch/Directorate/Service_____ Date

| Item of Expenditure |
|---|

Explanation of contents of 19__ budget expenditure:

Explanation of change from 19__ budget to 19__ budget:

9b

DEPARTMENT_____FISCAL 19___ BUDGET

EXPENDITURE COMMENT

Branch/Directorate/Service_____Date_____

| Item of Expenditure |
|---|

| Month | 19__<br>Budget | Brief Comments |
|---|---|---|
| January | | |
| February | | |
| March | | |
| April | | |
| May | | |
| June | | |
| July | | |
| August | | |
| September | | |
| October | | |
| November | | |
| December | | |
| TOTAL | | |

Special case

DEPARTMENT _____

O & M MONTHLY EXPENDITURE

FISCAL 19 ___ BUDGET

Branch/Directorate/Service _____    Date _____

($000)

| Expenses | JAN. | FEB. | MAR. | APR. | MAY | JUNE | JULY | AUG. | SEPT. | OCT. | NOV | DEC. | TOTAL |
|---|---|---|---|---|---|---|---|---|---|---|---|---|---|
| Personnel | | | | | | | | | | | | | |
| Salaries | | | | | | | | | | | | | |
| Travel | | | | | | | | | | | | | |
| Prof & Sp.Services | | | | | | | | | | | | | |
| Other trans & comm. | | | | | | | | | | | | | |
| Materiel & supplies | | | | | | | | | | | | | |
| Repairs & upkeep | | | | | | | | | | | | | |
| | | | | | | | | | | | | | |
| Total Expenses | | | | | | | | | | | | | |
| | | | | | | | | | | | | | |
| Capital | | | | | | | | | | | | | |
| | | | | | | | | | | | | | |
| | | | | | | | | | | | | | |
| Total Capital | | | | | | | | | | | | | |

10

DEPARTMENT _____

11

FISCAL 19____ BUDGET

SALARY SCHEDULE

Branch/Directorate/Service _____     Date _____

| | JAN. | FEB. | MAR. | APR. | MAY | JUNE | JULY | AUG. | SEPT. | OCT. | NOV. | DEC. | TOTAL |
|---|---|---|---|---|---|---|---|---|---|---|---|---|---|
| | | | | | | | | | | | | | |
| | | | | | | | | | | | | | |
| | | | | | | | | | | | | | |
| | | | | | | | | | | | | | |
| | | | | | | | | | | | | | |
| | | | | | | | | | | | | | |
| | | | | | | | | | | | | | |
| | | | | | | | | | | | | | |
| | | | | | | | | | | | | | |
| | | | | | | | | | | | | | |
| | | | | | | | | | | | | | |
| Total | | | | | | | | | | | | | |

DEPARTMENT _____

FISCAL 19 ___ BUDGET

CAPITAL EXPENDITURE SCHEDULE

Branch/Directorate/Service _____

Date _____

12

| Capital Item | JAN. | FEB. | MAR. | APR. | MAY | JUNE | JULY | AUG. | SEPT. | OCT. | NOV. | DEC. | TOTAL |
|---|---|---|---|---|---|---|---|---|---|---|---|---|---|
|  |  |  |  |  |  |  |  |  |  |  |  |  |  |
|  |  |  |  |  |  |  |  |  |  |  |  |  |  |
|  |  |  |  |  |  |  |  |  |  |  |  |  |  |
|  |  |  |  |  |  |  |  |  |  |  |  |  |  |
|  |  |  |  |  |  |  |  |  |  |  |  |  |  |
|  |  |  |  |  |  |  |  |  |  |  |  |  |  |
|  |  |  |  |  |  |  |  |  |  |  |  |  |  |
|  |  |  |  |  |  |  |  |  |  |  |  |  |  |
|  |  |  |  |  |  |  |  |  |  |  |  |  |  |
|  |  |  |  |  |  |  |  |  |  |  |  |  |  |
| Total |  |  |  |  |  |  |  |  |  |  |  |  |  |

**Summary A-Base Review at Departmental Library***

June 24, 1977

Zero A-Base Review, Departmental Library Services Branch

1. Objectives

The Departmental Library Services Branch derives its mandate
from the Department's objectives. The primary objective of
library services is to support the scientific, technical and
managerial information needs of DFE. Its secondary objective
is to provide environmental information on a national and
international scale primarily by reference, interlibrary
loan and nationally or internationally sponsored referral
services. The role and function of the Branch was defined in
the policy paper adopted by the Library Policy Committee and
senior management in January 1976. /Appendix 1, pp 10-10c/

2. The "jobs" that are outlined for the purposes of the review
are based on the roles and functions outlined in this paper and
are:

> Job #1  Provision of library services to users in the
> National Capital Area. [ **Decision package enclosed.** ]

> Job #2  Provision of "backup" services to libraries in
> the regions.

> Job #3  Coordination and network function (includes
> systems). [ **Decision package enclosed.** ]

> Job #4  Purchasing material for nonlibrary retention
> (i.e., for office use).

3. Resource allocation to the Departmental Library Services
Branch for the current and last two years were:

|  | 1975-76 | 1976-77t | 1977-78t |
|---|---|---|---|
| Man-years | X | X | X |
| $000 | X | X | X |
| In terms of $: | | | |
| Salaries | X | X | X |
| Other | X | X | X |
| Ratio of salary to other | X | X | X |

tOrganization charts attached.

*Decision Packages of Jobs 1 and 3 are included.

Various standards in the library literature are quoted as "acceptable" ratios of salary costs to total budgets:

>      CACUL: Guide to University Library Standards 1961-64   56%
>      Standards and specifications for Alberta government
>      libraries, 1975                                      60-80%

The Departmental Library's ratio shows a steady decrease from 1975 to 1977. Since the creation of the Departmental Library, 1976-77 was the most satisfactory year previous to the 20% man-year cut in April 1977. The resources were adequate and the proportion of salary versus O&M reflected an economical library operation.

4. Performance measurement and outputs

Library services are difficult to evaluate entirely by statistical methods. However, there are certain key areas that can be assessed. These are:

1. Accuracy, speed and depth of research in responding to information queries.

2. Attitude of library staff towards their clientele.

3. Promotion of the library's service program.

4. Use of library facilities and materials by the departmental staff.

5. Quality of the collection, i.e., its currency and relevance to the work of the Department.

6. Accountability to administration for funds and materials designated for library use.

In many of these areas the librarian and the administration must rely on "feedback" from departmental staff in evaluating service. User surveys may also be helpful as an indication of the users' perception of library services. /Appendix 2/

Some key areas lend themselves to statistical evaluation. Statistics are, for example, kept on loan transactions, reference queries, acquisition and cataloguing activities. These are periodically compared to statistics reported by government or university libraries of similar size. In this report, whenever such comparisons can be made usefully, they have been included. In June 1977 a committee including Headquarters and regional library representation was established in order to design departmentally acceptable performance measurement standards and uniform statistical reporting.

## WORK PROGRAM JOB DESCRIPTION FORM

Region:    National Capital Area

Directorate:  Departmental Management
              Services

Branch:    Departmental Library Services

Collator Code:  0580

Job Title:  Provision of library
            services to users in the
            National Capital Area

Job No.: 1

S.S.A.:

## R E S O U R C E   S U M M A R Y

|         | Man-years | | | | $000 | | | |
|---------|------|-------|-------|--------|-------|------|-------|-------|
|         | Off. | Supp. | Total | %Util. | O & M | Cap. | G & C | Total |
| 1975-76 | X    | X     | X     | X      | X     | X    | X     | X     |
| 1976-77 | X    | X     | X     | X      | X     | X    | X     | X     |

Note:  Only those with supervisory
duties are shown as officers.  All
others regardless of classification
or level have been shown as support
staff

## Job #1 Library service for National Capital Area users

Provision of library service to DFE staff in the National Capital Area necessary to support departmental objective. This objective is achieved by collecting, storing, organizing and making available published or unpublished material and scientific and technical information related to departmental programs. In addition to the primary (DFE) users, through interlibrary loans, reference and referral services, the library also serves other federal government departments, provincial and university libraries and, in justified cases, individual researchers and consultants. By its commitment to IRS/UNEP international referral service it answers queries in environmental matters originating from other countries.

## Basic information

| | | |
|---|---|---|
| 1. | Size of present collection | 250,000 items |
| 2. | Number of primary users | 3,000 (departmental staff in DFE) |
| 3. | Number of locations in National Capital Area served from PVM /Appendix 3/ | 18 |
| 4. | Number of libraries served (federal, provincial, university) | 140 |
| 5. | Number of "outside" users (researchers, consultants) | 200 |

| DESCRIPTION | TIME FRAME | COST | OUTPUT /June '76 - June '77 | PERFORMANCE MEASUREMENT; UNIT COST | RESULTS |
|---|---|---|---|---|---|
| Based on Collection Policy /Appendix 4/ select and acquire monographs, serials and government documents by purchase, gift or exchange for library retention. This activity includes screening review and gift material, bibliographic searching for duplication or dealer source, ordering, claiming, receiving, invoice verification and forwarding to cataloguing. | Continuous | X MY<br>x LS4<br>x LS3<br>x CR4<br>x CR3<br>x CR2<br>O&M<br>x$ | - x# monographic titles selected by library<br>- x# bibliographic searches<br>- x# serial titles selected<br>- x# periodical issues received and checked-in (i.e., kardexed)<br>- x# monographic items received<br>- x# invoices checked and authorized<br>- x# dealers notices, x# claims and x# orders typed and filed<br>- x# cancellation notices<br>- x# pieces of mail sorted | x# items acquired<br>Cost x$<br><br><br>UNIT COST X$ | Maintenance of a strong departmental collection.<br><br>x# subscriptions are maintained covering x# titles - x# monographs are added annually to collection. (Note that selection activity is shared between library staff and DFE users - final responsibility lying with the departmental library. All items are processed by bibliographic searchers). |
| Catalogue, classify, analyze and process library material according to Library of Congress scheme. Maintain catalogue records; compile and distribute monthly accessions list. | Continuous | X MY<br>x LS2<br>x CR4<br>x CR3<br>O&M<br>x$ | Catalogued<br><br>- x# monographic titles<br>- x# serial titles<br>- x# departmental publications | x# items catalogued and analyzed<br>x# items processed physically<br>Cost x$<br><br>Note: CACUL statistics quote $15-17 as average in 1961/64. Estimated to be at least $20 now.<br><br>UNIT COST X$ | Bibliographic control and access to library's content. The new system implemented in Dec '76 provides microfiche catalogues available for wide distribution. |
| Make library material available by direct loan, interlibrary loan and periodical "routing" to NCA users. This function also includes stack maintenance, photoduplication, duplication of microfiche, binding preparation and book repair. | Continuous | X. MY<br>x CR5<br>x CR3<br>x CR2<br>x CR3<br>O&M<br>X$ | - x# items on direct loan<br>- x# items lent on interlibrary loan<br>- x# borrowed on interlibrary loan<br>- x# issues corresponding to x# titles are routed to x# recipients<br>- x# items reshelved<br>- x# overdue notices sent out<br>- x# fiche copied (in lieu of loan) | x# items loaned<br>Cost x$<br><br><br><br><br>UNIT COST X$ | Making library material accessible at an adequate turn-around time. Waiting period for direct loan is 2 working days, for interlibrary loans the average is 10 working days.<br><br>The higher ILL lending figure indicates that DFE is a "net-lender" - this indicates a strong collection and by definition a national responsibility.<br><br>DFE is responsible for national distribution of EPA report material deposited in the Departmental Library Services Branch on microfiche. |
| Provide information service based on collection - this includes directional reference and in-depth searches. Supplement manual searches. Provide current awareness service (CAN/SDI profiles) and user orientation. Conduct user surveys and compile bibliographies on request. /Appendix 5 / | Continuous | X MY<br>x LS3<br>x LS2<br>x LS4<br>O&M<br>x$<br>Capital<br>x$ | - x# "quick" or directional questions<br>- x# reference questions based on collection<br>- x# searches on databases<br>- x# referrals from UNEP HQ (Nairobi)<br><br>N.B. Quantitative measurement of this area is complex. User surveys conducted show a high level of satisfaction with this service and note that it is highly professional. It is the most sensitive area of the library in terms of its direct and immediate exposure to users reaction. | x# transactions<br>Cost x$<br>Note: At the present time CISTI charges $20. per reference queries (manual or database). This cost is heavily subsidized by CISTI.<br><br><br><br>UNIT COST X$ | Time saving for research staff and managers - timely information at relatively low cost considering savings in users time. The unit cost is x$. If the research scientist needed to do search manually - it would take days or often weeks to achieve same result. |
| Integrate Fisheries collection in PVM (previously housed in Fontaine Bldg.) | Dec. '76 - May '77 | x# contract months<br>O&M<br>x$ | - cancellation of duplicate titles<br>- interfiling collection<br><br>Total of x# running feet | | Saving x# sq.ft. space allocation and x man-years - deleted May 1, 1977. (However, Fisheries & Marine Service plan to reinstate their own library after move to Sparks St. This will recreate the need for space, man-years and the duplication of library material). |
| Plan, organize, manage, monitor and supervise activities described in Job #1. Prepare policies, manuals and directives; plan and implement staff training; evaluate and improve library services. Coordinate activities with National Library and CISTI. Provide user orientation. | | x MY<br>X LS5<br>X LS3<br>X LS6<br>X AS2<br>X SEC2<br>O&M<br>X$ | - policies<br>- procedure manuals<br>- users' guides<br>- staffing actions<br>- appraisals<br>- budget<br>- resource allocation<br>- reports<br>- studies<br>- surveys | x officer man-years to x support staff: low ratio. | Teamwork - high level performance. |

## WORK PROGRAM JOB DESCRIPTION FORM

Region:  National Capital Area

Directorate:  Departmental Management
Services

Branch:  Departmental Library Services

Collator Code:  0580

Job Title:  Coordination and
network function

Job No.:  3

S.S.A.:

## R E S O U R C E   S U M M A R Y

|  | Man-years | | | | $000 | | | |
|---|---|---|---|---|---|---|---|---|
|  | Off. | Supp. | Total | %Util. | O & M | Cap. | G & C | Total |
| 1975-76 | X | X | X |  | XX |  |  | XX |
| 1976-77 | X | X | X |  | XX | X |  | XX |

## Job #3 Coordination and network function

The functions related to this area are described in the policy paper, point #1. These are:

> To coordinate the operation of library services throughout the Department and to provide functional guidance thereto (defined in Annex 2);
>
> --by advising management on departmental needs for library services, standards and quality
>
> --by designing, developing and maintaining a national system for Environment Canada libraries
>
> --by providing advice and guidance on the organization, classification, staffing, training and performance review of library personnel throughout the Department
>
> --by advising on the coordination of collection policies for departmental library units and by building collections in the headquarters library for subject areas where regional collections are inadequate or the material is too expensive for small libraries
>
> --by organizing regular meetings for Departmental Library staff.

Although the resources devoted to this activity might not reflect its importance, this is considered to be of a very high priority by the Library Policy Committee and the Departmental Library Services Branch. DFE operates the largest library network in the federal government. By building it into a network and coordinating its activities, a valuable national resource collection can be built and made available. It is in the Department's interest to coordinate activities of high unit cost, i.e., acquiring and cataloguing scientific/technical material. This objective prompted the Departmental Library to develop an automated system with record-keeping capabilities for a network as a whole.

The automated system ELIAS was developed in three years, 1975-77; cost of development was shared between the Departmental Library Services Branch and CASD. It is now being implemented in Headquarters, AES Downsview and the Quebec region. Total development cost was estimated at X$. 1976-77 was the highest cost period as most of the programming was done during this year. ELIAS was developed by the Department because the manual system was inefficient, had a high error rate and generated a great deal of repetitive tasks. For benefits of ELIAS and comments on the system, see Appendix #8.

| DESCRIPTION | TIME FRAME | COST | OUTPUT /June '76 – June '77 | PERFORMANCE MEASUREMENT; UNIT COST | RESULTS |
|---|---|---|---|---|---|
| Advising local management on services, standards, quality, staffing, collection building. Training library staff from regions and preparing material (video tape, booklets, procedure manuals). Workshops for DFE library staff. | Continuous | X MY<br><br>X   LS5<br>X   LS6<br>X   SEC2<br>X   LS3<br><br>O&M<br><br>X$<br><br>Capital<br><br>X$<br>(Micom Text Processor) | -  $_x$ policies - collection; role and function<br>-  $_{x\#}$ reports on:  organizations, physical plant; training; budget-ing<br>-  $_x$ selection boards in regions<br>- review of LS group classification across Canada /  $_{x\#}$ PAS reviewed in functional committee<br>- survey and directory in prepara-tion on scientific/technical collections in Canadian Govern-ment libraries<br>-  $_{x\#}$ trips to regions<br>-  $_{x\#}$ two day training sessions in database and SDI<br>-  $_{x\#}$ two day training sessions in regions on database searching and CAN/SDI profiles in Headquarters<br>-  $_{x\#}$ one week orientation programs<br>-  $_x$ information booklets<br>-  $_{x\#}$ newsletters published<br>-  $_x$ workshop (3 days) organized for all DFE librarians | UNIT COST   N A | Standardization, shared workload.<br><br>Text processor reduces repetitive typing work-load.<br><br>Professional develop-ment - better qualified library staff. |
| ELIAS development system analysis, programming, implementation in Headquarters and in two test regions:  AES Downsview;  Quebec Region, Ste Foy. /Appendix 9/ | June '75 – Aug. '77 | X MY<br><br>X CS3<br>(seconded to CASD)<br>X   LS5<br>X   SI2<br>X   AS2<br><br>O&M<br><br>X$<br><br>Capital<br><br>X$<br>(fiche readers) | Most important outputs<br>Author-title-subject catalogue on microfiche.<br>- circulation records<br>- on-order file, overdue notices, claims, notices, address file, periodical routing | Not fully known as yet.<br><br><br><br><br><br>UNIT COST   N A | Eliminate manual opera-tion in areas of order typing, claims, checking in, filing, overdue notices.<br><br>Capability of "union" catalogue, i.e., registry of total library holdings of Department. Eliminates duplication of work for participating libraries. Provides catalogue in-formation to any number of users on location.<br><br>All outputs on microfiche |
| Conversion of manual catalogue record.  /Appendix 10/ | April '77 – April '79 | X$ | Converting manual catalogue records into ELIAS | UNIT COST   N A | $_{x\#}$  catalogue records converted by 1979 cre-ating a departmental database. |

## A-Base Expenditure Review*

This report describes and compares the efforts of these two departments to find, from within their own expenditure base, the resources required to implement new program initiatives. Due to space limitations, we can include only the Executive Summary and the Table of Contents of this Report for the readers' convenience.

EXECUTIVE SUMMARY

In the current period of restraint. Ministers of the Treasury Board have been requesting departments to find resources within their existing budgets in order to undertake new program initiatives. The purpose of this report is to describe how two departments, Fisheries and Environment Canada (DFE) and Transport Canada, are attempting to find available resources through a comprehensive expenditure review. The report details the essential features of these two reviews and highlights aspects that may be of interest to other departments.

Reviews in Progress: The Fisheries and Environment review (the Zero A-Base Review) resulted from the Department's attempts to abide by the government's policy of restraint while fulfilling expanded responsibilities in areas such as fisheries jurisdiction and environmental protection. When Treasury Board Ministers recommended only 68 MY and $4M of a requested 357 MY and $22M to manage extended fisheries jurisdiction, the Deputy Minister, Mr. Seaborn, asked the Treasury Board Secretariat to help him design and manage a review of departmental expenditures that would indicate where resources might be made available. Work began late in 1976 and is to be completed by May, 1978. The Transport review was initiated by the Deputy Minister, Mr. Cloutier, as a comprehensive departmental effort to reduce program costs. While the Treasury Board Secretariat participates in both analysis and decision making, departmental personnel have designed and are implementing the review. Work began in mid 1977 and is scheduled to last approximately 12 months.

Principal Features: The most important aspect of this type of expenditure review is the strong commitment and active involvement of the deputy minister. In particular, the realization by managers that they must meet directly with the deputy to justify their expenditures has provided a significant impetus to the review process. Although the exact scope and nature of the DFE and Transport reviews are somewhat different, both reviews will provide a comprehensive overview of departmental activities. Furthermore, these reviews are both intended to generate a pool of resources without suggesting new areas of expenditure. In other words, this is not a planning exercise but only a way to free resources from within existing programs.

*A Report on Recent Experience in the Federal Government.* Canada, Treasury Board, Planning Branch, August 1978.

<u>Organization and Procedures</u>: The DFE and Transport reviews are
proceeding along similar lines. In each case, the department has
been divided into a number of reporting centres whose managers
are responsible directly to a senior management review committee.
Senior management uses small task forces of analysts to examine
the operations of each reporting centre and to recommend areas
of potential resource saving and other program improvements.
In addition, Transport is using task forces to examine specific
functions (personnel, finance, planning and telecommunications
and electronics) that involve a number of reporting centres.
The procedures used in these reviews are summarized in tabular
form on page (iv). This table identifies the responsibilities
of senior management, the task force and reporting centre managers
during the five major phases of the review: initiation, information gathering, task force analysis, senior management review
committee meetings and follow-up studies. The review process
is by no means, however, simply a number of mechanical procedures. Judgement has been an extremely important factor and
review procedures have remained flexible to accommodate specific
features of individual reporting centres.

<u>Resource Savings</u>: The overall level of resource savings from
such a review depends largely on a department's anticipated
resource requirements and constraints on the availability of
new resources. Although some savings are being achieved through
increased operating efficiency, any further savings involve
tradeoffs between existing programs and new program opportunities. Immediate man-year reductions at DFE have been approximately 3 per cent in areas where the review is complete; dollar
savings have been principally from associated salary reductions.
Total savings in those areas, including potential reductions that
could be realized as a result of follow-up studies, represent
more than 10 percent of man-year strength. At Transport, where
almost half the budget of the Department has been reviewed,
savings for the 1978/79 fiscal year represent 1.8 percent of
man-years and 2.5 percent of the O&M budget. Further savings
that may result from follow-up studies in the areas already
reviewed could represent an additional 1.5 percent of man-years
and 4 percent of the O&M budget.

<u>Other Benefits</u>: The benefits of these reviews are not strictly
related to belt tightening. Middle managers have appreciated
the opportunity to express their concerns directly to the deputy
and the deputy in turn has been able to gain a better apprecia-
tion of his programs and to assess his managers' capabilities.
(Mr. Seaborn has used this review as an important factor in
the performance appraisals of his SX group.) Also of benefit
has been a surfacing of broad issues limiting departmental
performance, such as problem interfaces with other departments
and restrictive government-wide policies or regulations. In

addition, the review has helped departments to respond to new government initiatives like the contracting-out policy and the Treasury Board's new policy on program evaluation. Finally, this review process has allowed senior management to avoid the traditional percentage reductions applied indiscriminately to all programs.

Costs: The cost of this type of review is not insignificant. At DFE, the Deputy Minister and two of his ADMs are personally meeting more than 50 reporting centre managers, devoting several hours to reviewing the program of each manager individually. A similar in-depth interview process is scheduled at Transport. A substantial amount of managers' time and a number of man-years of task force effort are also required. For one area of DFE, comprising approximately 2,500 man-years, the total cost of the review has been estimated at roughly $300,000 or 0.3 per cent of the total budget. Other costs may be imposed if personnel are forced to relocate as a result of the review, although these costs can be minimized by taking advantage of natural attrition, retraining, etc.

Limitations: A major limitation of this type of review is a lack of information to evaluate programs. In order to have a simultaneous overview of all departmental activities it is not possible to undertake in-depth analysis of specific programs without immediate access to such information. To some extent this problem can be offset by subsequent follow-up studies but, even so, the review process cannot hope to isolate all possible resource savings. Another limitation is that the results of the review apply to a single point in time and become less useful as program and personnel changes are made. To over-come this difficulty such a review would have to be undertaken on a cyclical basis, perhaps every 3 to 5 years.

Relationship to Treasury Board Policies on Program Evaluation and Program Performance Measurement: The purpose of these reviews may be related directly to the intent of the Treasury Board's policy (TB 77-44) which stresses the requirement of deputy heads to periodically subject all programs and supporting admin-istrative activities to in-depth evaluation. Many of the procedures and mechanisms described and the results obtained provide use-ful examples of how this policy may be appropriately applied. The Treasury Board policy on performance measurement (TB 76-25) is also relevant to this type of review process. At DFE, the Zero A-Base Review is resulting in the development of performance measurement information for most of the department's activities.

| | Review Procedures | | |
|---|---|---|---|
| Phases \ Participants | Senior Management Review Committee | Task Force | Reporting Centres |
| PHASE I: Initiation of the review | -allocates time for review<br>-chooses task force<br>-briefs managers<br>-emphasizes personnel incentives for resource saving (Transport only)<br>-establishes controls for resource transfers | -selects reporting centres<br>-prepares instructions for reporting centre managers<br>-briefs union representatives (Transport only)<br>-surveys related organizations (Transport only) | |
| PHASE II: Information gathering | -provides departmental objectives and priorities to task force | | -prepare a report to task force |
| PHASE III: Task force analysis | | -analyses reporting centres (and functions at Transport)<br>-interviews reporting centre managers<br>-prepares a report on each centre (and function at Transport) for senior management | |
| PHASE IV: Senior management review committee meetings | -reads task force reports<br>-interviews reporting centre managers<br>-decides on resource reductions, other immediate changes and follow-up studies | -briefs senior management before meetings<br>-answers questions concerning task force report<br>-records committee decisions | -provide an overview of reporting centre activities<br>-discuss task force recommendations |
| PHASE V: Follow-up studies | -oversees management of follow-up studies | | -prepare follow-up studies as required |

# TABLE OF CONTENTS

# Example Two
# Oregon State Library, Salem, Oregon

## 1979-81 Biennial Budget Preparation Manual*

This manual describes Oregon's adaptation of the zero-base budgeting system. It is 103 pages long and provides extensive instructions. For the reader's convenience, the Table of Contents is reproduced to illustrate the detailed coverage of the manual. The forms recommended for use in the Appendix section of the manual (pp. 63-103) are identical to those used by the State Library and are included in this example.

*Vol. 2, *Alternative Program Levels System (APLS)*, eds. Laurence R. Sprecher and Robert W. Smith (Salem, OR: Executive Department, State of Oregon, March 1978).

STATE OF OREGON

1979-81 BIENNIAL BUDGET
PREPARATION MANUAL

VOLUME 2

ALTERNATIVE PROGRAM LEVELS SYSTEM (APLS)


OREGON'S ADAPTATION OF THE
ZERO-BASE BUDGETING SYSTEM


Prepared by the
EXECUTIVE DEPARTMENT

Laurence R. Sprecher
Manager


Budget and Management Division
Robert W. Smith
Administrator


March 1978
Salem, Oregon

## SECTION 1 -- SYSTEM DESCRIPTION

## SECTION 2 -- GENERAL INFORMATION

SECTION THREE -- APLS BUDGET REQUEST

## APPENDIX -- FORMS

**1979-81 APLS Prepared by the Oregon
State Library\***

## CERTIFICATION

I hereby certify that the accompanying summary and detailed statements are true and correct to the best of my knowledge and belief and that the arithmetic accuracy of all numerical information has been verified.

| | |
|---|---|
| *Margaret S Oliver* | **Board Chairman** |
| Signature | Title |
| **OREGON STATE LIBRARY** | **State Library Building, Salem, Oregon 97310** |
| Agency Name | Agency Address |
| *Mary L. Johnston* | *Mally D. Hohestmm* |
| Approved (Board or Commission Member) | |
| *Nina Rae Cleveland* | *John Smith* |
| *Phyllis Clark* | |

NOTICE: Requests of those agencies headed by a multiple body must be approved by those bodies of official action and signed by a majority of the members. The requests of other agencies must be approved and signed by the agency administrator. Requests which are not properly signed will be returned.

105 BF 1

\*Selected pages are included here.

OREGON STATE LIBRARY

1979-81

## Table of Contents

BUDGET REPORT-Joint Committee on Ways and Means - 50th Legislative Assembly

| | Budget Page | LFO Analysis Page | Bill No. | Biennium |
|---|---|---|---|---|
Agency | II-43 | 2-43 | HB 5012 | 1977-79

**State Library**

Prepared by: (Executive Department)

Subcommittee No.  3

Elizabeth S. Hands *[signature]*

*[signature]*
Sen. Edward N. Fadeley        Chairman

Reviewed by: (Legislative Fiscal Office)

Rick Burke *[signature]*

Date  April 22, 1977

| Budget Description | 1975-77 Estimated Expenditures | 1977-79 Governor's Budget Recommendation | 1977-79 Committee Recommendation | Differences from Governor's Rec. |
|---|---|---|---|---|
| **STATE LIBRARY (OPERATING):** | | | | |
| General Fund | $1,697,395 | $2,130,963 | $2,087,366 | $-43,597 |
| Other Funds | 27,500 | 29,858 | 29,858 | -- |
| Federal Funds | 1,369,815 | 1,477,795 | 1,477,795 | -- |
| Total All Funds | $3,094,710 | $3,638,616 | $3,595,019 | $-43,597 |
| **POSITION SUMMARY:** | | | | |
| Positions | 71.00 | 71.00 | 71.00 | -- |
| Full-time equivalent positions | 69.00 | 71.00 | 71.00 | -- |

**SUMMARY OF SUBCOMMITTEE ACTION:**

The Subcommittee reduced the General Fund portion of the budget by $43,597 through the following actions:

**Library Services:** $-67,871 (Decision Package "7," page 44). Deletion of one position and some library acquisitions.

**Library Services to Blind and Physically Handicapped:** $434,274 (Decision Package "15," page 61). Addition of one position and some library materials.

**Library Development:** $-10,000 (Decision Package "5," page 80). Purchase of library materials for state institutions.

**Administration:** In approving level 3 the Subcommittee understands that some moneys will be used for staff development and training.

OREGON STATE LIBRARY

AGENCY NARRATIVE
1979-81

SERVICES TO
GOVERNMENT

Provides special reference services to officials,
agencies, and institutions of state government.
Provides resource materials and research services
for state legislators and their staff members.
Coordinates and develops state institutional
library services.

SERVICES TO
PUBLIC

Supplements existing resources and services of
public, school, academic, and special libraries.
Lends materials to Oregon residents without access
to local public library service. Provides special
reference and research assistance on all subjects
relating to Oregon. Provides special library
services for the blind and physically handicapped.

CONSULTANT
SERVICES

Advises public, special, and school libraries and
cities and counties on establishing, administering,
and supporting libraries. Prepares recommendations
to meet library needs of Oregon. Conducts or
arranges in-service training programs for librarians,
trustees, and local government officials. Prepares plans and makes recommendations encompassing
continuing education, resource sharing, and library
research on both an intrastate and an interstate
basis. Administers federal aid to public libraries
through the Library Services and Construction
Act. Administers state aid to public libraries
through ORS 357.740.

SPECIAL
SERVICES

Prepares Checklist of Official Publications of the
State of Oregon and distributes state documents
to designated depository libraries. (ORS 182.070)
Publishes an annual statistical Directory of
Oregon Libraries. Responds to national and regional
inquiries concerning the library needs, resources,
and development in Oregon. Coordinates the Oregon
Resource Library Network. Compiles and publishes
the Oregon Regional Union List of Serials. Operates the Oregon Library Media Jobline.

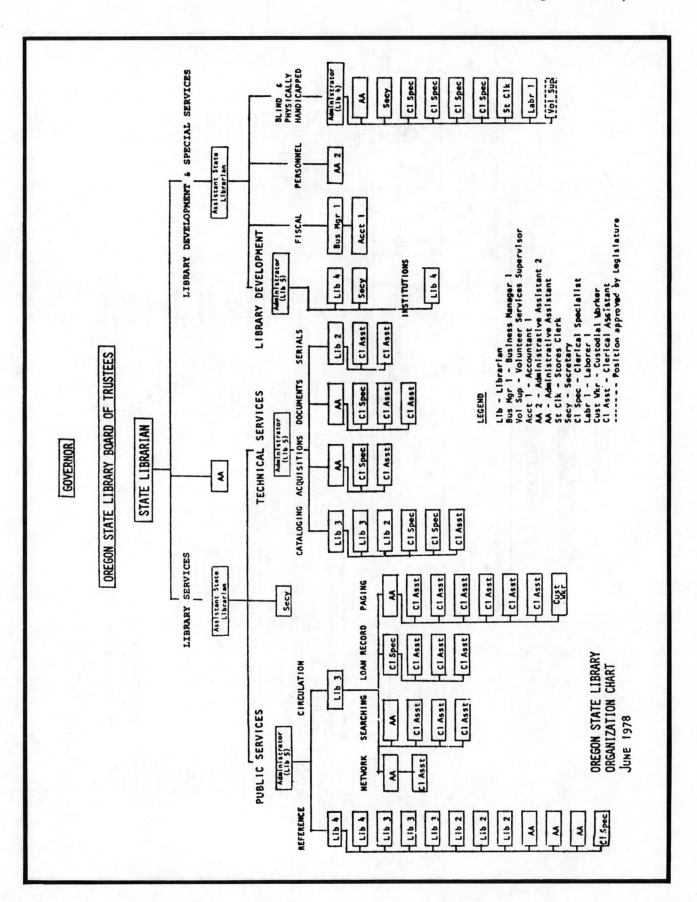

OREGON STATE LIBRARY
ORGANIZATION CHART
JUNE 1978

LEGEND

Lib - Librarian
Bus Mgr 1 - Business Manager 1
Vol Sup - Volunteer Services Supervisor
Acct 1 - Accountant 1
AA 2 - Administrative Assistant 2
AA - Administrative Assistant
St Clk - Stores Clerk
Secy - Secretary
Cl Spec - Clerical Specialist
Labr 1 - Laborer 1
Cust Wkr - Custodial Worker
Cl Asst - Clerical Assistant
----- Position approved by Legislature

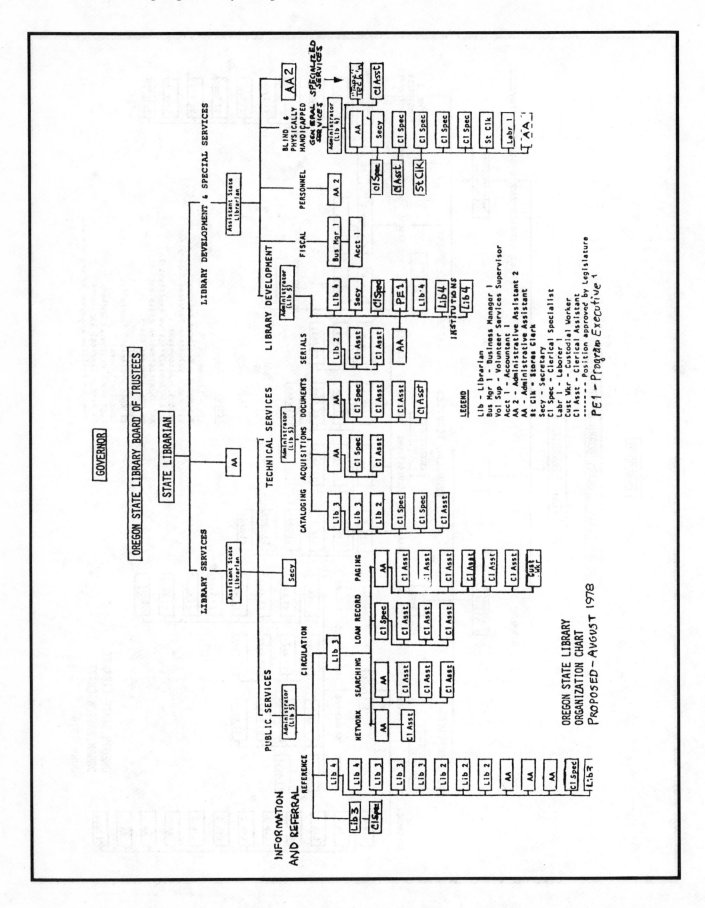

OREGON STATE LIBRARY
ORGANIZATION CHART
PROPOSED — AUGUST 1978

LEGEND

Lib — Librarian
Bus Mgr 1 — Business Manager 1
Vol Sup — Volunteer Services Supervisor
Acct 1 — Accountant 1
AA 2 — Administrative Assistant 2
AA — Administrative Assistant
St Clk — Stores Clerk
Secy — Secretary
Cl Spec — Clerical Specialist
Labr 1 — Laborer 1
Cust Wkr — Custodial Worker
Cl Asst — Clerical Assistant
------- Position approved by Legislature
PE1 — Program Executive 1

OREGON STATE LIBRARY

SPECIAL ANALYSIS

HOUSING COSTS

In 1977-79 Housing Costs for space in the State Library building were allocated to individual activities and Programs-01,
02, and 04.

In 1979-81 the Housing (category #11, Services and Supplies) has
been removed from Programs 02 and 04 and the entire amount
calculated in program 01 (Administration).

Housing is a noncontrollable Services and Supplies expense for
program managers and represents a disproportionate percent of
total budget. In calculating Reduced Level Budget, program related services and supplies were eroded because the 85 RLB
could not be applied to Housing.

A distortion still remains in Program 01.

The State Library's flexibility is limited and somewhat hampered
by the fact that stack space is dependent on number of books
rather than number of employes-and reading room space is dependent upon patrons.

Housing has been retained as a separately set out Services and
Supplies expense in Program 03, Library Services for the Blind
and Physically Handicapped, since the space in question is
leased for that operation only.

OREGON STATE LIBRARY

SPECIAL ANALYSIS

JOB SHARING

1977-79

On March 1, 1978, two clerical assistant employees in Technical Services (002-02) began a job sharing experience. The resultant vacancy was filled by hiring one new full-time clerical assistant.

To date, this is the only position of the 71 authorized that has utilized job sharing. However, the experience has been rewarding to the two employes involved and successful for the agency.

The success of job sharing and the successful use of flex-hours by many State Library employes have demonstrated to the State Library staff that job sharing can be a viable alternative for employes whose personal and financial circumstances warrant it.

STATE OF OREGON
EXECUTIVE DEPARTMENT

BIENNIAL BUDGET SUMMARY

105 BF 110

CONSOLIDATED SUMMARY OF REVENUES AND DISBURSEMENTS

| DESCRIPTION | 1975-77 Actual | 1977-79 Legis. Approved | 1977-79 Estimated | 1979-81 Adjusted Budget | Agency Request | 1979-81 Governor's Recommendation | Legislatively Approved |
|---|---|---|---|---|---|---|---|
| **Beginning Balances** | | | | | | | |
| Donation Funds | 11,287 | 7,000 | 13,282 | 11,282 | 11,282 | 11,282 | |
| Miscellaneous Receipts | 5,275 | 1,062 | 6,622 | 6,783 | 6,783 | 6,783 | |
| Federal Funds | - | | 211,731 | - | - | - | |
| Total | 16,562 | 8,062 | 231,635 | 18,065 | 18,065 | 18,065 | |
| General Fund Appropriations | 1,540,995 | 2,387,366 | 2,387,366 | 3,883,526 | 5,972,268 | 2,876,813 | |
| Emergency Fund allocations | | - | | - | - | - | |
| Approved salary adjustment 1977-79 | 156,400 | 43,115 | 43,115 | - | - | - | |
| Total General Fund | 1,697,395 | 2,430,481 | 2,430,481 | 3,883,526 | 5,972,268 | 2,876,813 | |
| **Other Funds Revenue** | | | | | | | |
| Interest Income | 1,470 | 1,500 | 2,697 | 1,000 | 1,000 | 1,000 | |
| Donations | 7,518 | 6,650 | 3,453 | 1,200 | 1,200 | 1,200 | |
| Other Revenues (Miscellaneous Receipts) | 19,847 | 22,146 | 21,869 | 20,100 | 20,100 | 20,100 | |
| Total Other Revenues | 28,835 | 30,296 | 28,019 | 22,300 | 22,300 | 22,300 | |

AGENCY   CODE   54300   TITLE   OREGON STATE LIBRARY
PROGRAM
SUBPROGRAM
ACTIVITY
Form 110

BIENNIAL BUDGET SUMMARY

Page 10

STATE OF OREGON
EXECUTIVE DEPARTMENT

BIENNIAL BUDGET SUMMARY

105 BF 110

CONSOLIDATED SUMMARY OF REVENUES AND DISBURSEMENTS (continued)

| DESCRIPTION | 1975-77 Actual | 1977-79 Legis. Approved | 1977-79 Estimated | 1979-81 Adjusted Budget | Agency Request | 1979-81 Governor's Recommendation | Legislatively Approved |
|---|---|---|---|---|---|---|---|
| Federal Funds Revenues | | | | | | | |
| Title I Services | 1,309,976 | 1,387,795 | 1,344,671 | 1,377,032 | 1,377,032 | 1,506,404 | |
| Approved salary adjustment funding | 130,633 | 47,831 | 47,831 | | | | |
| Title III Interlibrary Cooperation | 108,967 | 90,000 | 90,000 | 105,470 | 105,470 | 141,182 | |
| White House Conference | | 17,500 | 17,500 | - | - | - | |
| Total Federal Funds | 1,549,576 | 1,543,126 | 1,500,002 | 1,482,502 | 1,482,502 | 1,647,586 | |
| Funds Available | | | | | | | |
| General Fund | 1,697,395 | 2,430,481 | 2,430,481 | 3,883,526 | 5,972,268 | 2,876,813 | |
| Other Funds | 45,397 | 38,358 | 47,923 | 40,365 | 40,365 | 40,365 | |
| Federal Funds | 1,549,576 | 1,543,126 * | 1,711,733 * | | 1,482,502 | 1,647,586 | |
| Total | 3,292,368 | 4,011,965 | 4,190,137 | 3,923,891 | 7,495,135 | 4,564,764 | |
| Expenditures | | | | | | | |
| General Fund | 1,685,394 | 2,430,481 | 2,430,481 | 3,883,526 | 5,972,268 | 2,876,813 | |
| Other Funds | 25,493 | 29,858 | 29,858 | 23,500 | 23,500 | 33,365 | |
| Federal Funds | 1,337,754 | 1,543,126 | 1,711,733 | - | 1,482,502 | 1,647,586 | |
| Total | 3,048,641 | 4,003,465 | 4,172,072 | 3,907,026 | 7,478,270 | 4,557,764 | |

* Federal Funds (LSCA) in the estimated amount of $168,607 are available to the State Library. The Emergency Board will be requested to approve the expenditure limitation increase.

Page 11

BIENNIAL BUDGET SUMMARY

AGENCY    CODE 54300    TITLE OREGON STATE LIBRARY
PROGRAM
SUBPROGRAM
ACTIVITY
Form 110

STATE OF OREGON
EXECUTIVE DEPARTMENT

BIENNIAL BUDGET SUMMARY

105 BF 110

CONSOLIDATED SUMMARY OF REVENUES AND DISBURSEMENTS (continued)

| DESCRIPTION | 1975-77 Actual | 1977-79 Legis. Approved | 1977-79 Estimated | 1979-81 Adjusted Budget | Agency Request | 1979-81 Governor's Recommendation | Legislatively Approved |
|---|---|---|---|---|---|---|---|
| Ending Balances | | | | | | | |
| Reverts to: | | | | | | | |
| General Fund | 10,001 | | | | | | |
| Federal Government | 91 | | | | | - | |
| Carried forward: | | | | | | | |
| Donation Fund | 13,282* | 7,000* | 11,282* | 9,982* | 9,982* | 7,000 | |
| Miscellaneous Receipts | 6,622 | 1,500 | 6,783 | 6,883 | 6,883 | - | |
| Total Other Funds | 19,904 | 8,500 | 18,065 | 16,865 | 16,865 | 7,000 | |
| Federal Funds | 211,731 | | | | | | |

* $7,000 reserved for investments

AGENCY   CODE   54300   TITLE   OREGON STATE LIBRARY
PROGRAM
SUBPROGRAM
ACTIVITY

BIENNIAL BUDGET SUMMARY

Page 12

STATE OF OREGON
EXECUTIVE DEPARTMENT

BIENNIAL BUDGET SUMMARY

105 BF 110

CONSOLIDATED SUMMARY OF EXPENDITURES BY PROGRAM BY FUND

| DESCRIPTION | 1975-77 Actual | 1977-79 Legis. Approved | 1977-79 Estimated | 1979-81 Adjusted Budget | Agency Request | 1979-81 Governor's Recommendation | Legislatively Approved |
|---|---|---|---|---|---|---|---|
| **001 Administration** | | | | | | | |
| General Fund | 200,207 | 222,073 | 228,912 | 1,043,731 | 1,065,240 | 531,288 | |
| Other Funds | - | 2,737 | 2,737 | 100 | 100 | - | |
| Federal Funds | 187,492 | 220,451 | 227,290 | - | - | 488,869 | |
| Total | 387,699 | 445,261 | 458,939 | 1,043,831 | 1,065,340 | 1,020,157 | |
| **002 Library Services** | | | | | | | |
| General Fund | 1,114,561 | 1,398,971 | 1,412,872 | 2,178,948 | 2,310,992 | 1,314,592 | |
| Other Funds | 20,618 | 23,971 | 23,971 | 20,400 | 20,400 | 30,365 | |
| Federal Funds | 834,620 | 849,575 | 839,047 | - | - | 811,332 | |
| Total | 1,969,799 | 2,272,517 | 2,275,890 | 2,199,348 | 2,331,392 | 2,156,289 | |
| **003 Library Services for the Blind & Physically Handicapped** | | | | | | | |
| General Fund | 269,431 | 393,583 | 369,155 | 411,543 | 570,814 | 399,934 | |
| Other Funds | 4,875 | 3,150 | 3,150 | 3,000 | 3,000 | 3,000 | |
| Federal Funds | - | - | - | - | - | - | |
| Total | 274,306 | 396,733 | 372,305 | 414,543 | 573,814 | 402,934 | |

AGENCY          CODE          TITLE
PROGRAM         54300         OREGON STATE LIBRARY
SUBPROGRAM
ACTIVITY
Form 110

Page 13

BIENNIAL BUDGET SUMMARY

STATE OF OREGON
EXECUTIVE DEPARTMENT

BIENNIAL BUDGET SUMMARY

105 BF 110

## CONSOLIDATED SUMMARY OF EXPENDITURES BY PROGRAM BY FUND (continued)

| DESCRIPTION | 1975-77 Actual | 1977-79 Legis. Approved | 1977-79 Estimated | 1979-81 Adjusted Budget | Agency Request | 1979-81 Governor's Recommendation | Legislatively Approved |
|---|---|---|---|---|---|---|---|
| **004 Library Development** | | | | | | | |
| General Fund | 101,195 | 415,854 | 419,542 | 249,304 | 2,025,222 | 630,999 | |
| Other Funds | - | - | - | - | - | - | |
| Federal Funds | 315,642 | 473,100 | 645,396 | - | 1,482,502 | 347,385 | |
| Total | 416,837 | 888,954 | 1,064,938 | 249,304 | 3,507,724 | 978,384 | |
| **Summary** | | | | | | | |
| General Funds | 1,685,394 | 2,430,481 | 2,430,481 | 3,883,526 | 5,972,268 | 2,876,813 | |
| Other Funds | 25,493 | 29,858 | 29,858 | 23,500 | 23,500 | 33,365 | |
| Federal Funds | 1,337,754 | 1,543,126 | 1,711,733 | - | 1,482,502 | 1,647,586 | |
| Total | 3,048,641 | 4,003,465 | 4,172,072 | 3,907,026 | 7,478,270 | 4,557,764 | |

AGENCY    CODE   54300
PROGRAM
SUBPROGRAM    TITLE   OREGON STATE LIBRARY
ACTIVITY
Form 110

BIENNIAL BUDGET SUMMARY

STATE OF OREGON
EXECUTIVE DEPARTMENT

BIENNIAL BUDGET SUMMARY

105 BF 110

CONSOLIDATED SUMMARY OF EXPENDITURES BY CATEGORY BY FUND

| DESCRIPTION | 1975-77 Actual | 1977-79 Legis. Approved | 1977-79 Estimated | 1979-81 Adjusted Budget | Agency Request | 1979-81 Governor's Recommendation | Legislatively Approved |
|---|---|---|---|---|---|---|---|
| **Personal Services** | | | | | | | |
| General Fund | 953,954 | 1,186,209 | 1,192,609 | 2,398,704 | 2,811,062 | 1,485,119 | |
| Other Funds | - | - | - | - | - | - | |
| Federal Funds | 810,841 | 926,893 | 943,304 | - | 35,527 | 922,734 | |
| Total | 1,764,795 | 2,113,102 | 2,135,913 | 2,398,704 | 2,846,589 | 2,407,853 | |
| **Services and Supplies** | | | | | | | |
| General Fund | 363,485 | 542,238 | 535,838 | 1,001,127 | 1,090,576 | 611,084 | |
| Other Funds | 18,500 | 21,708 | 21,708 | 20,000 | 20,000 | 26,883 | |
| Federal Funds | 305,855 | 276,285 | 264,874 | - | 2,982 | 377,467 | |
| Total | 687,840 | 840,231 | 822,420 | 1,021,127 | 1,113,558 | 1,015,434 | |
| **Capital Outlay** | | | | | | | |
| General Funds | 367,955 | 402,034 | 402,034 | 483,695 | 470,630 | 435,610 | |
| Other Funds | 6,993 | 8,150 | 8,150 | 3,500 | 3,500 | 6,482 | |
| Federal Funds | 60,466 | 200 | 200 | - | 1,540 | - | |
| Total | 435,414 | 410,384 | 410,384 | 487,195 | 475,670 | 442,092 | |

Page 15

| AGENCY | CODE 54300 | TITLE OREGON STATE LIBRARY |
| PROGRAM | | |
| SUBPROGRAM | | |
| ACTIVITY | | |

FORM 110

BIENNIAL BUDGET SUMMARY

STATE OF OREGON
EXECUTIVE DEPARTMENT

BIENNIAL BUDGET SUMMARY

105 BF 110

CONSOLIDATED SUMMARY OF EXPENDITURES BY CATEGORY BY FUND (continued)

| DESCRIPTION | 1975-77 Actual | 1977-79 Legis. Approved | 1977-79 Estimated | 1979-81 Adjusted Budget | Agency Request | 1979-81 Governor's Recommendation | Legislatively Approved |
|---|---|---|---|---|---|---|---|
| **Special Payments** | | | | | | | |
| General Funds | - | 300,000 | 300,000 | - | 1,600,000 | 345,000 | |
| Other Funds | - | - | - | - | | - | |
| Federal Funds | 160,592 | 334,748 | 503,355 | - | 1,442,453 | 347,385 | |
| Total | 160,592 | 634,748 | 803,355 | - | 3,042,453 | 692,385 | |
| **Summary** | | | | | | | |
| General Funds | 1,685,394 | 2,430,481 | 2,430,481 | 3,883,526 | 5,972,268 | 2,876,813 | |
| Other Funds | 25,493 | 29,858 | 29,858 | 23,500 | 23,500 | 33,365 | |
| Federal Funds | 1,337,754 | 1,543,126 | 1,711,733 | - | 1,482,502 | 1,647,586 | |
| Total | 3,048,641 | 4,003,465 | 4,172,072 | 3,907,026 | 7,478,270 | 4,557,764 | |

Page 16

AGENCY   CODE 54300    TITLE OREGON STATE LIBRARY
PROGRAM
SUBPROGRAM
ACTIVITY
Form 110

BIENNIAL BUDGET SUMMARY

STATE OF OREGON
EXECUTIVE DEPARTMENT

BIENNIAL BUDGET SUMMARY

105 BF 110

### CONSOLIDATED SUMMARY BY CLASSIFICATION BY FUND

| DESCRIPTION | 1975-77 Actual | 1977-79 Legis. Approved | 1977-79 Estimated | 1979-81 Adjusted Budget | Agency Request | 1979-81 Governor's Recommendation | Legislatively Approved |
|---|---|---|---|---|---|---|---|
| **Reduced Level Budget** | | | | | | | |
| General Fund | - | - | | | 3,299,570 | 2,127,295 | |
| Other Funds | - | - | | | 23,500 | 33,365 | |
| Federal Funds | - | - | | | - | 1,130,171 | |
| Total | | | | | 3,323,070 | 3,290,831 | |
| **All Decision Packages** | | | | | | | |
| General Fund | | | | | 2,672,698 | 749,518 | |
| Other Funds | | | | | - | - | |
| Federal Funds | | | | | 1,482,502 | 517,415 | |
| Total | | | | | 4,155,200 | 1,266,933 | |
| **APLS Total** | | | | | | | |
| General Funds | 1,685,394 | 2,430,481 | 2,430,481 | 3,883,526 | 5,972,268 | 2,869,813 | |
| Other Funds | 25,493 | 29,855 | 29,858 | 23,500 | 23,500 | 33,365 | |
| Federal Funds | 1,337,754 | 1,543,126 | 1,711,733 | - | 1,482,502 | 1,647,586 | |
| Total | 3,048,641 | 4,003,465 | 4,172,072 | 3,907,026 | 7,478,270 | 4,557,764 | |
| Authorized positions * | 72 | 71 | 71 | 71 | 86 | 72 | |
| FTE positions * | 68.8 | 71 | 67 | 71 | 86 | 72 | |

*Does not include seven Board Members

BIENNIAL BUDGET SUMMARY

AGENCY    CODE  54300
PROGRAM    TITLE   OREGON STATE LIBRARY
SUBPROGRAM
ACTIVITY
Form 110

STATE OF OREGON
EXECUTIVE DEPARTMENT

APLS BUDGET SUMMARY

105 BF 125

| 1 BUDGET DATA | 1977-79 | | | | | | 1979-81 | | | | | |
|---|---|---|---|---|---|---|---|---|---|---|---|---|
| | 2 Legislatively Approved | 3 Estimated for Biennium | 4 Adjusted Budget | 5 Reduced Level Budget | 6 % Adj Budg | 7 Decision Package Subtotal | 8 Total Agency Request | 9 % Adj Budg | 10 Governor's Recommendation | 11 % Adj Budg | 12 Legislatively Approved | 13 % Adj Budg |
| **POSITION SUMMARY** | | | | | | | | | | | | |
| Authorized Positions | 71 | 71 | 71 | 57 | 80 | 29 | 86 | 121 | 72 | 100 | | |
| FTE Positions | 71 | 67 | 71 | 57 | 80 | 29 | 86 | 121 | 72 | | | |
| **14 EXPENDITURES BY CATEGORY** | | | | | | | | | | | | |
| Personal Services | 2,113,102 | 2,135,913 | 2,398,704 | 1,977,110 | 82 | 869,479 | 2,846,589 | 119 | 2,407,853 | 100 | | |
| Services and Supplies | 840,231 | 822,420 | 1,021,127 | 954,065 | 93 | 159,493 | 1,113,558 | 109 | 1,015,434 | 99 | | |
| Capital Outlay | 35,384 | 35,384 | 31,195 | 21,895 | 70 | 43,775 | 65,670 | 210 | 32,092 | 103 | | |
| Special Payments | 639,748 | 803,355 | | | | 3,042,453 | 3,042,453 | | 692,385 | | | |
| 15 Library Materials | 375,000 | 375,000 | 456,000 | 370,000 | 81 | 40,000 | 410,000 | 90 | 410,000 | 90 | | |
| 16 TOTAL | 4,003,465 | 4,172,072 | 3,907,026 | 3,323,070 | 85 | 4,155,200 | 7,478,270 | 195 | 4,557,764 | 116 | | |
| **EXPENDITURES BY FUND** | | | | | | | | | | | | |
| General Fund | 2,430,481 | 2,430,481 | 2,401,024 | 3,299,570 | 137 | 2,672,698 | 5,972,268 | 249 | 2,876,813 | 119 | | |
| Other Funds | 29,858 | 29,858 | 23,500 | 23,500 | 100 | - | 23,500 | - | 33,365 | 142 | | |
| Federal Funds | 1,543,126 | 1,711,733 | 1,482,502 | - | - | 1,482,502 | 1,482,502 | - | 1,647,586 | 111 | | |
| 17 TOTAL | 4,003,465 | 4,172,072 | 3,907,026 | 3,323,070 | 85 | 4,155,200 | 7,478,270 | 191 | 4,557,764 | 116 | | |
| **18 ACCOMPLISHMENTS/WORKLOAD MEASURES** | | | | | | | | | | | | |
| Programs administered | 4 | 4 | 4 | 4 | 100 | - | 4 | 100 | 4 | 100 | | |
| Major publications | 4 | 4 | 4 | 4 | 100 | - | 4 | 100 | 4 | 100 | | |
| Communications publications | 30 | 30 | 30 | 15 | 50 | 15 | 30 | 100 | 30 | 100 | | |
| *Reference requests received | 48,000 | 67,989 | 84,000 | 50,000 | 60 | 41,000 | 91,000 | 108 | 84,000 | 100 | | |
| Title requests received | 238,000 | 236,452 | 236,500 | 185,000 | 78 | 63,000 | 248,000 | 105 | 242,000 | 102 | | |
| Items circulated | 636,000 | 500,060 | 500,000 | 340,000 | 70 | 265,000 | 605,000 | 102 | 500,000 | 100 | | |
| *Photocopies provided | 46,000 | 82,462 | 20,000 | 14,000 | 70 | 7,000 | 21,000 | 105 | 20,000 | 100 | | |
| On-line searches | 800 | 2,462 | 3,400 | 3,400 | 100 | 1,200 | 4,600 | 135 | 3,400 | 100 | | |

19 *Definition to change for 1979-81 biennium.

AGENCY  CODE 54300  TITLE OREGON STATE LIBRARY
PROGRAM
SUBPROGRAM
ACTIVITY

Form 125

Page 18

APLS BUDGET SUMMARY

STATE OF OREGON
EXECUTIVE DEPARTMENT

APLS BUDGET SUMMARY

105 BF 125a

| BUDGET DATA | 1977-79 | | Adjusted Budget | Reduced Level Budget | % Adj. Budg. | Decision Package Subtotal | 1979-81 | | Governor's Recommendation | % Adj. Budg. | Legislatively Approved | % Adj. Budg. |
| 1 | 2 Legislatively Approved | 3 Estimated for Biennium | 4 | 5 | 6 | 7 | 8 Total Agency Request | 9 % Adj. Budg. | 10 | 11 | 12 | 13 |
| --- | --- | --- | --- | --- | --- | --- | --- | --- | --- | --- | --- | --- |
| ACCOMPLISHMENTS/WORKLOAD MEASURES (Continued) | | | | | | | | | | | | |
| Information & referral requests | - | - | - | - | - | 14,000 | 14,000 | - | - | - | | |
| Requests forwarded to PNBC resource & other libraries | 18,000 | 13,988 | 16,000 | 16,000 | 100 | - | 16,000 | 100 | 16,000 | 100 | | |
| Books acquired | 19,400 | 20,421 | 21,500 | 19,000 | 88 | 2,500 | 21,500 | 100 | 21,500 | 100 | | |
| Items cataloged | 28,000 | 22,062 | 25,000 | 23,000 | 92 | 2,800 | 25,800 | 103 | 25,500 | 102 | | |
| Documents added | 64,000 | 63,863 | 80,000 | 80,000 | 100 | - | 80,000 | 100 | 80,000 | 100 | | |
| Oregon documents acquired for distribution | 2,000 | 2,012 | 2,500 | 2,500 | 100 | 500 | 3,000 | 120 | 2,500 | 100 | | |
| Volumes microfilmed | - | - | - | - | - | 2,500 | 2,500 | - | - | - | | |
| *Average circulation per individual client per quarter | - | 9 | 9 | 6 | 67 | 6 | 12 | 133 | - | - | | |
| *Increase in net number of clients per quarter | - | 100 | 100 | 50 | 50 | 75 | 125 | 125 | - | - | | |
| Library items circulated | 636,000 | 500,060 | 500,000 | 340,000 | 67 | 265,000 | 605,000 | 133 | 500,000 | 100 | | |
| Number of new materials produced and circulated | - | - | - | - | - | 240 | 240 | - | - | - | | |
| Public library contacts | 170 | 193 | 193 | 155 | 80 | 370 | 525 | 272 | 350 | 181 | | |
| In-depth library consultation | 160 | 52 | 52 | 40 | 77 | 125 | 165 | 317 | 95 | 182 | | |
| Institutional visits | 300 | 333 | 333 | 325 | 98 | - | 325 | 98 | 325 | 100 | | |

14 *New workload measures for 1979-81. Workload measures have been changed to be compatible with the Library of Congress.

Page 19

AGENCY      CODE        TITLE
            54300       OREGON STATE LIBRARY
PROGRAM _____
SUBPROGRAM _____
ACTIVITY _____

Form 125a

APLS BUDGET SUMMARY

STATE OF OREGON
EXECUTIVE DEPARTMENT

APLS BUDGET SUMMARY

105 BF 125a

| BUDGET DATA | 1977-79 | | 4 Adjusted Budget | 5 Reduced Level Budget | 6 % Adj. Budg. | 7 Decision Package Subtotal | 1979-81 | | 10 Governor's Recommendation | 11 % Adj. Budg. | 12 Legislatively Approved | 13 % Adj. Budg. |
|---|---|---|---|---|---|---|---|---|---|---|---|---|
| | 2 Legislatively Approved | 3 Estimated for Biennium | | | | | 8 Total Agency Request | 9 % Adj. Budg. | | | | |
| ACCOMPLISHMENTS/WORKLOAD MEASURES (Continued) | | | | | | | | | | | | |
| Communication contacts | 3,600 | 5,483 | 5,483 | 4,200 | 77 | 7,050 | 11,250 | 205 | 7,975 | 138 | | |
| Meetings and workshops | 152 | 286 | 286 | 155 | 54 | 320 | 475 | 166 | 355 | 124 | | |
| Documents completed | 4 | 4 | 4 | 4 | 100 | 12 | 16 | 400 | 14 | 350 | | |
| Grants processed and monitored | 25 | 199 | 199 | - | - | 598 | 598 | 301 | 300 | 150 | | |
| Reports written | 10 | 3 | 3 | 1 | 33 | 10 | 11 | 367 | - | - | | |
| Workshops conducted | - | 10 | 10 | - | - | 74 | 74 | 74 | - | - | | |
| Evaluations | - | - | - | - | - | 40 | 40 | - | - | - | | |
| Materials purchased | 9,405 | 10,161 | 10,161 | 10,000 | 98 | 5,000 | 15,000 | 148 | 10,000 | 98 | | |
| Per capita grants awarded | - | - | - | - | - | 300 | 300 | - | - | - | | |

14

APLS BUDGET SUMMARY

Page 20

AGENCY      CODE    54300
PROGRAM
SUBPROGRAM
ACTIVITY

TITLE
OREGON STATE LIBRARY

Form 125a

STATE OF OREGON
EXECUTIVE DEPARTMENT

PRIORITY TABLE

105 BF 120

| Rank 1 | Page Ref. 2 | DECISION PACKAGES 3 | AMOUNTS BY PACKAGE | | | | | CUMULATIVE TOTALS | | | | |
|---|---|---|---|---|---|---|---|---|---|---|---|---|
| | | | General 4 | Other 5 | Federal 6 | Total 7 | FTE 8 | General 9 | Other 10 | Federal 11 | Total 12 | FTE 13 |
| RLB | 40 | Administration | 985,237 | 100 | | 985,337 | 6 | 985,237 | 100 | | 985,337 | 6 |
| RLB | 66,83 93 | Library Services | 1,784,400 | 20,400 | | 1,804,800 | 40 | 2,769,637 | 20,500 | | 2,790,137 | 46 |
| RLB | 112 | Blind & Phys. Handicapped | 345,779 | 3,000 | | 348,779 | 8 | 3,115,416 | 23,500 | | 3,138,916 | 54 |
| RLB | 145 166 | Library Development | 184,154 | | | 184,154 | 3 | 3,299,570 | | | 3,323,070 | 57 |
| 1 | 68 | Limited Reference Service (02-01 DP-1) | 131,792 | | | 131,792 | 4 | 3,431,362 | | | 3,454,862 | 61 |
| 2 | 85 | Library Materials (02-02 DP-1) | 69,256 | | | 69,256 | 1 | 3,500,618 | | | 3,524,118 | 62 |
| 3 | 70 | Standard Reference Service (02-01 DP-2) | 150,768 | | | 150,768 | 5 | 3,651,386 | | | 3,674,886 | 67 |
| 4 | 147 | Library Development, Current Level (04-01 DP-1) | 54,920 | | | 54,920 | 1 | 3,706,306 | | | 3,729,806 | 68 |
| 5 | 114 | Limited Service (03-01 DP-1) | 58,559 | | | 58,559 | 2 | 3,764,865 | | | 3,788,365 | 70 |
| 6 | 42 | Personnel & Publications (01 DP-1) | 43,454 | | | 43,454 | 1 | 3,808,319 | | | 3,831,819 | 71 |
| 7 | 149 | Children's Services (04-01 DP-2) | 74,968 | | | 74,968 | 2 | 3,883,287 | | | 3,906,787 | 73 |
| 8 | 72 | Government Information Coordinator (02-01 DP-3) | 56,827 | | | 56,827 | 1 | 3,940,114 | | | 3,963,614 | 74 |

(continued)

PRIORITY TABLE

AGENCY     CODE  54300       TITLE  OREGON STATE LIBRARY
PROGRAM
SUBPROGRAM
ACTIVITY

Form 120

[X] AGENCY REQUEST
[ ] GOVERNOR'S RECOMMENDATION
[ ] LEGISLATIVELY APPROVED

Page  21

STATE OF OREGON
EXECUTIVE DEPARTMENT

PRIORITY TABLE

105 BF 120

| Rank 1 | Page Ref. 2 | DECISION PACKAGES 3 | AMOUNTS BY PACKAGE | | | | | CUMULATIVE TOTALS | | | | |
|---|---|---|---|---|---|---|---|---|---|---|---|---|
| | | | General 4 | Other 5 | Federal 6 | Total 7 | FTE 8 | General 9 | Other 10 | Federal 11 | Total 12 | FTE 13 |
| | | (continued) | | | | | | | | | | |
| 9 | 151 | Continuing Education (04-01 DP-3) | 51,130 | | | 51,130 | 1 | 3,991,244 | | | 4,014,744 | 75 |
| 10 | 116 | Workload Increase (03-01 DP-2) | 78,634 | | | 78,634 | 3 | 4,069,878 | | | 4,093,378 | 78 |
| 11 | 125 | Specialized Services (03-02 DP-1) | 87,842 | | | 87,842 | 2 | 4,157,720 | | | 4,181,220 | 80 |
| 12 | 44 | Administrative Support (01 DP-2) | 33,549 | | | 33,549 | 1 | 4,191,269 | | | 4,214,769 | 81 |
| 13 | 168 | Institutional Library Materials (04-02 DP-1) | 20,000 | | | 20,000 | 0 | 4,211,269 | | | 4,234,769 | 81 |
| 14 | 87 | State Documents and Preservation (02-02 DP-2) | 46,924 | | | 46,924 | 1 | 4,258,193 | | | 4,281,693 | 82 |
| 15 | 46 | Air conditioning (01 DP-3) | 3,000 | | | 3,000 | 0 | 4,261,193 | | | 4,284,693 | 82 |
| 16 | 74 | State Government Information and Referral (02-01 DP-4) | 71,025 | | | 71,025 | 2 | 4,332,218 | | | 4,355,718 | 74 |
| 17 | 153 | LSCA Grants (04-01 DP-4) | 40,050 | | 1,482,502 | 1,522,552 | 2 | 4,372,268 | | 1,482,502 | 5,878,270 | 86 |
| 18 | 155 | State Aid-Establishment Grants (04-01 DP-5) | 300,000 | | | 300,000 | 0 | 4,672,268 | | | 6,178,270 | 86 |
| 19 | 157 | State Aid-Per Capita (04-01 DP-6) | 1,300,000 | | | 1,300,000 | 0 | 5,972,268 | 23,500 | 1,482,502 | 7,478,270 | 86 |
| | | | 5,972,268 | 23,500 | 1,482,502 | 7,478,270 | 86* | 5,972,268 | 23,500 | 1,482,502 | 7,478,270 | 86* |

* Does not include 7 Board members

AGENCY CODE 54300 TITLE OREGON STATE LIBRARY
PROGRAM
SUBPROGRAM
ACTIVITY
Form 120

[X] AGENCY REQUEST
[ ] GOVERNOR'S RECOMMENDATION
[ ] LEGISLATIVELY APPROVED

Page 22

PRIORITY TABLE

STATE OF OREGON
EXECUTIVE DEPARTMENT

PRIORITY TABLE

105 BF 120

| Rank 1 | Page Ref. 2 | DECISION PACKAGES 3 | AMOUNTS BY PACKAGE | | | | | CUMULATIVE TOTALS | | | | |
|---|---|---|---|---|---|---|---|---|---|---|---|---|
| | | | General 4 | Other 5 | Federal 6 | Total 7 | FTE 8 | General 9 | Other 10 | Federal 11 | Total 12 | FTE 13 |
| RLB | 41 | Administration | 507,598 | - | 469,666 | 977,264 | 6 | 507,598 | - | 469,666 | 977,264 | 6 |
| RLB | 67 | Public Services | 392,311 | 24,883 | 383,111 | 800,305 | 22 | 899,909 | 24,883 | 852,777 | 1,777,569 | 28 |
| RLB | 84 | Technical Services | 647,394 | 5,482 | 277,394 | 930,270 | 16 | 1,547,303 | 30,365 | 1,130,171 | 2,707,839 | 44 |
| RLB | 94 | Network Services | 55,606 | - | - | 55,606 | 2 | 1,602,909 | 30,365 | - | 2,763,445 | 46 |
| RLB | 113 | Blind & Phys. Handicapped | 342,089 | 3,000 | - | 345,089 | 8 | 1,944,998 | 33,365 | - | 3,108,534 | 54 |
| RLB | 146 | Statewide Library Develop. | 84,112 | - | - | 84,112 | 2 | 2,029,110 | - | - | 3,192,646 | 56 |
| RLB | 167 | Institutional Lib. Develop. | 98,185 | - | - | 98,185 | 1 | 2,127,295 | - | - | 3,290,831 | 57 |
| 1 | 69 | Limited Reference Service | 65,383 | - | 64,543 | 129,926 | 4 | 2,192,678 | - | 1,194,714 | 3,420,757 | 61 |
| 2 | 86 | Library Materials | 55,031 | - | 12,918 | 67,949 | 1 | 2,247,709 | - | 1,207,632 | 3,488,706 | 62 |
| 3 | 71 | Standard Reference Service | 73,867 | - | 73,366 | 147,233 | 5 | 2,321,576 | - | 1,208,998 | 3,635,939 | 67 |
| 4 | 148 | Current Consultant Service | 53,942 | - | - | 53,942 | 1 | 2,375,518 | - | - | 3,689,881 | 68 |
| 5 | 115 | Blind — Limited Service | 57,845 | - | - | 57,845 | 2 | 2,433,363 | - | - | 3,747,726 | 70 |
| 6 | 43 | Personnel & Publications | 23,690 | - | 19,203 | 42,893 | 1 | 2,457,053 | - | 1,300,201 | 3,790,619 | 71 |
| 9 | 152 | Continuing Education | 49,760 | - | - | 49,760 | 1 | 2,506,813 | - | - | 3,840,379 | 72 |

(continued)

AGENCY
PROGRAM
SUBPROGRAM
ACTIVITY

CODE  54300

TITLE  OREGON STATE LIBRARY

Form 120

[] AGENCY REQUEST
[X] GOVERNOR'S RECOMMENDATION
[] LEGISLATIVELY APPROVED

Page 23

PRIORITY TABLE

STATE OF OREGON
EXECUTIVE DEPARTMENT

PRIORITY TABLE

105 BF 120

| Rank 1 | Page Ref. 2 | DECISION PACKAGES 3 | AMOUNTS BY PACKAGE | | | | | CUMULATIVE TOTALS | | | | |
|---|---|---|---|---|---|---|---|---|---|---|---|---|
| | | | General 4 | Other 5 | Federal 6 | Total 7 | FTE 8 | General 9 | Other 10 | Federal 11 | Total 12 | FTE 13 |
| | | (continued) | | | | | | | | | | |
| 14 | 88 | State Documents & Preservation | 25,000 | - | - | 25,000 | - | 2,531,813 | - | - | 3,865,379 | 72 |
| 17 | 154 | LSCA Grants | - | - | 347,385 | 347,385 | - | 2,531,813 | - | 1,647,586 | 4,212,764 | 72 |
| 18 | 156 | State Aid Grants | 345,000 | 0 | - | 345,000 | - | 2,876,813 | 33,365 | 1,647,586 | 4,557,764 | 72 |
| | | TOTAL | 2,876,813 | 33,365 | 1,647,586 | 4,557,764 | 72 | 2,876,813 | 33,365 | 1,647,586 | 4,557,764 | |

AGENCY    CODE   54300    TITLE   OREGON STATE LIBRARY
PROGRAM
SUBPROGRAM
ACTIVITY

Form 120

[] AGENCY REQUEST
[X] GOVERNOR'S RECOMMENDATION
[] LEGISLATIVELY APPROVED

Page 24

PRIORITY TABLE

STATE OF OREGON
EXECUTIVE DEPARTMENT

PRIORITY TABLE

105 BF 120

| Rank 1 | Page Ref. 2 | DECISION PACKAGES 3 | AMOUNTS BY PACKAGE | | | | | CUMULATIVE TOTALS | | | | |
|---|---|---|---|---|---|---|---|---|---|---|---|---|
| | | | General 4 | Other 5 | Federal 6 | Total 7 | FTE 8 | General 9 | Other 10 | Federal 11 | Total 12 | FTE 13 |
| | | | | | | | | | | | | |

AGENCY    CODE  54300

TITLE
OREGON STATE LIBRARY

PROGRAM
SUBPROGRAM
ACTIVITY

Form 120

[ ] AGENCY REQUEST
[ ] GOVERNOR'S RECOMMENDATION
[X] LEGISLATIVELY APPROVED

Page  25

PRIORITY TABLE

STATE OF OREGON
EXECUTIVE DEPARTMENT

PRIORITY TABLE

105 BF 120

| Rank 1 | Page Ref. 2 | DECISION PACKAGES 3 | AMOUNTS BY PACKAGE | | | | CUMULATIVE TOTALS | | | | |
|---|---|---|---|---|---|---|---|---|---|---|---|
| | | | General 4 | Other 5 | Federal 6 | Total 7 | FTE 8 | General 9 | Other 10 | Federal 11 | Total 12 | FTE 13 |

AGENCY   CODE   54300
PROGRAM
SUBPROGRAM
ACTIVITY

Form 120

TITLE
OREGON STATE LIBRARY

[] AGENCY REQUEST
[] GOVERNOR'S RECOMMENDATION
[X] LEGISLATIVELY APPROVED

Page 26

PRIORITY TABLE

STATE OF OREGON
EXECUTIVE DEPARTMENT

FINANCIAL AID TO LOCAL GOVERNMENT

105 BF 104

| 1 Statutory Authority | 2 Fund Source | 3 Purpose of Grant or Payments | 4 Page No. | 5 Recipient | 6 1975-77 Actual | 7 1977-79 Estimated | 8 Agency Request | 9 1979-81 Governor's Recommendation | 10 Legislatively Approved |
|---|---|---|---|---|---|---|---|---|---|
| ORS 357.740 - 357.770 | G | **State Aid-Establishment** Grants to local public libraries for purchase of materials, equipment, furniture, and minor building repairs. Larger grants for extending public library service into new areas and for interlibrary resource sharing. | 155 | Cities Counties Total | | 190,000 110,000 300,000 | 200,000 100,000 300,000 | 230,000 115,000 345,000 | |
| ORS 357.015, 357.031, 357.035 Federal Library Services and Construction Act, Title I Services | F | **Library Development** Grants for the development of library activities emphasizing statewide projects benefitting improvement of public library services. | 153 | Cities Counties Other Governments Total | - 30,000 - 30,000 | 2,000 23,000 58,976 83,976 | 810,000 | 53,000 56,085 30,000 139,085 | |
| ORS 357.015, 357.031, 357.035 Federal Library Services and Construction Act, Title III, Interlibrary Cooperation | F | **Interlibrary Cooperation** Grants for the development of library services involving public and other types of libraries. | 153 | Cities Counties Total | 19,898 17,988 37,884 | - 60,000 60,000 | 60,000 | - - - | |
| None | G | **State Aid — Per Capita** Financial support to local governments with public libraries at $.25 per capita per year to be expended for library purposes. | 157 | Cities ) Counties ) Other Governments ) | - - | - - | 1,300,000 | - - | |

FINANCIAL AID TO LOCAL GOVERNMENT

AGENCY     CODE  54300
PROGRAM
SUBPROGRAM
ACTIVITY
Form 104

TITLE    OREGON STATE LIBRARY

PROGRAM NARRATIVE

LIBRARY SERVICES

1979-81

This program exists to provide state government with a centralized collection of reference and information resources together
with the professional and clerical staff to interpret this collection; to supplement the resources of local libraries; to provide
library materials and services to individuals who do not have
access to a local library; to collect and disseminate publications of Oregon state government agencies and the legislature
to selected Oregon depository libraries; and to provide the
technical staff and processes for organizing all of the materials
acquired for effective and efficient use. (ORS 357.005 (2) (c),
(d), (e), (f), (j); and (3); and ORS 357.015 (6)).

The vast number of programs that agencies of state government
must administer requires a versatile, up-to-date collection of
books, periodicals, documents, and information databases if
these programs are to be planned and implemented effectively
and efficiently. A strong centralized library and information
service is needed to provide state government agencies and the
legislature with access to this proliferating universe of information.

There is a pressing need to begin a planned program to restore and
preserve the unique information resources of the State Library,
particularly document and Oregon-related materials. An information and referral service will facilitate citizen access to
information about and from state government agencies.

54300     OREGON STATE LIBRARY
  002     Library Services

STATE OF OREGON
EXECUTIVE DEPARTMENT

BIENNIAL BUDGET SUMMARY

105 BF 110

SUMMARY OF REVENUES AND DISBURSEMENTS

| DESCRIPTION | 1975-77 Actual | 1977-79 Legis. Approved | 1977-79 Estimated | 1979-81 Adjusted Budget | Agency Request | 1979-81 Governor's Recommendation | Legislatively Approved |
|---|---|---|---|---|---|---|---|
| **Beginning Balances** | | | | | | | |
| Miscellaneous Receipts | 2,875 | 1,062 | 4,085 | 6,783 | 6,783 | 6,783 | |
| Donation Fund | 8,074 | 7,000 | 12,085 | 9,782 | 9,782 | 9,782 | |
| Total Beginning Balances | 10,949 | 8,062 | 16,170 | 16,565 | 16,565 | 16,565 | |
| General Fund Appropriation | 1,033,864 | 1,380,753 | 1,394,654 | 2,178,948 | 2,310,992 | 1,314,592 | |
| Approved salary adjustment | 83,308 | 18,218 | 18,218 | | | | |
| Total General Fund | 1,117,172 | 1,398,971 | 1,412,872 | 2,178,948 | 2,310,992 | 1,314,592 | |
| **Revenues** | | | | | | | |
| Other Revenues | 19,710 | 19,409 | 21,669 | 20,000 | 20,000 | 20,000 | |
| Interest Income | 1,470 | 1,500 | 2,697 | 600 | 600 | 800 | |
| Donations | 4,659 | 2,000 | - | - | - | - | |
| Total Other Revenues | 25,839 | 22,909 | 24,366 | 20,600 | 20,600 | 20,800 | |
| **Federal Library Services & Construction Act** | | | | | | | |
| Title I Services | 746,953 | 812,511 | 801,983 | - | - | 811,332 | |
| Approved salary adjustment | 87,667 | 37,064 | 37,064 | - | - | - | |
| Total | 834,620 | 849,575 | 839,047 | - | - | 811,332 | |

AGENCY — CODE 5400 — TITLE OREGON STATE LIBRARY
PROGRAM — 002 — Library Services
SUBPROGRAM
ACTIVITY
Form 110

BIENNIAL BUDGET SUMMARY

STATE OF OREGON
EXECUTIVE DEPARTMENT

BIENNIAL BUDGET SUMMARY

105 BF 110

## SUMMARY OF REVENUES AND DISBURSEMENTS (continued)

| DESCRIPTION | 1975-77 Actual | 1977-79 Legis. Approved | 1977-79 Estimated | 1979-81 Adjusted Budget | Agency Request | 1979-81 Governor's Recommendation | Legislatively Approved |
|---|---|---|---|---|---|---|---|
| Total Funds Available | | | | | | | |
| General Fund | 1,117,172 | 1,398,971 | 1,412,872 | 2,178,948 | 2,310,992 | 1,314,592 | |
| Other Funds | 36,788 | 30,971 | 40,536 | 37,165 | 37,165 | 37,365 | |
| Federal Funds | 834,620 | 849,575 | 839,047 | - | - | 811,332 | |
| Total | 1,988,580 | 2,279,517 | 2,292,455 | 2,216,113 | 2,348,157 | 2,163,289 | |
| Total Expenditures | | | | | | | |
| General Fund | 1,114,561 | 1,398,971 | 1,412,872 | 2,178,948 | 1,310,992 | 1,314,592 | |
| Other Funds | 20,618 | 23,971 | 23,971 | 20,400 | 20,400 | 30,365 | |
| Federal Funds | 834,620 | 849,575 | 839,047 | - | - | 811,332 | |
| Total | 1,969,799 | 2,272,517 | 2,275,890 | 2,199,348 | 2,331,392 | 2,156,289 | |
| Ending Balances | | | | | | | |
| Reverts to: | | | | | | | |
| General Fund | 2,611 | | | | | | |
| Federal Government | - | | | | | | |
| Carried forward: | | | | | | | |
| Miscellaneous Receipts | 4,085 | - | 6,783 | 6,883 | 6,883 | - | |
| Donation Funds | 12,085 | 7,000 | 9,782 | 9,882 | 9,882 | 7,000 | |

AGENCY CODE 54300
PROGRAM 002
SUBPROGRAM
ACTIVITY

TITLE OREGON STATE LIBRARY
Library Services

BIENNIAL BUDGET SUMMARY

STATE OF OREGON
EXECUTIVE DEPARTMENT

BIENNIAL BUDGET SUMMARY

105 BF 110

## SUMMARY OF EXPENDITURES BY CATEGORY BY FUND

| DESCRIPTION | 1975-77 Actual | 1977-79 Legis. Approved | 1977-79 Estimated | 1979-81 Adjusted Budget | Agency Request | 1979-81 Governor's Recommendation | Legislatively Approved |
|---|---|---|---|---|---|---|---|
| **Personal Services** | | | | | | | |
| General Fund | 561,880 | 688,040 | 690,397 | 1,545,951 | 1,666,546 | 789,591 | |
| Other Funds | - | - | - | - | - | - | |
| Federal Funds | 596,053 | 688,039 | 690,406 | - | - | 736,198 | |
| Total | 1,157,933 | 1,376,079 | 1,380,803 | 1,545,951 | 1,666,546 | 1,525,789 | |
| **Services and Supplies** | | | | | | | |
| General Fund | 199,004 | 332,466 | 344,010 | 164,382 | 213,771 | 102,348 | |
| Other Funds | 18,500 | 18,971 | 18,971 | 19,900 | 19,900 | 26,883 | |
| Federal Funds | 238,567 | 161,536 | 148,641 | - | - | 75,134 | |
| Total | 456,071 | 512,973 | 511,622 | 184,282 | 233,671 | 204,365 | |
| **Capital Outlay** | | | | | | | |
| General Fund | 353,677 | 378,465 | 378,465 | 468,615 | 430,675 | 422,653 | |
| Other Funds | 2,118 | 5,000 | 5,000 | 500 | 500 | 3,482 | |
| Federal Funds | - | - | - | - | - | - | |
| Total | 355,795 | 383,465 | 383,465 | 469,115 | 431,175 | 426,135 | |

AGENCY CODE 54300
PROGRAM 002
SUBPROGRAM
ACTIVITY
Form 110

TITLE OREGON STATE LIBRARY
Library Services

BIENNIAL BUDGET SUMMARY

Page 51

STATE OF OREGON
EXECUTIVE DEPARTMENT

BIENNIAL BUDGET SUMMARY

105 BF 110

## SUMMARY OF EXPENDITURES BY CLASSIFICATION BY FUND

| DESCRIPTION | 1975-77 Actual | 1977-79 Legis. Approved | 1977-79 Estimated | 1979-81 Adjusted Budget | Agency Request | 1979-81 Governor's Recommendation | Legislatively Approved |
|---|---|---|---|---|---|---|---|
| **Reduced Level Budget** | | | | | | | |
| General Fund | | | | | 1,784,400 | 1,095,311 | |
| Other Funds | | | | | 20,400 | 30,365 | |
| Federal Funds | | | | | - | 660,505 | |
| Total | | | | | 1,804,800 | 1,786,181 | |
| **All Decision Packages** | | | | | | | |
| General Fund | | | | | 526,592 | 219,281 | |
| Other Funds | | | | | - | - | |
| Federal Funds | | | | | - | 150,827 | |
| Total | | | | | 526,592 | 370,108 | |
| **Summary** | | | | | | | |
| General Fund | 1,114,561 | 1,398,971 | 1,412,872 | 2,178,948 | 2,310,992 | 1,314,592 | |
| Other Funds | 20,618 | 23,971 | 23,971 | 20,400 | 20,400 | 30,365 | |
| Federal Funds | 834,620 | 849,575 | 839,047 | - | - | 811,332 | |
| Total | 1,969,799 | 2,272,517 | 2,275,890 | 2,199,348 | 2,331,392 | 2,156,289 | |
| Authorized positions | 50 | 50 | 50 | 50 | 54 | 50 | |
| FTE positions | 48.9 | 50 | 47 | 50 | 54 | 50 | |

AGENCY  CODE  54300
PROGRAM  002
SUBPROGRAM
ACTIVITY

TITLE
OREGON STATE LIBRARY
Library Services

BIENNIAL BUDGET SUMMARY

Page 52

STATE OF OREGON
EXECUTIVE DEPARTMENT

APLS BUDGET SUMMARY

105 BF 125

| BUDGET DATA | 1977-79 | | | | | | 1979-81 | | | | | |
|---|---|---|---|---|---|---|---|---|---|---|---|---|
| | 2 Legislatively Approved | 3 Estimated for Biennium | 4 Adjusted Budget | 5 Reduced Level Budget | 6 % Adj. Budg. | 7 Decision Package Subtotal | 8 Total Agency Request | 9 % Adj. Budg. | 10 Governor's Recommendation | 11 % Adj. Budg. | 12 Legislatively Approved | 13 % Adj. Budg. |
| **1 POSITION SUMMARY** | | | | | | | | | | | | |
| Authorized Positions | 50 | 50 | 50 | 40 | 80 | 14 | 54 | 108 | 50 | 100 | | |
| FTE Positions | 50 | 47 | 50 | 40 | 80 | 14 | 54 | 108 | 50 | 100 | | |
| **14** | | | | | | | | | | | | |
| **EXPENDITURES BY CATEGORY** | | | | | | | | | | | | |
| Personal Services | 1,376,079 | 1,380,803 | 1,545,951 | 1,260,642 | 82 | 405,904 | 1,666,546 | 108 | 1,525,789 | 99 | | |
| Services and Supplies | 512,973 | 511,622 | 184,282 | 160,063 | 87 | 73,608 | 233,671 | 126 | 204,365 | 111 | | |
| Capital Outlay | 8,465 | 8,465 | 13,115 | 14,095 | 107 | 7,080 | 21,175 | 161 | 16,135 | 123 | | |
| Special Payments | - | - | - | - | - | - | - | - | - | - | | |
| 15 Library Materials | 375,000 | 375,000 | 456,000 | 370,000 | 81 | 40,000 | 410,000 | 90 | 410,000 | 88 | | |
| 16 TOTAL | 2,272,517 | 2,275,890 | 2,199,348 | 1,804,800 | 82 | 526,592 | 2,331,392 | 106 | 2,156,289 | 98 | | |
| **EXPENDITURES BY FUND** | | | | | | | | | | | | |
| General Fund | 1,398,971 | 1,412,872 | 2,178,948 | 1,784,400 | 82 | 526,592 | 2,310,992 | 106 | 1,314,592 | 60 | | |
| Other Funds | 23,971 | 23,971 | 20,400 | 20,400 | - | - | 20,400 | - | 30,365 | 149 | | |
| Federal Funds | 849,575 | 839,047 | - | - | - | - | - | - | 811,332 | - | | |
| 17 TOTAL | 2,272,517 | 2,275,890 | 2,199,348 | 1,804,800 | 82 | 526,592 | 2,331,392 | 106 | 2,156,289 | 98 | | |
| **18 ACCOMPLISHMENTS/WORKLOAD MEASURES** | | | | | | | | | | | | |

See following page.

**19**

| AGENCY | CODE 54300 | TITLE OREGON STATE LIBRARY |
|---|---|---|
| PROGRAM | 002 | Library Services |
| SUBPROGRAM | | |
| ACTIVITY | | |

Form 125

APLS BUDGET SUMMARY

STATE OF OREGON
EXECUTIVE DEPARTMENT

PLS BUDGET SUMMARY

105 BF 125a

| BUDGET DATA 1 | 1977-79 | | Adjusted Budget 4 | Reduced Level Budget 5 | % Adj. Budg. 6 | Decision Package Subtotal 7 | 1979-81 | | % Adj. Budg. 9 | Governor's Recommendation 10 | % Adj. Budg. 11 | Legislatively Approved 12 | % Adj. Budg. 13 |
|---|---|---|---|---|---|---|---|---|---|---|---|---|---|
| | Legislatively Approved 2 | Estimated for Biennium 3 | | | | | Total Agency Request 8 | | | | | | |
| **ACCOMPLISHMENTS/WORKLOAD MEASURES (Continued)** | | | | | | | | | | | | | |
| *Reference requests received | 48,000 | 67,989 | 84,000 | 50,000 | 60 | 41,000 | 91,000 | | 108 | 84,000 | 100 | | |
| Title requests received | 238,000 | 236,452 | 236,500 | 185,000 | 78 | 63,000 | 248,000 | | 105 | 241,000 | 102 | | |
| Items circulated | 236,000 | 200,060 | 200,000 | 140,000 | 70 | 65,000 | 205,000 | | 102 | 200,000 | 100 | | |
| *Photocopies provided | 46,000 | 82,462 | 20,000 | 14,000 | 70 | 7,000 | 21,000 | | 105 | 20,000 | 100 | | |
| On-line searches | 800 | 2,462 | 3,400 | 3,400 | 100 | 1,200 | 4,600 | | 135 | 3,400 | 100 | | |
| Information & referral requests | - | - | - | - | - | 14,000 | 14,000 | | - | - | | | |
| Requests forwarded to PNBC resource & other libraries | 18,000 | 13,988 | 16,000 | 16,000 | 100 | - | 16,000 | | 100 | 16,000 | 100 | | |
| Books acquired | 19,400 | 20,421 | 21,500 | 19,000 | 88 | 2,500 | 21,500 | | 100 | 21,500 | 100 | | |
| Items cataloged | 28,000 | 22,062 | 25,000 | 23,000 | 92 | 2,800 | 25,800 | | 103 | 25,500 | 102 | | |
| Documents added | 64,000 | 63,863 | 80,000 | 80,000 | 100 | - | 80,000 | | 100 | 80,000 | 100 | | |
| Oregon documents acquired for distribution | 2,000 | 2,012 | 2,500 | 2,500 | 100 | 500 | 3,000 | | 120 | 2,500 | 100 | | |
| Volumes microfilmed | - | - | - | - | - | 2,500 | 2,500 | | - | 2,500 | | | |

*Definition to change for 1979-81 biennium

14

| AGENCY | CODE | 54300 |
|---|---|---|
| PROGRAM | | 002 |
| SUBPROGRAM | | |
| ACTIVITY | | |

TITLE  OREGON STATE LIBRARY
Library Services

Form 125a

Page 54

APLS BUDGET SUMMARY

DECISION UNITS

LIBRARY SERVICES

1979-81


002-01    PUBLIC SERVICES

Provides direct patron access to the materials and information resources of the State Library through the
reference, circulation, and interlibrary loan services.


002-02    TECHNICAL SERVICES

Provides support services to Public and Network Services
by acquiring, cataloging, and processing all library
materials; by distributing the State Library Catalog;
and by coordinating the Oregon Regional Union List of
Serials.


002-03    NETWORK SERVICES

Provides all Oregon public libraries and their patrons
with access to the resources of other major Oregon
libraries through the Resource Library Network, and
to library resources throughout the Northwest through
the Pacific Northwest Bibliographic Center.


54300            OREGON STATE LIBRARY
  002            Library Services

STATE OF OREGON
EXECUTIVE DEPARTMENT

PRIORITY TABLE

105 BF 120

| Rank 1 | Page Ref. 2 | DECISION PACKAGES 3 | AMOUNTS BY PACKAGE | | | | | CUMULATIVE TOTALS | | | | |
|---|---|---|---|---|---|---|---|---|---|---|---|---|
| | | | General 4 | Other 5 | Federal 6 | Total 7 | FTE 8 | General 9 | Other 10 | Federal 11 | Total 12 | FTE 13 |
| 1 | 68 | 002-01-DP1 Limited Reference Service | 131,792 | | | 131,792 | 4 | 131,792 | | | 131,792 | 4 |
| 2 | 85 | 002-02-DP1 Library Materials | 69,256 | | | 69,256 | 1 | 201,084 | | | 201,084 | 5 |
| 3 | 70 | 002-01-DP2 Standard Reference Service | 150,768 | | | 150,768 | 5 | 351,816 | | | 351,816 | 10 |
| 4 | 72 | 002-01-DP3 Gov't Information Coordinator | 56,827 | | | 56,827 | 1 | 408,643 | | | 408,643 | 11 |
| 5 | 87 | 002-02-DP2 State Documents and Preservation | 46,924 | | | 46,924 | 1 | 455,567 | | | 455,567 | 12 |
| 6 | 74 | 002-01-DP4 State Government Information & Referral | 71,025 | | | 71,025 | 2 | 526,592 | | | 526,592 | 14 |
| | | | 526,592 | | | 526,592 | 14 | 526,592 | | | 526,592 | 14 |

AGENCY   CODE 54300
PROGRAM   002
SUBPROGRAM
ACTIVITY

TITLE
OREGON STATE LIBRARY
Library Services

[X] AGENCY REQUEST
[] GOVERNOR'S RECOMMENDATION
[] LEGISLATIVELY APPROVED

Page 56

Form 120

PRIORITY TABLE

STATE OF OREGON
EXECUTIVE DEPARTMENT

PRIORITY TABLE

*105 BF 120

| Rank 1 | Page Ref. 2 | DECISION PACKAGES 3 | AMOUNTS BY PACKAGE | | | | | CUMULATIVE TOTALS | | | | |
|---|---|---|---|---|---|---|---|---|---|---|---|---|
| | | | 4 General | 5 Other | 6 Federal | 7 Total | 8 FTE | 9 General | 10 Other | 11 Federal | 12 Total | 13 FTE |
| 1 | 69 | Limited Reference Service | 65,383 | - | 64,543 | 129,926 | 4 | 65,383 | | 64,543 | 129,926 | 4 |
| 2 | 86 | Library Materials | 55,031 | - | 12,918 | 67,949 | 1 | 120,414 | | 77,461 | 197,875 | 5 |
| 3 | 71 | Standard Reference Service | 73,867 | - | 73,366 | 147,233 | 5 | 194,281 | | 150,827 | 345,108 | 10 |
| 5 | 88 | State Documents and Preservation | 25,000 | - | - | 25,000 | 0 | 219,281 | - | 150,827 | 370,108 | 10 |
| | | TOTAL | 219,281 | - | 150,827 | 370,108 | 10 | 219,281 | | 150,827 | 370,108 | 10 |

AGENCY        CODE    54300
PROGRAM               002
SUBPROGRAM
ACTIVITY

TITLE
OREGON STATE LIBRARY
Library Services

Form 120

[] AGENCY REQUEST
[X] GOVERNOR'S RECOMMENDATION
[] LEGISLATIVELY APPROVED

Page 57

PRIORITY TABLE

STATE OF OREGON
EXECUTIVE DEPARTMENT

PRIORITY TABLE

105 BF 120

| Rank 1 | Page Ref. 2 | Decision Packages 3 | Amounts by Package | | | | | Cumulative Totals | | | | |
|---|---|---|---|---|---|---|---|---|---|---|---|---|
| | | | 4 General | 5 Other | 6 Federal | 7 Total | 8 FTE | 9 General | 10 Other | 11 Federal | 12 Total | 13 FTE |
| 1 | 68 | Limited Reference Service | 131,792 | | | 131,792 | 4 | 131,792 | | | 131,792 | 4 |
| 2 | 70 | Standard Reference Service | 150,768 | | | 150,768 | 5 | 282,560 | | | 282,560 | 9 |
| 3 | 72 | Government Information Coordinator | 56,827 | | | 56,827 | 1 | 339,387 | | | 339,387 | 10 |
| 4 | 74 | State Government Information & Referral | 71,025 | | | 71,025 | 2 | 410,412 | | | 410,412 | 12 |
| | | | 410,412 | | | 410,412 | 12 | 410,412 | | | 410,412 | 12 |

|  | CODE | TITLE |
|---|---|---|
| AGENCY | 54300 | OREGON STATE LIBRARY |
| PROGRAM | 002 | Library Services |
| SUBPROGRAM | 01 | Public Services |
| ACTIVITY | | |

Form 120

[X] AGENCY REQUEST
[] GOVERNOR'S RECOMMENDATION
[] LEGISLATIVELY APPROVED

Page 59

PRIORITY TABLE

STATE OF OREGON
EXECUTIVE DEPARTMENT

PRIORITY TABLE

105 BF 120

| Rank 1 | Page Ref. 2 | DECISION PACKAGES 3 | AMOUNTS BY PACKAGE | | | | | CUMULATIVE TOTALS | | | | |
|---|---|---|---|---|---|---|---|---|---|---|---|---|
| | | | General 4 | Other 5 | Federal 6 | Total 7 | FTE 8 | General 9 | Other 10 | Federal 11 | Total 12 | FTE 13 |
| 1 | 69 | Limited Reference Service | 65,383 | - | 64,543 | 129,926 | 4 | 65,383 | - | 64,543 | 129,926 | 4 |
| 2 | 71 | Standard Reference Service | 73,867 | - | 73,366 | 147,233 | 5 | 139,250 | - | 137,909 | 277,159 | 9 |
| | | | 139,250 | - | 137,909 | 277,159 | 9 | 139,250 | - | 137,909 | 277,159 | |

AGENCY    CODE   54300
PROGRAM   002
SUBPROGRAM   01
ACTIVITY

Form 120

TITLE
OREGON STATE LIBRARY
Library Services
Public Services

[] AGENCY REQUEST
[X] GOVERNOR'S RECOMMENDATION
[] LEGISLATIVELY APPROVED

Page 60

PRIORITY TABLE

STATE OF OREGON
EXECUTIVE DEPARTMENT

APLS BUDGET SUMMARY

105 BF 125

| BUDGET DATA | 1977-79 | | Adjusted Budget | Reduced Level Budget | %Adj. Budg. | 1979-81 | | %Adj. Budg. | Governor's Recommendation | %Adj. Budg. | Legislatively Approved | %Adj. Budg. |
|---|---|---|---|---|---|---|---|---|---|---|---|---|
| | Legislatively Approved (2) | Estimated for Biennium (3) | (4) | (5) | (6) | Decision Package Subtotal (7) | Total Agency Request (8) | (9) | (10) | (11) | (12) | (13) |
| **POSITION SUMMARY** | | | | | | | | | | | | |
| Authorized Positions | 30.5 | 30.5 | 31 | 22 | 71 | 12 | 34 | 110 | 31 | 100 | | |
| FTE Positions | 30.5 | 30.5 | 31 | 22 | 71 | 12 | 34 | 110 | 41 | 100 | | |
| **EXPENDITURES BY CATEGORY** | | | | | | | | | | | | |
| Personal Services | 855,964 | 857,689 | 964,480 | 711,360 | 74 | 366,374 | 1,077,734 | 112 | 963,839 | 100 | | |
| Services and Supplies | 418,257 | 416,108 | 105,210 | 90,147 | 86 | 39,558 | 129,705 | 123 | 103,035 | 98 | | |
| Capital Outlay | 6,958 | 6,958 | 9,200 | 9,200 | 100 | 4,480 | 13,680 | 149 | 10,540 | 115 | | |
| Special Payments | - | - | - | - | - | - | - | - | - | - | | |
| **TOTAL** | 1,281,179 | 1,280,755 | 1,078,890 | 810,207 | 76 | 410,412 | 1,221,119 | 113 | 1,077,464 | 100 | | |
| **EXPENDITURES BY FUND** | | | | | | | | | | | | |
| General Fund | 720,048 | 732,055 | 1,064,890 | 796,707 | 75 | 410,412 | 1,207,119 | 113 | 531,561 | 50 | | |
| Other Funds | 18,971 | 18,971 | 14,000 | 14,000 | 100 | - | 14,000 | 100 | 24,883 | 178 | | |
| Federal Funds | 542,160 | 529,729 | - | - | - | - | - | - | 521,020 | - | | |
| **TOTAL** | 1,281,179 | 1,280,755 | 1,078,890 | 810,207 | 76 | 410,412 | 1,221,119 | 113 | 1,077,464 | 100 | | |
| **ACCOMPLISHMENTS/WORKLOAD MEASURES** | | | | | | | | | | | | |
| *Reference requests rec'd | 48,000 | 67,989 | 84,000 | 50,000 | 60 | 41,000 | 91,000 | 108 | 84,000 | 100 | | |
| Title requests received | 238,000 | 236,452 | 236,500 | 185,000 | 78 | 63,000 | 248,000 | 105 | 241,000 | 102 | | |
| Items circulated | 236,000 | 200,060 | 200,000 | 140,000 | 70 | 65,000 | 205,000 | 102 | 200,000 | 100 | | |
| *Photocopies provided | 46,000 | 82,462 | 20,000 | 14,000 | 70 | 7,000 | 21,000 | 105 | 20,000 | 100 | | |
| Online searches | 800 | 2,426 | 3,400 | 3,400 | 100 | 1,200 | 4,600 | 135 | 3,400 | 100 | | |
| Information and referral requests | - | - | - | - | - | 14,000 | 14,000 | - | - | - | | |

*Definition to change for 1979-81 biennium

| | CODE | TITLE |
|---|---|---|
| AGENCY | 54300 | OREGON STATE LIBRARY |
| PROGRAM | 002 | Library Services |
| SUBPROGRAM | 01 | Public Services |
| ACTIVITY | | |

Form 125

APLS BUDGET SUMMARY

STATE OF OREGON
EXECUTIVE DEPARTMENT

DECISION UNIT SUMMARY

105 BF 130

| BUDGET DATA | 1979-81 Reduced Level Budget | Decision Packages in Priority Order Within the Unit | | | | | | | | Subtotal of Decision Packages | Total For Decision Unit |
|---|---|---|---|---|---|---|---|---|---|---|---|
| | 2 | (1) 3 | (2) 4 | (3) 5 | (4) 6 | (5) 7 | (6) 8 | (7) 9 | (8) 10 | 11 | 12 |
| **POSITION SUMMARY** | | | | | | | | | | | |
| Authorized Positions | 22 | 4 | 5 | 1 | 2 | | | | | 12 | 34 |
| FTE Positions | 22 | 4 | 5 | 1 | 2 | | | | | 12 | 34 |
| **EXPENDITURES BY CATEGORY** | | | | | | | | | | | |
| Personal Services | 711,360 | 127,659 | 139,123 | 38,407 | 61,185 | | | | | 366,374 | 1,077,734 |
| Services and Supplies | 90,147 | 3,293 | 11,145 | 17,920 | 7,200 | | | | | 39,558 | 129,705 |
| Capital Outlay | 9,200 | 840 | 500 | 500 | 2,640 | | | | | 4,480 | 13,680 |
| Special Payments | - | - | - | - | - | | | | | - | - |
| **TOTAL** | 810,707 | 131,792 | 150,768 | 56,827 | 71,025 | | | | | 410,412 | 1,221,119 |
| **EXPENDITURES BY FUND** | | | | | | | | | | | |
| General Fund | 796,707 | 131,792 | 150,768 | 56,827 | 71,025 | | | | | 410,412 | 1,207,119 |
| Other Funds | 14,000 | - | - | - | - | | | | | - | 14,000 |
| Federal Funds | - | - | - | - | - | | | | | - | - |
| **TOTAL** | 810,707 | 131,792 | 150,768 | 56,827 | 71,025 | | | | | 410,412 | 1,221,119 |
| **ACCOMPLISHMENTS/WORKLOAD MEASURES** | | | | | | | | | | | |
| Reference requests rec'd | 50,000 | 21,000 | 13,000 | 7,000 | - | | | | | 41,000 | 91,000 |
| Title requests received | 185,000 | 36,000 | 20,000 | 7,000 | - | | | | | 63,000 | 248,000 |
| Items circulated | 140,000 | 30,000 | 30,000 | 5,000 | - | | | | | 65,000 | 205,000 |
| Photocopies provided | 14,000 | 3,000 | 3,000 | 1,000 | - | | | | | 7,000 | 21,000 |
| On-line searches | 3,400 | - | 1,200 | - | - | | | | | 1,200 | 4,600 |
| Information & referral requests | - | - | - | - | 14,000 | | | | | 14,000 | 14,000 |

| | CODE | | TITLE | |
|---|---|---|---|---|
| AGENCY | 54300 | | OREGON STATE LIBRARY | |
| PROGRAM | 002 | | Library Services | |
| SUBPROGRAM | 01 | | Public Services | |
| ACTIVITY | | | | |

Form 130

[X] AGENCY REQUEST
[ ] GOVERNOR'S RECOMMENDATION
[ ] LEGISLATIVELY APPROVED

DECISION UNIT SUMMARY

Page 6.3

STATE OF OREGON
EXECUTIVE DEPARTMENT

DECISION UNIT SUMMARY

105 BF 130

| BUDGET DATA | 1979-81 Reduced Level Budget | Decision Packages in Priority Order Within the Unit | | | | | | | | Subtotal of Decision Packages | Total For Decision Unit |
|---|---|---|---|---|---|---|---|---|---|---|---|
| | 2 | (1) | (2) | (3) | (4) | (5) | (6) | (7) | (8) | 11 | 12 |
| 1 POSITION SUMMARY | | 3 | 4 | 5 | 6 | 7 | 8 | 9 | 10 | | |
| Authorized Positions | 22 | 4 | 5 | | | | | | | 9 | 31 |
| FTE Positions | 22 | 4 | 5 | | | | | | | 9 | 31 |
| 13 EXPENDITURES BY CATEGORY | | | | | | | | | | | |
| Personal Services | 700,958 | 125,793 | 137,088 | | | | | | | 262,881 | 963,839 |
| Services and Supplies | 90,147 | 3,293 | 9,645 | | | | | | | 12,938 | 103,085 |
| Capital Outlay | 9,200 | 840 | 500 | | | | | | | 1,340 | 10,540 |
| Special Payments | - | - | - | | | | | | | - | - |
| 14 TOTAL | 800,305 | 129,926 | 147,233 | | | | | | | 277,159 | 1,077,464 |
| 15 EXPENDITURES BY FUND | | | | | | | | | | | |
| General Fund | 392,311 | 65,383 | 73,867 | | | | | | | 139,250 | 531,561 |
| Other Funds | 24,883 | - | - | | | | | | | - | 24,883 |
| Federal Funds | 383,111 | 64,543 | 73,366 | | | | | | | 137,909 | 521,020 |
| 16 TOTAL | 800,305 | 129,926 | 147,233 | | | | | | | 277,159 | 1,077,464 |
| 17 ACCOMPLISHMENTS/WORKLOAD MEASURES | | | | | | | | | | | |
| Reference requests rec'd | 50,000 | 21,000 | 13,000 | | | | | | | 34,000 | 84,000 |
| Title requests received | 185,000 | 36,000 | 20,000 | | | | | | | 56,000 | 241,000 |
| Items circulated | 140,000 | 30,000 | 30,000 | | | | | | | 60,000 | 200,000 |
| Photocopies provided | 14,000 | 3,000 | 3,000 | | | | | | | 6,000 | 20,000 |
| on-line searches | 3,400 | | | | | | | | | | 3,400 |
| Information & referral | | | | | | | | | | | |
| 18 requests | | | | | | | | | | | |

| | CODE | TITLE |
|---|---|---|
| AGENCY | 54300 | OREGON STATE LIBRARY |
| PROGRAM | 002 | Library Services |
| SUBPROGRAM | 01 | Public Services |
| ACTIVITY | | |

Form 130

[ ] AGENCY REQUEST
[X] GOVERNOR'S RECOMMENDATION
[ ] LEGISLATIVELY APPROVED

Page 64

DECISION UNIT SUMMARY

STATE OF OREGON
EXECUTIVE DEPARTMENT

REDUCED LEVEL/DECISION PACKAGE

105 BF 135

PURPOSE

Provide library materials, reference and information services to state agencies and the legislature; to Oregon citizens who do not have access to a public library; and to other libraries in the state. Provide interlibrary loan, interlibrary reference, and referral to Oregon resource libraries and PNBC (Pacific Northwest Bibliographic Center).

HOW ACCOMPLISHED

State government employes send requests by interagency mail, the telephone, or in person. Other libraries and individuals without local library service are served by mail. Individuals come to the State Library to do research.

The State Library will provide library materials, reference service and interlibrary loan to all types of library users. Average turn-around time for mail requests will be increased. Interlibrary reference and information questions and assistance to individuals who use the library for personal research will be limited. Current awareness publications will be curtailed.

ALTERNATIVES

The State Library is the only Oregon library with an obligation to serve the state government and all Oregon citizens. There is no alternative to this service.

The only alternative to increased turnaround time for requests for library materials and limitations on reference and information service is to eliminate service to a whole class of library users. This was rejected since it would make the services of the State Library completely unavailable to some Oregon citizens.

IMPACT: Positive and Negative

Providing library services to all current users insures that Oregon citizens will continue to have access to the materials and services of the State Library. Services to state government will be fully maintained. However, increasing turnaround time and limiting reference service for mail requests will have a negative impact on local libraries. Increased turnaround time at the State Library will mean that it takes longer for local libraries to receive the materials they have requested for their users. Some users will receive the materials too late to be useful to them. Local libraries will be under pressure to purchase more materials. Limitations on the time spent on reference and information questions will mean that users with more complicated information needs will not get service. Limitations on assistance for individuals using the library for research will mean longer waits for service. Specialized assistance for users of the genealogy and Oregon collections will no longer be available.

ACCOMPLISHMENTS/WORKLOAD

| MEASURES | 1977-79 | | | 1979-81 | | |
|---|---|---|---|---|---|---|
| | 6 First Year | 7 Second Year | 8 Biennium | 9 Agency Request | 10 Governor's Recom. | 11 Legislatively Approved |
| * Reference requests received | 32,989 | 35,000 | 67,989 | 50,000 | 50,000 | |
| Title requests received | 118,452 | 118,000 | 236,452 | 185,000 | 185,000 | |
| Items circulated | 100,060 | 100,000 | 200,060 | 140,000 | 140,000 | |
| * Photocopies provided | 41,462 | 41,000 | 82,462 | 14,000 | 14,000 | |
| On-line searches | 426 | 2,000 | 2,426 | 3,400 | 3,400 | |
| * Definition to change for the 1979-81 biennium | | | | | | |

| | CODE | TITLE |
|---|---|---|
| AGENCY | 54300 | OREGON STATE LIBRARY |
| PROGRAM | 002 | Library Services |
| SUBPROGRAM | 01 | Public Services |
| ACTIVITY | | |

Form 135

[X] Reduced Level Budget or [ ] Decision Package Number _____

Description _____

Page 66

REDUCED LEVEL/DECISION PACKAGE

STATE OF OREGON
EXECUTIVE DEPARTMENT

REDUCED LEVEL/DECISION PACKAGE

105 BF 135a

1 AGENCY COMMENTS:

2 EXECUTIVE DEPARTMENT COMMENTS:

3 RELATED DECISION PACKAGES

| Pkg. No. | Page | Title | Amount | FTE |
|---|---|---|---|---|

| 4 BUDGET DATA | 1977-79 5 Estimated for Biennium | 1979-81 6 Agency Request | 7 Governor's Recommendation | 8 Legislatively Approved |
|---|---|---|---|---|
| POSITION SUMMARY | | | | |
| Authorized Positions | 30.5 | 22 | 22 | |
| 9 FTE Positions | 30.5 | 22 | 22 | |
| EXPENDITURES BY CATEGORY | | | | |
| Personal Services | 857,689 | 711,360 | 700,958 | |
| Services and Supplies | 416,108 | 90,147 | 90,147 | |
| Capital Outlay | 6,958 | 9,200 | 9,200 | |
| Special Payments | - | - | - | |
| 10 TOTAL | 1,280,755 | 810,707 | 800,305 | |
| 11 EXPENDITURES BY FUND | | | | |
| General Fund | 732,055 | 796,707 | 392,311 | |
| Other Funds | 18,971 | 14,000 | 24,883 | |
| 12 Federal Funds | 529,729 | - | 383,111 | |
| 13 TOTAL | 1,280,755 | 810,707 | 800,305 | |
| 14 REVENUE INFORMATION | | | | |

| AGENCY | CODE | TITLE |
|---|---|---|
| | 54300 | OREGON STATE LIBRARY |
| PROGRAM | 002 | Library Services |
| SUBPROGRAM | 01 | Public Services |
| ACTIVITY | | |

16

[k] Reduced Level Budget or [ ] Decision Package Number _____
Description _____

| PRIORITY | Agency Request | Governor's Recommendation | Legislatively Approved |
|---|---|---|---|
| Agency Wide _____ of ___ | _____ of ___ | _____ of ___ | |

17 REDUCED LEVEL/DECISION PACKAGE

Page 67

Form 135a

STATE OF OREGON
EXECUTIVE DEPARTMENT

REDUCED LEVEL/DECISION PACKAGE

105 BF 135

**PURPOSE**

Improve reference and information service to libraries and individuals without local library service.

Improve turnaround time on requests from libraries for materials listed in the book and microfiche catalogs of the State Library.

1

**HOW ACCOMPLISHED**

Add 2 reference librarians and 2 clerical assistants in the Circulation Section. Limitations on interlibrary reference would be removed but turnaround time would average 5 days, instead of the current 3 days. Turnaround time on title requests verified in the catalog would be 1 day, but turnaround time on unverified requests would average 4 instead of the current 2 days. Current awareness publications will still be curtailed. Service to individuals using the library for research will continue to be limited.

2

**ALTERNATIVES**

The State Library is the only Oregon library with an obligation to serve the state government and all Oregon citizens. There is no alternative to this service.

The only alternative to increased turnaround time for requests for library materials and limitations on reference and information service is to eliminate service to a whole class of library users. This was rejected since it would make the services of the State Library completely unavailable to some Oregon citizens.

3

**IMPACT: Positive and Negative**

This package would result in improved service to local libraries. Local library users will get fast and efficient service if they know exactly what they want, and if what they want is owned by the State Library. Users who request materials which require bibliographic searching or who need reference assistance will have to wait longer for service. Thus, the unique resources of the State Library will not be utilized in the most efficient or effective manner. The lack of current awareness publications will mean that local libraries will not fully be aware of the services and materials available for their users.

4

**ACCOMPLISHMENTS/WORKLOAD**
**MEASURES**

5

| | 6 First Year | 7 1977-79 Second Year | 8 Biennium | 9 Agency Request | 10 1979-81 Governor's Recom. | 11 Legislatively Approved |
|---|---|---|---|---|---|---|
| * Reference requests received | | | | 21,000 | 21,000 | |
| Title requests received | | | | 36,000 | 36,000 | |
| Items circulated | | | | 30,000 | 30,000 | |
| * Photocopies provided | | | | 3,000 | 3,000 | |
| * Definition to change for the 1979-81 biennium | | | | | | |

| AGENCY | CODE 54300 | TITLE OREGON STATE LIBRARY |
|---|---|---|
| PROGRAM | 002 | Library Services |
| SUBPROGRAM | 01 | Public Services |
| ACTIVITY | | |

Form 135

[ ] Reduced Level Budget or [X] Decision Package Number  01

Description  Limited Reference Service

Page  68

REDUCED LEVEL/DECISION PACKAGE

STATE OF OREGON
EXECUTIVE DEPARTMENT

REDUCED LEVEL/DECISION PACKAGE

105 BF 135a

**1 AGENCY COMMENTS:**

This package includes current positions and services.

**2 EXECUTIVE DEPARTMENT COMMENTS:**

| 4 BUDGET DATA | 5 1977-79 Estimated for Biennium | 6 Agency Request | 7 Governor's Recommendation | 8 Legislatively Approved |
|---|---|---|---|---|
| POSITION SUMMARY | | | | |
| Authorized Positions | | 4 | 4 | |
| 9 FTE Positions | | 4 | 4 | |
| EXPENDITURES BY CATEGORY | | | | |
| Personal Services | | 127,659 | 125,793 | |
| Services and Supplies | | 3,293 | 3,293 | |
| Capital Outlay | | 840 | 840 | |
| Special Payments | | - | - | |
| 10 | | | | |
| 11 TOTAL | | 131,792 | 129,926 | |
| EXPENDITURES BY FUND | | | | |
| General Fund | | 131,792 | 65,383 | |
| Other Funds | | - | - | |
| 12 Federal Funds | | - | 64,543 | |
| 13 TOTAL | | 131,792 | 129,926 | |
| 14 REVENUE INFORMATION | | | | |

**3 RELATED DECISION PACKAGES**

| Pkg. No. | Page | Title | Amount | FTE |
|---|---|---|---|---|

| | |
|---|---|
| AGENCY | CODE 54300 | TITLE OREGON STATE LIBRARY |
| PROGRAM | 002 | Library Services |
| SUBPROGRAM | 01 | Public Services |
| ACTIVITY | | |

[ ] Reduced Level Budget or [x] Decision Package Number ___01___

Description  Limited Reference Service

16

| PRIORITY | | Agency Request | Governor's Recommendation | Legislatively Approved |
|---|---|---|---|---|
| | Agency Wide | 1 of 19 | of | of |
| 17 | | | REDUCED LEVEL/DECISION PACKAGE | |

Form 135a

Page 69

STATE OF OREGON
EXECUTIVE DEPARTMENT

REDUCED LEVEL/DECISION PACKAGE

105 BF 135

**PURPOSE**

Restore all services to libraries, individuals without local library service, and individuals who use the library for research to current levels.

1

**IMPACT: Positive and Negative**

This package would result in fast and efficient service to all types of users of the State Library.

**HOW ACCOMPLISHED**

Add one librarian and one administrative assistant in the Reference Section. Add two clerical assistants and one custodial worker in the Circulation Section.

Turnaround time for mail requests will be restored to current levels. Service to individuals who use the library for research will be restored to the current level. Current awareness publications will be resumed.

2

**ALTERNATIVES**

The State Library is the only Oregon library with an obligation to serve the state government and all Oregon citizens. There is no alternative to this service.

3

**ACCOMPLISHMENTS/WORKLOAD MEASURES**

5

| | 1977-79 | | | 1979-81 | | |
| --- | --- | --- | --- | --- | --- | --- |
| 4 | First Year 6 | Second Year 7 | Biennium 8 | Agency Request 9 | Governor's Recom. 10 | Legislatively Approved 11 |
| * Reference requests received | | | | 13,000 | 13,000 | |
| Title requests received | | | | 20,000 | 20,000 | |
| Items circulated | | | | 30,000 | 30,000 | |
| * Photocopies provided | | | | 3,000 | 3,000 | |
| * Definition will be changed for the 1979-81 biennium | | | | | | |

| | CODE | TITLE |
| --- | --- | --- |
| AGENCY | 54300 | OREGON STATE LIBRARY |
| PROGRAM | 002 | Library Services |
| SUBPROGRAM | 01 | Public Services |
| ACTIVITY | | |

[1] Reduced Level Budget or [X] Decision Package Number 02

Description Standard Reference Service

Page 70

Form 135

REDUCED LEVEL/DECISION PACKAGE

STATE OF OREGON
EXECUTIVE DEPARTMENT

REDUCED LEVEL/DECISION PACKAGE

105 BF 135a

**1 AGENCY COMMENTS:**

This package includes current positions and services.

**2 EXECUTIVE DEPARTMENT COMMENTS:**

| 4 BUDGET DATA | 5 1977-79 Estimated for Biennium | 6 Agency Request | 7 Governor's Recommendation | 8 Legislatively Approved |
|---|---|---|---|---|
| | | | 1979-81 | |
| 9 POSITION SUMMARY | | | | |
| Authorized Positions | | 5 | 5 | |
| FTE Positions | | 5 | 5 | |
| EXPENDITURES BY CATEGORY | | | | |
| Personal Services | | 139,123 | 137,088 | |
| Services and Supplies | | 11,145 | 9,645 | |
| Capital Outlay | | 500 | 500 | |
| Special Payments | | - | | |
| 10    11 TOTAL | | 150,768 | 147,233 | |
| EXPENDITURES BY FUND | | | | |
| General Fund | | 150,768 | 73,867 | |
| Other Funds | | - | - | |
| 12 Federal Funds | | - | 73,366 | |
| 13 TOTAL | | 150,768 | 147,233 | |
| REVENUE INFORMATION | | | | |
| 14 | | | | |

**3 RELATED DECISION PACKAGES**

| Pkg. No. | Page | Title | Amount | FTE |
|---|---|---|---|---|

| | | |
|---|---|---|
| AGENCY | CODE | TITLE |
| | 54300 | OREGON STATE LIBRARY |
| PROGRAM | 002 | Library Services |
| SUBPROGRAM | 01 | Public Services |
| ACTIVITY | | |
| 16 | | |

[ ] Reduced Level Budget or [x] Decision Package Number ___02___

Description   Standard Reference Service

| PRIORITY | Agency Request | Governor's Recommendation | Legislatively Approved |
|---|---|---|---|
| Agency Wide 3 of 19 | | of | of |
| 17 | | | REDUCED LEVEL/DECISION PACKAGE |

Page ___71___

16

Form 135a

STATE OF OREGON
EXECUTIVE DEPARTMENT

REDUCED LEVEL/DECISION PACKAGE

105 BF 135

**PURPOSE**

1. Expand and improve the specialized reference and information service provided to state agencies and the legislature.
2. Expand the computer assisted reference service provided to state agencies and the legislature.
3. Establish direct access to the Oregon Legislative Information System (OLIS).

**HOW ACCOMPLISHED**

Add a Government Information Coordinator to coordinate library services to state agencies. Government information needs will be studied and ways to meet them will be developed. This will include the promotion of greater usage of current services by state agencies and the planning and implementation of improvements to current services. Computer assisted reference service will be doubled, increasing the amount of information available to state agencies and the legislature. Use of the OLIS system will provide direct access to the Oregon Constitution, Oregon Revised Statutes, newly introduced measures, and measure status history.

**ALTERNATIVES**

State agencies could develop their own libraries, purchase data processing equipment, acquire and index specialized information sources and hire professional staff. This would be much less efficient and much more expensive than continuing to develop a strong centralized information service for state government in the State Library.

**IMPACT: Positive and Negative**

1. The specialized information which state agencies need in order to accomplish their objectives continues to grow.
2. The use of the State Library by the legislature is increasing during both the Session and the interim.
3. This package will enable the State Library to meet these needs.

**ACCOMPLISHMENTS/WORKLOAD MEASURES**

| | 1977-79 | | | 1979-81 | | |
|---|---|---|---|---|---|---|
| | First Year 6 | Second Year 7 | Biennium 8 | Agency Request 9 | Governor's Recom. 10 | Legislatively Approved 11 |
| * Reference requests received | | | | 7,000 | — | |
| Title requests received | | | | 7,000 | — | |
| Items circulated | | | | 5,000 | — | |
| * Photocopies provided | | | | 1,000 | — | |
| On-line searches | | | | 1,200 | — | |
| * Definition to change for the 1979-81 biennium | | | | | | |

| CODE | | TITLE |
|---|---|---|
| AGENCY | 54300 | OREGON STATE LIBRARY |
| PROGRAM | 002 | Library Services |
| SUBPROGRAM | 01 | Public Services |
| ACTIVITY | | |

[ ] Reduced Level Budget or [X] Decision Package Number 03

Description Government Information Coordinator

Page 72

REDUCED LEVEL/DECISION PACKAGE

Form 135

STATE OF OREGON
EXECUTIVE DEPARTMENT

REDUCED LEVEL/DECISION PACKAGE

105 BF 135a

1 AGENCY COMMENTS:

2 EXECUTIVE DEPARTMENT COMMENTS:

| 4 BUDGET DATA | 5 1977-79 Estimated for Biennium | 6 Agency Request | 1979-81 7 Governor's Recommendation | 8 Legislatively Approved |
|---|---|---|---|---|
| POSITION SUMMARY | | | | |
| Authorized Positions | | 1 | 1 | |
| 9 FTE Positions | | 1 | 1 | |
| EXPENDITURES BY CATEGORY | | | | |
| Personal Services | | 38,407 | | |
| Services and Supplies | | 17,920 | | |
| Capital Outlay | | 500 | | |
| Special Payments | | - | | |
| 10 TOTAL | | 56,827 | - | |
| 11 EXPENDITURES BY FUND | | | | |
| General Fund | | 56,827 | - | |
| Other Funds | | - | | |
| 12 Federal Funds | | - | | |
| 13 TOTAL | | 56,827 | - | |
| 14 REVENUE INFORMATION | | | | |

3 RELATED DECISION PACKAGES

Pkg. No.    Page    Title                          Amount    FTE

16 [ ] Reduced Level Budget or [X] Decision Package Number   03

Description   Government Information Coordinator

| PRIORITY | Agency Request | Governor's Recommendation | Legislatively Approved |
|---|---|---|---|
| Agency Wide 8 of 19 | | of | |

17 REDUCED LEVEL/DECISION PACKAGE

AGENCY       CODE    TITLE
             54300   OREGON STATE LIBRARY
PROGRAM      002     Library Services
SUBPROGRAM   01      Public Services
ACTIVITY

Page  73

Form 135a

STATE OF OREGON
EXECUTIVE DEPARTMENT

REDUCED LEVEL/DECISION PACKAGE

105 BF 135

### PURPOSE

Provide an information and referral service for citizens who need information about and/or from Oregon state government.

1

### HOW ACCOMPLISHED

Two staff members will be hired, a librarian 3 and a clerical specialist. They will compile a subject index file to services provided by Oregon state government agencies. They will publicize the service with press releases and by the preparation of a brochure. They will answer questions directly from citizens.

2

### ALTERNATIVES

The Department of General Services currently maintains an in-WATS line for the use of citizens seeking information from state government. This directory assistance operation serves well as long as the request is fairly straightforward and background information is not necessary. Newspapers generally have "help" columns which also help to fill the citizen's need for information about state services. Neither of these, however, is a substitute for an in-depth, one-stop information service which the State Library could provide with its strong collection of Oregon state documents, materials published about the state of Oregon, and a trained staff of reference librarians.

3

### IMPACT: Positive and Negative

A state government information and referral center at the State Library would free state agencies of the necessity of answering routine questions about their organization, statutory authority, general activities, and other subjects for which information is provided in printed form. Thus, agency time need only be spent on more complicated questions which would be the result of an informed referral by the State Library. The State Library already answers many questions about state government. The availability of staff to supplement published information with an information and referral file would improve the quality of service which the library staff can provide.

4

### ACCOMPLISHMENTS/WORKLOAD MEASURES

5

| | 6 First Year | 7 Second Year 1977-79 | 8 Biennium | 9 Agency Request | 10 Governor's Recom. 1979-81 | 11 Legislatively Approved |
|---|---|---|---|---|---|---|
| Information and referral requests received | | | | 14,000 | — | |

| AGENCY | CODE 54300 | TITLE OREGON STATE LIBRARY |
|---|---|---|
| PROGRAM | 002 | Library Services |
| SUBPROGRAM | 01 | Public Services |
| ACTIVITY | | |

Form 135

[ ] Reduced Level Budget or [X] Decision Package Number  04

Description  State Government Information and Referral

Page  "74

REDUCED LEVEL/DECISION PACKAGE

STATE OF OREGON
EXECUTIVE DEPARTMENT

REDUCED LEVEL/DECISION PACKAGE

105 BF 135a

1 AGENCY COMMENTS:

2 EXECUTIVE DEPARTMENT COMMENTS:

| BUDGET DATA | 1977-79 Estimated for Biennium (5) | 1979-81 Agency Request (6) | Governor's Recommendation (7) | Legislatively Approved (8) |
|---|---|---|---|---|
| 4 POSITION SUMMARY | | | | |
| Authorized Positions | | 2 | - | |
| 9 FTE Positions | | 2 | - | |
| EXPENDITURES BY CATEGORY | | | | |
| Personal Services | | 61,185 | | |
| Services and Supplies | | 7,200 | | |
| Capital Outlay | | 2,640 | | |
| Special Payments | | - | | |
| 10 | | | | |
| 11 TOTAL | | 71,025 | - | |
| EXPENDITURES BY FUND | | | | |
| General Fund | | 71,025 | | |
| Other Funds | | - | | |
| 12 Federal Funds | | - | | |
| 13 TOTAL | | 71,025 | - | |
| 14 REVENUE INFORMATION | | | | |

3 RELATED DECISION PACKAGES
Pkg. No.    Page    Title        Amount    FTE

15

| AGENCY | CODE 54300 | TITLE OREGON STATE LIBRARY |
|---|---|---|
| PROGRAM | 002 | Library Services |
| SUBPROGRAM | 01 | Public Services |
| ACTIVITY | | |

[ ] Reduced Level Budget or [x] Decision Package Number   04
Description   State Government Information & Referral

16

| PRIORITY | Agency Request | Governor's Recommendation | Legislatively Approved |
|---|---|---|---|
| Agency Wide 16 of 19 | of | | |

17

REDUCED LEVEL/DECISION PACKAGE

Page   75

Form 135a

# Example Three
# Lockwood Library, State University of New York at Buffalo, New York

## Background Information

Lockwood Library is the graduate social sciences and humanities library of the SUNY at Buffalo library system. It is comparable in size to a number of medium-sized academic libraries. It has several departments, branches, and special collections.

The ZBB techniques were used by Lockwood's reference and collection development staff to analyze their activities and operations as part of the university library's staff justification project. Their experience on ZBB was reported at the first National Conference of the American College and Research Libraries in Boston, November 8-11, 1978, and published later in the Proceedings of the Conference.[*]

## Librarian's Comment on ZBB Experience

Ms. Diane C. Parker, Head of Reference and Acting Head of Lockwood Library, commented that

Lockwood Library's formal zero base budgeting project occurred in August-September, 1977. It was our unit's method of doing a staff utilization analysis required of all units in our University Libraries System. The project was an extremely time consuming process, one that we probably won't repeat. There were specific short-range benefits that made it worthwhile at the time. There also have been long-range benefits in terms of skills and attitudes. In planning for this fiscal year, the Director of Libraries asked all units in our library systems to use zero base budgeting in formulating our Temporary Services (student assistant) budget. No one was required to use ZBB forms, but everyone was required to justify a budget from a zero base. Historical justifications were eliminated. Our own unit was able to demonstrate that we have been underfunded for years, and we received a considerable improvement (an increase from $82,000 to $102,000).

In formulating this year's budget (1979/80), the department heads who had participated in the original project were able to develop precise requests which could be easily explained and justified. One person voluntarily linked his request to a complete reanalysis of his department operations. He felt he did a much better job of it the second time around!

ZBB will continue to have its influence on the University Libraries system. The Director of Libraries has scheduled a ZBB review of our acquisitions budget. Of course, decision packages will be inappropriate. The import factor is attitudinal — eliminating historical justifications. Funds will be reallocated according to present program needs.

In general, Lockwood references and collection development staff members found their ZBB experience successful in that it gave them complete and precise data immediately useful for their staff justification. It also raised many fundamental questions in their minds regarding various library services and forced them to reexamine their operations more precisely and carefully.

---

[*]Diane C. Parker and Eric J. Carpenter, "Zero-Base Budget Approach to Staff Justification for a Combined Reference and Collection Development Department," in *New Horizons for Academic Libraries*, eds. Robert D. Stueart and Richard D. Johnson (New York: K. G. Saur, 1979), pp. 472-82.

## Sample ZBB Materials Prepared by Lockwood Reference Staff

### FORM USED FOR ZERO-BASE BUDGETING

Lockwood Library
Budget Analysis & Planning

| (1) Package Name | (2) Department or Branch | (3) Activity | (4) Dept. Rank | (5) Unit Rank |
|---|---|---|---|---|
| (1 of  ) | | | | |

(6) Statement of Purpose as Related to the Department or Branch

(7) Statement of Purpose as Related to Lockwood Library

(8) Description of Actions (Operations)

(9) Achievements from Actions

(10) Consequences of not Approving Actions

   (a)  For the Department or Branch

   (b)  t or Lockwood Library

| (11) Quantitative Package Measures | FY 1974/5 | FY 1975/6 | FY 1976/7 | FY (projected) 1977/8 |
|---|---|---|---|---|
| | | | | |

(12) Resources Required: Staff

| | 1975/6 | 1976/7 | 1977/8 |
|---|---|---|---|
| Professional | | | |
| Paraprofessional | | | |
| Secretarial | | | |
| Clerical | | | |
| Students | | | |

Resources Required: Dollars Budgeted

| | 1975/6 | 1976/7 | 1977/8 |
|---|---|---|---|
| OTPS Supplies | | | |
| Contractual | | | |
| Capital outlay | | | |
| Travel | | | |
| ACQUISITIONS | | | |

Prepared by:_____ Title: _____ Date:_____ Page 1 of ___

Lockwood Library
Budget Analysis & Planning

| (1) Package Name | (2) Department or Branch | (3) Activity | (4) Dept. Rank | (5) Unit Rank |
|---|---|---|---|---|
|  |  |  |  |  |

(13) Alternatives (Different Levels of Effort) and Cost

Dept. Rank:

Unit  Rank:

Dept. Rank:

Unit  Rank:

(14) Alternatives (Different ways of Performing the Same Function, Activity, or Operation)

(a)

(b)

(c)

| (15) Sources of Funds (in dollars) | | FY 1974/5 | FY 1975/6 | FY 1976/7 | FY 1977/8 |
|---|---|---|---|---|---|
| Operational: | State |  |  |  |  |
|  | Federal |  |  |  |  |
|  | Other |  |  |  |  |
| Grants: | State |  |  |  |  |
|  | Federal |  |  |  |  |
|  | Other |  |  |  |  |
| Capital & Lease | State |  |  |  |  |
|  | Federal |  |  |  |  |
|  | Other |  |  |  |  |
| Endowments: |  |  |  |  |  |

Prepared by: _____  Title: _____  Date: _____  Page 2 of__

Reference Department
Lockwood Library
Budget Analysis and Planning
October 7, 1977

Materials submitted:

1. List of Decision Packages

2. Twelve Decision Packages

3. Summary of Staff Allocations by Package and by Type of Staff-Table 1

4. Summary of Staff Allocations by Broad Activity and by Type of Staff-Table 2

5. Gross Staff Allocations by Job Descriptions for Reference and Collection Development

   A. Distribution-Table 3

   B. Summary-Table 4

6. Job Description for Reference (16) and Collection Development (2) [This is not included.]

7. Standard Job Description for Librarians; Reference Department and Collection Development [This is not included.]

Reference Department
Lockwood Library
Budget Analysis and Planning
September 30, 1977


                    List of Decision Packages


Number              Package Name                    Priority

    1.        Reference service-desk                1 [ enclosed. ]
    2.        Reference collection-selection        1
    3.        Reference collection-maintenance      1
    4.        Reference service-subject specialization   2
    5.        Library instruction; In-house publications  2
    6.        Liaison; Academic departments         2
    7.        Computersearch                        3 [ enclosed. ]
    8.        Administration                        4
    9.        Vertical file                         5
   10.        Telephone directories                 6
   11.        Corporate annual reports              7
   12.        Professional service                  8

Lockwood Library
Budget Analysis & Planning

Package #1

| (1) Package Name<br><br>Reference Service -<br>Desk     (1 of 7) | (2) Department or<br>Branch<br><br>Reference | (3) Activity<br>Information service<br>given during scheduled<br>hours at the desk. | (4) Dept.<br>Rank<br><br>1 | (5)  Unit<br>Rank |
|---|---|---|---|---|

(6) Statement of Purpose as Related to the Department or Branch. This is a primary function of the Department. Information service is available 'on demand' according to the individual patron's immediate need.

(7) Statement of Purpose as Related to Lockwood Library. The service helps patrons make full use of all the collections and services that exist in the library.

(8) Description of Actions (Operations)

        see addendum.

(9) Achievements from Actions. Patrons are helped to use the library effectively.

(10) Consequences of not Approving Actions

    (a) For the Department or Branch. A major component of the Department's service program would be lost.

    (b) For Lockwood Library. The focal point of responsive, professional service to users would be eliminated. Patrons would have difficulty in using the library.

| (11) Quantitative Package Measures | FY<br>1974/5 | FY<br>1975/6 | FY<br>1976/7 | FY (projected)<br>1977/8 Amherst |
|---|---|---|---|---|
| Number of reference questions | 34,396 | 33,591 | 43,888 | 41,989 |
| Number of reference service hours at desk | 3,416 | 3,264 | 3,106 | 4,142 |
| Number of manhours at reference desks | 4,436 | 4,829 | 4,185 | 5,922 |

| (12) Resources Required: Staff Amherst | | | | Resources Required: Dollars Budgeted | | | |
|---|---|---|---|---|---|---|---|
| | 1975/6 | 1976/7 | 1977/8 | | 1975/6 | 1976/7 | 1977/8 |
| Professional | 2.68 | 2.32 | 3.43 | OTPS Supplies | $100.00 | $100.00 | $100.00 |
| Paraprofessional | .32 | -- | -- | Contractual | | | |
| Secretarial | .10 | .10 | .10 | Capital outlay | | | |
| Clerical | --- | -- | -- | Travel | | | |
| Students | --- | .13 | .13 | ACQUISITIONS   see Reference collection, Selection. | | | |
| | | | 262 hrs/yr | | | | |

Prepared by: D. Parker        Title: Head of Reference      Date: 9/30/77    Page 1 of 7

Lockwood Library
Budget Analysis & Planning                              Package #1

| (1)   Package Name<br><br>Reference Service- desk | (2)   Department or<br>Branch<br><br>Reference | (3)   Activity<br>Information service given<br>during scheduled hours at<br>the reference desk. | (4)   Dept.<br>Rank<br><br>1 | (5) Unit<br>Rank |
|---|---|---|---|---|

(13) Alternatives (Different Levels of Effort) and Cost

|   | Increasing level of service:<br>It would be desirable to increase desk service hours to midnight on heavy study<br>nights (i.e. Monday – Thursday and Sunday). This was done in 1973/4 by hiring<br>library school students and giving them special training. It may be necessary<br>to increase the number of persons who work during evening hours or on weekends.<br>Because of reduced visual control from the desk and reduced proximity to the<br>reference collection, it may be necessary to have a student at the desk during<br>busy hours to give simple directions, take messages and assure patrons that<br>professional staff are nearby and will be available soon. |
|---|---|
| Dept. Rank:<br><br>Unit   Rank: | |
| Dept. Rank:<br><br>Unit   Rank: | Decreasing level of service:<br>Service hours could be reduced by opening the desk at 9 a.m. instead of 8 a.m.<br>Costs could be cut by having only one person on the desk from 9–10 a.m. and<br>4–5 p.m. This rearrangement may be necessary if service is scheduled for Main<br>Street Campus. |

(14) Alternatives (Different ways of Performing the Same Function, Activity, or Operation)

(a) Staff the desk partly with paraprofessionals; easier to do in a "core reference"
situation.
(b) Develop A-V capability to answer frequently asked questions.

(c)

| (15)   Sources of Funds (in dollars) | | FY<br>1974/5 | FY<br>1975/6 | FY<br>1976/7 | FY Amherst<br>1977/8 |
|---|---|---|---|---|---|
| Operational: | State | | | 34,371 | 52,957 |
| | Federal | | | | |
| | Other | | | | |
| Grants: | State | | | | |
| | Federal | | | | |
| | Other | | | | |
| Capital &<br>Lease | State | | | | |
| | Federal | | | | |
| | Other | | | | |
| Endowments: | | | | | |

Prepared by: D. Parker_____      Title: Head of Reference___ Date: 9/30/77___ Page 2 of 7

Package #1

Reference Department
Lockwood Library
Budget Analysis & Planning

ADDENDUM

Package name:

Reference Service - Desk

(8)  The reference staff gives information, assists and instructs individual users doing
library research, refers users to information sources and services outside the
Department, schedules appointments for on-line computer searches and follows up on
questions which cannot be answered right away at the desk.  For effective referral
service, the staff maintains an awareness of the collections and services available
throughout the University Libraries; except for an initial orientation period for
new staff members, no time is allocated for this liaison work which usually is part
of reference desk work.

(11)  (a)  The projected number of reference questions is calculated by using the 1975/6
figure and adding 25% (the typical increase experienced by many new libraries.)
The 1976/7 figure was based on sampling and is deemed too high.

$$\begin{array}{r} 33,591 \\ + 8,398 \\ \hline 41,989 \end{array}$$

(11)  (b)  Amherst service-hours are calculated at full service throughout the year.  The
figure would be reduced if there are weekend closings.  The assumption is
made that there will be full summer sessions.

July 4th
May  30th
Dec. 25th         $\begin{array}{r} 14 \\ \times 5 \\ \hline 70 \end{array}$ service-hours     $\begin{array}{r} 22 \\ \times 5 \\ \hline 110 \end{array}$ man-hours
Jan. 1st
Sept. 4th

For 6 holidays:  70 deducted from total service-hours; 110 for man-hrs.

$$\begin{array}{rr} \text{Service} & \text{Manhours} \\ 52 & 116 \\ \times 81 & \times 52 \\ \hline 52 & 232 \\ 416 & 580 \\ \hline 4212 & 6032 \\ - 70 & -110 \\ \hline 4142 & 5922 \end{array}$$

(11)  (c)  Lockwood/Amherst Reference Service Schedule

A.  Desk

1.  Service-hours/week

| | | |
|---|---|---|
| Monday - Thursday | 8 - 10 | 56 hours |
| Friday | 8 - 5 | 9 hours |
| Saturday | 9 - 5 | 8 hours |
| Sunday; 30 weeks | 2 - 10 | 8 hours |
| Sunday; 22 weeks | 2-5; 6-10 | (7) |
| | | 81(80) hours |

Package #1

Reference Department
Lockwood Library
Budget Analysis & Planning

ADDENDUM

Package name:
Reference Service—Desk

(11)  (c)

A.

2.  Man=Hours/week

| | | |
|---|---|---|
| Monday - Friday  (2 people from 9-5) | 96 | |
| Saturday        (2 people including CBS; see II below) | 8 | |
| Sunday; 30 weeks  2-10 | 12 | |
| 2-4:30; 2 people; 5 hours | | |
| 4:30-6:30; 1 person; 2 hours | | |
| 6:30-8; 2 people; 3 hours | | |
| 8-10; 1 person; 2 hours | | |
| Sunday; 22 weeks 2-5; 6-10 | | (7) |
| | 116 | (111) hours |

B.  Computersearch

| | | |
|---|---|---|
| Monday - Friday     9-5 | 40 | |
| Saturday         11-12; 2-5 | 4 | |
| (Covers lunch hour at the reference | 44 | hours |

desk; works at desk when no appointments
are scheduled)

C.  Totals

| Service=Hours | | Man=Hours | |
|---|---|---|---|
| 81 | (80) | 116 | (111) |
| 44 | | 44 | |
| 125 | (122) | 160 | (156) |

(11)  (d)    Assignment of Reference Service Manhours at Amherst

| | Desk | Computer | Total |
|---|---|---|---|
| Head of Reference | 5 | | 5 |
| Anthropology | 11 | | 11 |
| Business | 5 | 6 | 11 |
| Education | 4 | 7 | 11 |
| English (substitute for EJC) | 5 | 8 | 13 |
| Geography (.5 FTE) | 5 | | 5 |
| History | 11 | | 11 |
| Library Science | 4 | 7 | 11 |
| Political Science | 9 | | 9 |
| Psychology/Computer | 0 | 11 | 11 |
| Sociology | 4 | 7 | 11 |
| Spanish, etc. | 11 | | 11 |
| Reference (.5 FTE Art) | 16 | | 16 |
| Reference/Microforms | 24 | | 24 |
| | 116 | 44 | 160 |

Page 4 of 7

Package #1

Reference Department
Lockwood Library
Budget Analysis & Planning

ADDENDUM

Package name:
Reference Service — Desk

(11) (e)  If there is no subject librarian for Library Science, or if service on
Main Street Campus is scheduled, then planned service hours would need
to be adjusted downward to provide fewer service hours at Amherst Campus.

(11) (f)  (1)  For the purpose of translating a professional FTE to annual service
hours and vice versa, it has been assumed that a professional staff
member receives four weeks of annual leave and is therefore at work
only 48 weeks out of the year.  Approximately 1800 manhours are
available per year, per FTE.

$$\begin{array}{r} 37.5 \\ \times\ 48 \\ \hline 1{,}800.0 \end{array}$$

(2)  For the purpose of translating student hours to FTE's, the annual
number of hours was divided by 52, and the results of that calculation
were divided by 37.5.

(12) Distribution of Reference/Instruction FTE's

(a)  FTE's available

| Job Description | % allocated to Reference/Instruction % | % allocated to <u>scheduled</u> service % | Hours | % allocated to reference follow-up subject reference, or instruction % | Hours |
|---|---|---|---|---|---|
| Head of Reference | 20% | 14% | 5 hrs. | 6% | 2 hrs. |
| Anthropology | 45 | 29 | 11 | 16 | 6 |
| Business | 45 | 29 | 11 | 16 | 6 |
| Education | 45 | 29 | 11 | 16 | 6 |
| English (sub. for EJC) | 40 | 35 | 13 | 5 | 2 |
| Geography (.5 FTE) | 20 | 14 | 5 | 6 | 2 |
| History | 45 | 29 | 11 | 16 | 6 |
| Library Science | 50 | 29 | 11 | 21 | 8 |
| Political Science | 35 | 24 | 9 | 11 | 4 |
| Psychology/Computer | 40 | 29 | 11 | 11 | 4 |
| Sociology | 45 | 29 | 11 | 16 | 6 |
| Spanish | 45 | 29 | 11 | 16 | 6 |
| Reference (.5 FTE Art) | 45 | 43 | 16 | 2 | 1 |
| Reference/Microforms | 80 | 64 | 24 | 16 | 6 |
| Head of Collec. Develop. | 4 | -- | -- | 4% | 1.5 |
| | 604% or 226.5 hrs. | 427% or | 160 hrs. | 178% or | 66.5 hrs. |

Package #1

Reference Department
Lockwood Library
Budget Analysis & Planning

ADDENDUM

Package name:
Reference Service — Desk

(11) (b) FTE's allocated to reference follow-up, subject specialty reference and
instruction.

| Job Description | % available for all these functions | | Reference follow-up | | Subject Reference | | Instruction | |
|---|---|---|---|---|---|---|---|---|
| | % | Hours/week | % | Hours/week | % | Hours/week | % | Hours/week |
| Head of Reference | 6 | 2 | | .5 | | 0 | | 1.5 |
| Anthropology | 16 | 6 | | 1 | | 2 | | 3 |
| Business | 16 | 6 | | 1 | | 2 | | 3 |
| Education | 16 | 6 | | 1 | | 2 | | 3 |
| English (sub.for EJC) | 5 | 2 | | 1 | | 0 | | 1 |
| Geography | 6 | 2 | | .5 | | .5 | | 1 |
| History | 16 | 6 | | 1 | | 2 | | 3 |
| Library Science | 21 | 8 | | 1 | | 3 | | 4 |
| Political Science | 11 | 4 | | .5 | | 1.5 | | 2 |
| Psychology/Computer | 11 | 4 | | 0 | | 2 | | 2 |
| Sociology | 16 | 6 | | 1 | | 2 | | 3 |
| Spanish | 16 | 6 | | 1 | | 2 | | 3 |
| Reference (.5 FTE)Art | 2 | 1 | | 1 | | 0 | | 0 |
| Reference/Microforms | 16 | 6 | | 2 | | 2 | | 2 |
| Head of Coll.Develop. | 4 | 1.5 | | 0 | | 1 | | 0.5 |
| | 178% or | 66.5 hrs. | 33% or | 12.5 hrs. | 59% or | 22 hrs. | 85% or | 32 hrs. |

|  |  |  |  |
|---|---|---|---|
| .333 | 1800 | 1800 | 1800 |
| .587 | x1.78 | x.33 | x.59 |
| +.853 | 3204 | 594 hrs/yr | 1,062 hrs/yr |
| 1.773 | | | |

```
                      .333    1800            1800             1800              1800
                      .587    x1.78           x.33             x.59              x.85
                     +.853    3204            594 hrs/yr      1,062 hrs/yr      1,530 hrs/yr.
                     1.773

                              48              48               48                48
                              x66.5           x12.5            x22               x32
                              3192            600 hrs/yr      1056 hrs./yr      1536 hrs./yr.
```

(11) (c) FTE's allocated by broad function

```
        Reference desk: scheduled 3.10
                        follow up   .33
                        subtotal            3.43
        Computersearch                      1.17
        Subject referral                     .59
        Instruction                          .85
                            Total           6.04
```

(12) (d) The projection for professional staff needed at Amherst includes time for
following up reference questions received at the reference desk; figures for
1975/6 and 1976/7 do not include this factor.

Page 6 of 7

Reference Department
Lockwood Library
Budget Analysis & Planning

### ADDENDUM

Package name:
Reference Service — Desk

(15)   Average salaries per FTE

|  | 1976/7 | 1977/8 |
|---|---|---|
| Professional | 14,262 | 15,147.87 |
| Secretarial | 9,137 | 10,002.00 |
| Clerical (.5) | 3,735 | 3,900.00 |
| Student | 2.30/hour | 2.30/hour |

Lockwood Library
Budget Analysis & Planning

Package #7

| (1)  Package Name Computersearch (1 of 4) | (2)  Department or Branch Reference | (3)  Activity Computer searching of bibliographic data bases. | (4)  Dept. Rank 3 | (5)  Unit Rank |
|---|---|---|---|---|

(6)  Statement of Purpose as Related to the Department or Branch. Expands research capabilities for social sciences data bases.

(7)  Statement of Purpose as Related to Lockwood Library. Gives Lockwood clientele more effective access to social sciences literature; is especially appropriate for comprehensive literature searches or current material needed for graduate and faculty research.

(8)  Description of Actions (Operations) see Package addendum.

(9)  Achievements from Actions. A bibliography tailored to the needs of the patron is produced. Definitions of new terms are found more easily.

(10)  Consequences of not Approving Actions

   (a)  For the Department or Branch. Service capabilities would be decreased. Some information would be virtually inaccessible.

   (b)  For Lockwood Library. Patrons would have to spend more time doing manual searches. The number of interlibrary loan requests might decrease.

| (11)  Quantitative Package Measures | FY 1974/5 | FY 1975/6 | FY 1976/7 | FY (projected) 1977/8 Amherst |
|---|---|---|---|---|
| Number of searches done | --- | 486 (8 months) | 842 | 1,480 |
| Scheduled service hours | --- | 800 (8 months) | 1300 | 2,288 |

| (12)  Resources Required:  Staff | 1975/6 | 1976/7 | 1977/8 Amherst |
|---|---|---|---|
| Professional | .445 | .67 | 1.17 |
| Paraprofessional | | | |
| Secretarial | .02 | .03 | .05 |
| Clerical | | | |
| Students | | | |

| Resources Required:  Dollars Budgeted | 1975/6 | 1976/7 | 1977/8 |
|---|---|---|---|
| OTPS  Supplies | | 300 | 400 |
| Contractual | 10,817.33 | 9,500 | |
| Capital outlay | | | 1,800 |
| Travel | | | 100 |
| ACQUISITIONS | | | 50 |

Prepared by:  D. Parker     Title: Head of Reference     Date: 9/30/77     Page 1 of 4

Lockwood Library
Budget Analysis & Planning                                      Package #7

| (1)  Package Name<br><br>Computersearch | (2)  Department or<br>Branch<br>Reference | (3)  Activity<br><br>Computer searching of<br>bibliographic data bases. | (4)  Dept.<br>Rank<br><br>3 | (5)  Unit<br>Rank |
|---|---|---|---|---|

(13) Alternatives (Different Levels of Effort) and Cost

> 1. Service at no charge to the user; a modest number of P.A. and ABI searches
>    could be done at no charge to the user with an increase in budget of
>    $4,500/year for royalty fees and printing charges.

Dept. Rank:

Unit Rank:

More of the cost of the service could be charged to the user, but this might
make the service too expensive for most users.

Dept. Rank:

Unit Rank:

(14) Alternatives (Different ways of Performing the Same Function, Activity, or Operation)

> (a) Some (not all) of the same work could be done manually by the patron; the library
>     wouldn't have sufficient staff to replace this service.
>
> (b)
>
> (c)

| (15)  Sources of Funds (in dollars) | | FY<br>1974/5 | FY<br>1975/6 | FY<br>1976/7 | FY Amherst<br>1977/8 |
|---|---|---|---|---|---|
| Operational: | State | | | 20,947 | 28,123 |
| | Federal | | | | |
| | Other | | | | |
| Grants: | State | | | | |
| | Federal | | | | |
| | Other | | | | |
| Capital &<br>Lease | State | | | | |
| | Federal | | | | |
| | Other | | | | |
| Endowments: | | | | | |

Prepared by: D. Parker          Title: Head of Reference     Date: 9/30/77     Page 2 of 4

Reference Department                                        Package #7
Lockwood Library
Budget Analysis & Planning

<u>ADDENDUM</u>

Package name: Computersearch


(8)  Description of Actions: (a) Appointments and initial interviews are made at the
     reference desk.  The patron is scheduled for an hour's block of time at a later date.
     At the time of the search, the librarian doing the search interviews the patron in
     depth to determine the perimeters of the search topic.  The searcher signs on at the
     computer terminal and does an on-line search with the patron present to help evaluate
     the results.  An offline search may also be requested.  The librarian determines and
     collects the search fee.  The librarian explains the results and advises the patron
     of additional library resources.

     (b)  Computersearch is also used as a reference tool to find definitions of new
          terms which do not yet appear in dictionaries or to identify garbled citations.

(11) Quantitative Package Measures

     (a)  The projection of 1,500 searches is based solely on the increase in service
          hours.  However, the number of searches could go down since there is a fee
          for <u>all</u> searches as of September, 1977.  On the other hand, at Amherst we will
          be closer to the Education Departments which use the service heavily.

     (b)  The number of service hours are gross figures, not adjusted downward to reflect
          holidays, hours cancelled for staff meetings, demonstrations, training sessions, etc.

(12) (a)  Resources required:  staff

                    44 hours
                     x52
          1800 $\overline{)2288}$
                   1.27 FTE

     (b)  Resources required

                1975/6
             8817.33  data base subscriptions and use
             2000     royalty fees
              300     paper and ink
            11,117.33

                1977/78
              100      forms & supplies
             7,500     data base subscriptions
             2,000     long-line rentals
             1,800     terminal purchase
              300      paper
            $11,700

```
Reference Department                                        Package #7
Lockwood Library
Budget Analysis & Planning
                              ADDENDUM

Package name: Computersearch


(15)  Sources of funds


      1976/7:
                  $  9,555.54  professional staff
                      274.11   secretarial staff
                   11,117.33   equipment, etc.
                  $ 20,946.98

      1977/8:

                  $ 16,686.54  professional staff
                      500.10   secretarial staff
                   11,800.00
                  $ 28,986.64

      Amherst:

                  $17,723      professional staff
                      500      secretarial
                      400      supplies, etc.
                    9,500      contractual
                   28,123
```

Reference Department
Lockwood Library
Budget Analysis & Planning
September 30, 1977

SUMMARY OF STAFF ALLOCATIONS BY PACKAGE AND BY TYPE OF STAFF — Table 1

| Priority | Package | Activity | Staff allocations in FTE's | | | | | Total FTE for each package |
|---|---|---|---|---|---|---|---|---|
| | | | Professional | Para-professional | Secretarial | Clerical | Student | |
| 1 | Reference service -- desk | Information service | 3.43 | - | .10 | - | .13 262 hrs. | 3.66 |
| 1 | Reference collection -- selection | Information service and Collection Development | [.20] | - | - | - | - | [.20] |
| 1 | Reference collection -- maintenance | Information service and Collection Development | .05 | - | - | .48 | 1.62 3,165 hrs | 2.15 |
| 2 | Reference service -- subject specialization | Information Service | .59 | - | - | - | - | .59 |
| 2 | Library instruction; In-house publications | Instruction | .85 | - | .24 | - | .20 398 hrs. | 1.29 |
| 2 | Liaison -- academic departments | Instruction (also information service and Collection Development) | See, Collection Development Liaison | - | See, Reference, Administrative | - | - | - |
| 3 | Computersearch | Information service | 1.17 | - | .05 | - | - | 1.22 |
| 5 | Vertical file | Information service | [.04] | - | - | - | .40 780 hrs. | .40 [.04] |
| 6 | Telephone directories | Information service | [.02] | - | - | - | .27 520 hrs. | .27 [.02] |
| 7 | Corporate annual reports | Information service | - | - | .08 | .02 | .13 260 hrs. | .23 |
| 8 | Administration | Administration | 1.71 [.30] | - | .40 | - | .03 52 hrs. | 2.14 [.30] |
| 9 | Professional service | Professional service | .71 | - | .13 | - | - | .84 |
| | TOTALS BY TYPE OF STAFF | | 8.51 | - | 1.00 | .50 | 2.78 | 12.79 |

SUMMARY OF STAFF ALLOCATIONS BY BROAD ACTIVITY AND BY TYPE OF STAFF — Table 2

| Activity | Professional | Para-Professional | Secretarial | Clerical | Student | Totals by type of activity |
|---|---|---|---|---|---|---|
| Information service | 5.24 [.26] | - | .23 | .50 | 2.55 | 8.52 [.26] |
| Instruction | .85 | - | .24 | - | .20 | 1.29 |
| Administration | 1.71 [.30] | - | .40 | - | .03 | 2.14 [.30] |
| Professional service | .71 | - | .13 | - | - | .84 |
| TOTALS BY TYPE OF STAFF | 8.51 | - | 1.00 | .50 | 2.78 | 12.79 |

Note: Numbers in brackets are not included in totals;
.26 is part of Collection Development;
.30 is administrative workload currently performed
by M. Lopez but not included in his job description.

Reference Department
Lockwood Library
Budget Analysis & Planning
September 30, 1977

GROSS STAFF ALLOCATIONS BY JOB DESCRIPTIONS

A. DISTRIBUTION -- Table 3

| Position | Information service and instruction | Collection Development | Administration (and/or 50% of "other") | Professional Service (50% of "Other") | Other Lockwood Departments |
|---|---|---|---|---|---|
| Head of Reference | .20 | .05 | .70 | .05 | - |
| Anthropology | .45 | .45 | .05 | .05 | - |
| Business | .45 | .45 | .05 | .05 | - |
| Education | .45 | .45 | .05 | .05 | - |
| English (substitute for EJC) | .40 | .40 | .15 | .05 | - |
| Geography (.50) | .20 | .20 | .05 | .05 | .50 AED |
| History | .45 | .45 | .05 | .05 | - |
| Library Studies (.90) | .50 | .30 | .05 | .05 | .10 LSL |
| Political Science (.80) | .35 | .35 | .05 | .05 | .20 Documents |
| Psychology/Computer | .40 | .30 | .25 | .05 | - |
| Sociology | .45 | .45 | .05 | .05 | - |
| Spanish | .45 | .45 | .05 | .05 | - |
| Reference (.50) | .45 | - | .025 | .025 | .50 Art |
| Reference/Microforms | .85 | - | .10 | .05 | - |
| Head of Collection Development | .04 | .90 | .03 | .03 | - |
| Reference secretary | .47 | - | .40 | .13 | - |
| Reference clerk (.50) | .50 | - | - | - | - |
| Collection Development clerk | - | 1.00 | - | - | - |
| Other selectors for Collection Development | - | AED .30<br>Art .50<br>Classics )<br>French ) .027<br>Non-Eur. )<br>Langs. ) .20<br>DOCs )<br>Italian .093<br>Polish .107<br>Slavic .20 | - | - | - |

Gross Staff Allocations by Job Descriptions (continued)

B.  SUMMARY -- Table 4

| Total FTE's by type of activity and type of staff | Information service and Instruction | Collection Development | Administration | Professional service | Totals by type of staff |
|---|---|---|---|---|---|
| Professional | 6.09 | 6.627 | 1.71 | .71 | 15.137 |
| Secretarial | .47 | - | .40 | .13 | 1.00 |
| Clerical | .50 | 1.00 | - | - | 1.50 |
| Student | 2.76 | .32 | .03 | - | 3.11 |
| Totals by type of activity | 9.82 | 7.947 | 2.14 | .84 | 20.747  Grand total |

**Sample ZBB Materials Prepared by Lockwood Collection Development Staff**

Collection Development
Lockwood Library
Budget Analysis and Planning
October 7, 1977


List of Decision Packages


| Number | Package Name | Activity | Priority |
|--------|--------------|----------|----------|
| 1 | Liaison Work | Liaison with Academic Dept. | I |
| 2 | Liaison Work | Liaison with CTS and other LML Depts. | II |
| 3 | Liaison Work | Liaison with other SUNYAB Libraries Libraries outside SUNYAB | III |
| 4 | Collection Policy Develop. | Preparation of Written Policy Statements | III |
| 5 | Collection Evaluation | Collection Evaluation | II |
| 6 | Bibliographic Search- ing | Bibliographic Searching | II |
| 7 | Selection | Choosing Materials | I |
| 8 | Selection | File maintenance for Selection | I |
| 9 | Selection | Coordination of Selection [ **enclosed.** ] | I |
| 10 | Selection | De-Selection: Serials (a) cancellation of serials (b) weeding | II IV |
| 11 | Selection | Gift and Exchange | III |
| 12 | Ordering | Preparation of Orders | I |
| 13 | Budgeting | Preparation, Justification & Allocation | II |

| 14 | Budgeting | Monitoring Expenditures | I |
| 15 | Work with Collections | Transfers | IV |
| 16 | Work with Collections | Collection Maintenance; Repair, Discard, Replacement | IV |
| 17 | Administration | Policy Preparation & Implementation [**enclosed.**] | I |
| 18 | Administration | Personnel | III |
| 19 | Administration | Design & Monitoring of Routines | III |
| 20 | Administration | Clerical Support for Administration | III |
| 21 | Professional Service | Service to Libraries & Libraries Faculty | IV |
| 22 | Professional Service | Service to SUNYAB and Community | IV |
| 23 | Professional Service | Service to Library Professions | IV |

```
            COLLECTION DEVELOPMENT DECISION PACKAGES - PRIORITY


PRIORITY I

        1.   Liaison with Academic Dept.

        7.   Choosing Materials

        9.   Coordination of Selection [enclosed.]

       12.   Preparation of Requests

       14.   Monitoring of Expenditures

       17.   Policy Preparation & Implementation

PRIORITY II

        2.   Liaison with CTS

        5.   Collection Evaluation

        6.   Bibliographic Searching

        8.   File Maintenance for Selection

       13.   Preparation & Allocation

PRIORITY III

        3.   Liaison with Other Libraries

        4.   CD Policy Statements

       11.   Gift and Exchange

       18.   Personnel

       19.   Design & Monitor Routines

       20.   Clerical Support for Administration

PRIORITY IV

       10.   De-selection cancellation weeding

       15.   Transfers

       16.   Maintenance
```

COLLECTION DEVELOPMENT ACTIVITIES AND STAFF COSTS OF EACH

| Activity Number | Package | Activity | Percent of time | STAFF COSTS FTE Professional | | 77-78/78-79 | |
|---|---|---|---|---|---|---|---|
| | | | | 77/78 | 78/79 | clerical | student |
| 7 | Selection | Choosing materials | 35 | 2.144 | 2.319 | | |
| 1 | Liaison | Liaison with academic dept. | 10 | .612 | .662 | | |
| 9 | Selection | Coordination of Selection | 6 | .367 | .397 | | |
| 12 | Ordering | Preparation of requests | 4 | .245 | .265 | | .032 |
| 14 | Budget | Monitoring of expenditures | 4 | .245 | .265 | | |
| 17 | Administration | Policy preparation and Implementation | 4 | .245 | .265 | | |
| 8 | Selection | File maintenance for selection | 2 | .123 | .133 | .35 | .032 |
| 6 | Searching | Bibliographic Searching | 6 | .367 | .397 | .10 | .128 |
| 2 | Liaison | Liaison with CTS | 6 | .367 | .397 | | |
| 5 | Evaluation | Collection Evaluation | 5 | .306 | .331 | | .064 |
| 13 | Budget | Preparation & Allocation | 3 | .183 | .198 | | |
| 4 | | CD Policy Statements | 3 | .183 | .198 | | |
| 3 | Liaison | Liaison with other libraries | 1 | .061 | .066 | | |
| 11 | Selection | Gift and Exchange | 1 | .061 | .066 | .05 | .016 |
| 18 | Administration | Personnel | 6 | .367 | .397 | | |
| 19 | Administration | Design & monitor Routines | 2 | .123 | .133 | | |
| 20 | Administration | Clerical Support for Administration | | – | – | .25 | .032 |
| 10 | Selection | De-selection cancellations weeding | 1 | .061 | .066 | | |
| 15 | Collection Work | Transfers | .5 | .030 | .033 | .05 | |
| 16 | Collection Work | Maintenance | .5 | .030 | .033 | .10 | .016 |
| | | TOTALS | 100% | 6.120 | 6.621 | 1.00 | .320 |

Lockwood Library
Budget Analysis & Planning

Activity # 9

| (1) Package Name | (2) Department or Branch | (3) Activity | (4) Dept. Rank | (5) Unit Rank |
|---|---|---|---|---|
| Selection  3 of 5  (1 of  ) | Collection Development | Coordination of Selection | Priority I | |

(6)  Statement of Purpose as Related to the Department or Branch facilitates purchase of needed materials not selected by subject librarians for their specific areas; Head of CD selects materials for areas not covered by other selectors; selectors also assist with this coverage.

(7)  Statement of Purpose as Related to Lockwood Library insures support of academic programs not covered by individual selectors; prevents gaps in collection; provides unified, coherent selection program.

(8)  Description of Actions (Operations) selectors submit proof slips, etc. to each other and to the Head of CD who reviews all orders.  proof slip bin is reviewed by all selectors; Head of CD consults with selectors to insure that gaps in coverage of subject areas & publishing output are filed. selectors and Head of CD select for subject areas not covered as necessary.

(9)  Achievements from Actions materials otherwise overlooked by selectors are purchased; all academic programs served by library are covered because gaps are filled; unified selection program is insured.

(10)  Consequences of not Approving Actions

(a)  For the Department or Branch selectors are unaware of materials overlooked by others.  necessary materials are not purchased.  subject areas not covered by selectors are neglected and funds are not spent.

(b)  For Lockwood Library gaps will appear in collections.  academic programs not served by a particular selector or fund are neglected; funds are not spent.

| (11) Quantitative Package Measures | FY 1975/76 | FY 1976/77 | FY 1977/78 | FY (projected) 1978/79 |
|---|---|---|---|---|
| 1.  number of programs not served by a single selector on a permanent basis | 6 | 6 | *7 | 7 |
| 2.  number of areas (funds) covered by Head of CD on temporary basis | | | 7 | 7 |
| | | | * Latin American studies added | |

(12)  Resources Required:  Staff

| | 1975/6 | 1976/7 | 1977/8 | 78/79 |
|---|---|---|---|---|
| Professional | | | .397 | .397 |
| Paraprofessional | | | | |
| Secretarial | | | | |
| Clerical | | | | |
| Students | | | | |

Resources Required:  Dollars

| OTPS | | 1975/6 | 1976/7 | Budgeted 1977/8 |
|---|---|---|---|---|
| | Supplies | | | |
| | Contractual | | | |
| | Capital outlay | | | |
| ACQUISITIONS | Travel | | | |

Prepared by: Eric Carpenter        Title: Head, Collection        Date: 10/7/77    Page 1 of 2
                                          Development

Lockwood Library
Budget Analysis & Planning

| (1)  Package Name | (2)  Department or Branch | (3)  Activity | (4)  Dept. Rank | (5)  Unit Rank |
|---|---|---|---|---|
| Selection | Collection Development | coordination of selection | Priority I | |

(13)  Alternatives (Different Levels of Effort) and Cost

Dept. Rank:

Unit  Rank:

current staffing patterns, frequent staff turnover due to resignations sabbaticals, re-assignments etc. necessitate a consistently high level of effort for this activity. collections for 80 academic programs must be developed and 33 accounts (not including endowments) must be monitored and spent.

Dept. Rank:

Unit  Rank;

(14)  Alternatives (Different ways of Performing the Same Function, Activity, or Operation)

(a) combine funds on appropriation review to consolidate efforts and make coordination easier

(b) change staffing pattern (see attachment to activity #7 choosing materials)

(c)

| (15)  Sources of Funds (in dollars) | | FY 1974/5 | FY 1975/6 | FY 1976/7 | FY 1977/8 |
|---|---|---|---|---|---|
| Operational: | State | | | | |
| | Federal | | | | |
| | Other | | | | |
| Grants: | State | | | | |
| | Federal | | | | |
| | Other | | | | |
| Capital & Lease | State | | | | |
| | Federal | | | | |
| | Other | | | | |
| Endowments: | | | | | |

Prepared by: __Eric Carpenter__    Title: _Head, Collection Development_    Date: _10/7/77_    Page 2 of 2

Lockwood Library
Budget Analysis & Planning

Activity #17

| (1) Package Name<br>Administration<br>(1 of 4 ) | (2) Department or<br>Branch<br>Collection<br>Development | (3) Activity<br>Policy Preparation<br>and Implementation | (4) Dept.<br>Rank<br>Priority I | (5) Unit<br>Rank |
|---|---|---|---|---|

**(6) Statement of Purpose as Related to the Department or Branch** to provide leadership in policy making for collection development; to coordinate the work of the subject librarians in this area; to insure smooth operations involving collection development

**(7) Statement of Purpose as Related to Lockwood Library** to provide direction by setting policy on development; disposition, and maintenance of collections. Those policies help fulfill the library's mission by building collections of materials needed by faculty and students.

**(8) Description of Actions (Operations).** The Head of Collection Development studies relevant documents, consults with selectors, department heads, and others; prepares written reports and policy statements; and conducts individual and group meetings to discuss policy development and implementation.

**(9) Achievements from Actions.** Decisions regarding collection development matters are made; policies are formulated and implemented; leadership is provided on collection development matters; activities of subject librarians are coordinated

**(10) Consequences of not Approving Actions**

**(a) For the Department or Branch.** decisions on CD matters are not made; policies remain unformulated. disputes among selectors and between them and CTS arise.

**(b) For Lockwood Library** lack of leadership in collection development causes collections to grow erratically. Friction arises between individual selectors and CTS cause dissension. Library becomes unresponsive to faculty and students causing tension.

| (11) Quantitative Package Measures | FY | FY | FY | FY (projected |
|---|---|---|---|---|
| | | | | |

| (12) Resources Required: Staff | 1975/6 | 1976/7 | 1977/8 | 78/79 | | Resources Required: | Dollars 1975/6 | Budgeted 1976/7 | 1977/8 |
|---|---|---|---|---|---|---|---|---|---|
| Professional | | | .245 | .265 | OTPS Supplies | | | | |
| Paraprofessional | | | | | Contractual | | | | |
| Secretarial | | | | | Capital outlay | | | | |
| Clerical | | | | | Travel | | | | |
| Students | | | | | ACQUISITIONS | | | | |

Prepared by: Eric Carpenter    Title: Head, Collection Development    Date: 10/7/77    Page 1 of 2

Lockwood Library
Budget Analysis & Planning

| (1)   Package Name | (2)   Department or Branch | (3)   Activity | (4)   Dept. Rank | (5)  Unit Rank |
|---|---|---|---|---|
| administration | collection Development | Policy Preparation and Implementation | Priority I | |

**(13) Alternatives (Different Levels of Effort) and Cost**

Dept. Rank:

Unit Rank:

Effort is provided for this administrative activity primarily by the Head of Collection Development. It is an daily activity involving constant consultation and decision making on large issues and the disposition of single volumes. Subject librarians participate by attendance at meetings and provision of advice on policy matters.

Dept. Rank:

Unit Rank;

**(14)   Alternatives (Different ways of Performing the Same Function, Activity, or Operation)**

(a)  decentralize policy making further; use committees of selectors to make policy.

(b)  centralize policy making for reference and collection development by having one administrator for both areas. This method has been used in some libraries

(c)  (U. of Wisconsin Madison, SUNY-Albany).

| (15)   Sources of Funds (in dollars) | | FY 1974/5 | FY 1975/6 | FY 1976/7 | FY 1977/8 |
|---|---|---|---|---|---|
| Operational: | State | | | | |
| | Federal | | | | |
| | Other | | | | |
| Grants: | State | | | | |
| | Federal | | | | |
| | Other | | | | |
| Capital & Lease | State | | | | |
| | Federal | | | | |
| | Other | | | | |
| Endowments: | | | | | |

Prepared by: Eric Carpenter          Title: Head, Collection     Date: 10/7/77     Page 2 of 2
                                                  Development

# Example Four
# Ryerson Polytechnical Institute Library, Toronto, Ontario, Canada

## Background Information on the Library

Ryerson Polytechnical Institute Library, opened in 1974, supports more than 30 programs in Arts, Applied Arts, Business, Community Services and Technology of the Institute. It serves approximately 600 full-time faculty, and 10,000 full-time and 22,000 part-time students. The Library has a collection of over 200,000 volumes and currently subscribes to about 2,000 periodicals. An automated batch circulation system was installed when the library opened in 1974, and conversion to an online system in Fall 1979 was planned.

In the year 1977/78, there were 674,858 library users and 184,937 volumes were charged out.

## Librarian's Comment on ZBB Experience

Director John North stated:

The whole experience was valuable in making us understand the workings of our system. Each department head broke down his/her area into functions, and they were centrally merged. Ranking was done by *all* librarians, in council, with little dispute.

Although it would be a nuisance to repeat each year, it would be a good exercise for internal use on an occasional basis.

We feel that, properly applied, ZBB can only benefit librarians and libraries—especially in academic institutions.

RYERSON POLYTECHNICAL INSTITUTE


ZERO-BASE BUDGETTING MANUAL


November 28, 1977

RYERSON POLYTECHNICAL INSTITUTE


ZERO-BASE BUDGETTING MANUAL


CONTENTS


1. Letter of Introduction from the President

2. Definition and Purpose of Zero-Base Budgetting (Z.B.B.)

3. General Philosophy and Procedures of Z.B.B.

   (a)  Concept of Decision Packages

   (b)  Formulation of Decision Packages

   (c)  Decision Package Ranking

4. Instructions and Z.B.B. Forms

   -    Decision Package - Non-Teaching - Form ZB1
                         - Teaching     - Form ZB1A (to follow)

   -    Decision Package Instructions

   -    Decision Package Rankings

5. Z.B.B. Parameters

   -    Non-Teaching

   -    Teaching (to follow)

6. Process Flow for Z.B.B. and How it Fits Into the Overall
   1978/79 Budget Process-(a) Budget Process,
                          (b) Organisational
                              Structure for
                              Zero-Base Budgetting

7. Calendar of Events

8. Resources Available to Assist You in the Z.B.B. Preparation

9. Examples of Decision Package Activities

RYERSON POLYTECHNICAL INSTITUTE
ZERO-BASE BUDGETTING MANUAL

## 1.  Letter of Introduction from the President

On Wednesday, the Board of Governors acting on the advice of
the Finance Committee has accepted the recommendation that
Ryerson proceed with a process known as zero-base budgetting
in developing its response to the provincial announcement of
reduced increases in funding for the next year.  This is believed
necessary particularly in view of the expectation that this
restraint will continue for at least two further fiscal years.

This policy of restraint can only be sensibly addressed by
a thorough review of every activity in the Institute, both
academic and support, to determine its value in relation to
student learning at Ryerson.  Across-the-board reductions in
the light of these pressures would be highly unfair, inequitable
and destructive.  Zero-base budgetting assumes a commitment to
reallocation within Ryerson as well as the acceptance of the
need to reduce the over-all budget levels.  In the context
of this process, no single on-going activity should be viewed
as essential--every activity must be reviewed, analyzed and evaluated.

This will be a difficult time-consuming process, demanding the
capacity to make tough decisions at every level.  The Institute
must know what the impact on student learning would be if
a particular activity is reduced in terms of the resources
available.  We know that the level of provincial support will
demand an over-all reduction in the well below 1977-78 levels
in dollar terms.  The above analysis will reveal the priority
rating of each activity being carried out at Ryerson.

In the academic area, it will probably mean significant reductions
in number of courses, changes in size of classes and laboratories,
reduced hours of timetabled instruction.  These are the activities
which can provide the level of cost reduction which will make
Ryerson a financially viable institution in future years.

The reality is that fewer people will be needed at this reduced
level of activity.  The faculty and support staff fully realize
this fact.  Along with the efforts to deal with the financial
crisis must come a strategy to cope with the impact on people.
The human reality is being discussed by members of the administration,
the R.F.A. and the R.S.A.  The whole emphasis is in the direction
of reducing the impact on the lives of members of the Ryerson
Community to the greatest extent possible.

One final point.  Zero-base budgetting does not replace the
normal budget system initiated last year involving faculty,
staff and administration, a process which will proceed as soon
as the appropriate information is available.  The intense analysis
projected of all activities and the ranking of them by priority
will facilitate the compilation of the 1978-79 Institute budget.

RYERSON POLYTECHNICAL INSTITUTE


ZERO-BASE BUDGETTING MANUAL


2.   Definition and Purpose of Zero-Base Budgetting (Z.B.B.)

Z.B.B. has been defined as follows:

> "Rather than tinker endlessly with the existing budget, one starts from
> base zero and views all activities and priorities afresh, and creates
> a new and better set of allocations for the upcoming budget year."

The manager of the budget must be able to justify each activity's projected
level of expenditure and no level is taken for granted.  Z.B.B. is a
management tool which can be used to review, analyze and evaluate activities.

The process has three steps:

    (a)  Describe — each separate activity in a "decision package;"

    (b)  Evaluate — and rank all these packages using a cost-benefit approach;
        and

    (c)  Allocate — resources accordingly.

During December 1977 and January 1978 (a) and (b) above will be completed and
after review will be submitted to the Board of Governors at the January Board
Meeting.  During February 1978 (c) above will be incorporated in the budget
procedures and after review will be submitted to the Board of Governors at

...2

(No. 2 continued)                    - 2 -

the February Board Meeting.  In other words Z.B.B. will be incorporated in
the 1978/79 budget process as the <u>initial</u> step that will enable us to more
fairly allocate the limited resources available to us.  Z.B.B. will allow
the manager of a budget activity to:

(a)  Identify all activities in his area and requires that each

     manager evaluate and consider the need for that activity and

     to consider different levels of effort*for that activity and

     to consider alternative ways of performing that activity;

(b)  After evaluating his activities in depth and evaluating

     alternatives the manager will be able to communicate his

     analysis and recommendations to higher management for review

     and consideration for future budget allocations.

---

*In ZBB Effort means the amount of the activity not how hard people
 work at it.

RYERSON POLYTECHNICAL INSTITUTE

ZERO-BASE BUDGETTING MANUAL

3.    General Philosophy and Procedures of Z.B.B.

(a)    Concept of Decision Packages

A decision package identifies a discrete activity in a definitive
manner for management evaluation and comparison with other
activities, including consequences of not performing that activity,
alternative courses of action, and cost and benefits.  Decision
packages will be defined at the current level and at a level below
the current level.  (No level taken for granted.)

When preparing decision packages one must consider alternatives
which include:

(i) Different ways of performing the same activity; and

(ii) Different levels of effort of performing the activity.

In (i) the manager* identifies alternative ways of performing a
function and the best alternative is chosen and the others are
discarded.  It is important that if an alternative to the current
way of performing the activity is chosen, that this way is clearly
identified as the recommended way and all other ways (including the
current way) are shown as alternatives, giving a brief explanation
as to why they were not chosen.

———————
*At Ryerson, manager is synonymous with support staff member, faculty member,
chairman or director who is primarily responsible for a specific activity.

...2

(No. 3 continued)                    - 2 -

       In (ii) the manager must establish the minimum level of effort
required and additional levels of effort be identified as
separate decision packages.  The consequences of not performing
the activity should also be clearly stated.

       Both types of alternatives should be considered in identifying
and evaluating each activity.  Managers will usually identify
different ways of performing the activity first, and then
evaluate different levels of effort for performing the activity
in the way or method chosen.

(b)  Formulation of Decision Packages

       To begin developing decision packages, the manager will be expected
to start by identifying the current year's activities in their
area.  The manager will take the 1977/78 level of expenditure and
identify the activities that create this expense, and calculate
or estimate the cost of each function.  The manager at this stage
will not be concerned with the "inflationary" items of expense
for the following year since they will be taken into account by
the budget office where applicable; i.e. salary increases July 1,
1978, inflationary increases for supplies, etc.  In summary, the
manager will review his activities in 1977/78 dollar levels and
view the requirements for 1978/79 in those terms.  However, if he
can foresee people, or other resource reductions, then they should be

                                                      ...3

(No. 3 continued)                    - 3 -

stated.  At the conclusion of the formulation stage the manager

will have identified the proposed activities, which will fall

into three categories:

    (i) Different ways and/or different levels of effort for

       performing the function;

   (ii) "Business as Usual" where there are no logical alternatives;

     or

 (iii) the present method and level of effort is recommended.

The manager is now ready to rank those packages.

(c)  Decision Package Ranking

At different levels there may well be different rankings, however

ranking must be done at the department level, divisional level, and

the institutional level.  The purpose of the ranking is to provide

management with a technique to allocate limited resources by

answering:

    (i) What activities should we (or must we) fund? and

   (ii) How much should we allocate to those activities?

Management can try to answer those questions by taking the decision

packages identified and rank them in order of decreasing benefit to

the Institution.  Management can then identify both the benefits to

be gained at each expenditure level and the consequences of non-

approval of that activity.                          ...4

(No. 3 continued)                    - 4 -

It should be noted that ranking will be initiated at the lowest level of management and will be reviewed at higher organizational levels and used as a guide for merging those rankings from an institutional point of view.

In order to minimise the difficulty and time consumed in ranking decision packages, it is imperative that the manager does not concentrate on ranking packages that have high priority (legal, essential, etc.) but rather concentrates on the discretionary activities and the alternative levels associated with that activity.

4.    Instructions and Z.B.B. Forms

This consists of:

        Decision Package - Non-Teaching - Form ZB1

        Decision Package - Teaching    - Form ZB1A    [ not included. ]

        Decision Package Instructions  - Form ZB1

        Decision Package Instructions  - Form ZB1A    [ not included. ]

        Decision Package Rankings

RYERSON POLYTECHNICAL INSTITUTE DECISION PACKAGE          FORM Z.B.1

NON-TEACHING

ACTIVITY AS IT IS CURRENTLY BEING PERFORMED

| 1) ACTIVITY NAME | 2) DEPARTMENT | 3) BUDGET CENTRE NO. | 4) YEAR | 5) RANKING | NUMBER OF ACTIVITIES |
|---|---|---|---|---|---|
| | | | 1977/78 | 1  2  3  4<br>Dept. _____<br>Div. _____<br>Inst. _____ | _____<br>_____<br>_____ |

6) STATEMENT OF PURPOSE

7) DESCRIPTION OF ACTIVITY

| 8) FACTOR THAT AFFECTS CHANGE IN THE ACTIVITY | EST. OF % CHANGE IN 1978/79 | | |
|---|---|---|---|
| | + | - | SAME AS 77/78 |
| | | | |

9) ACTIVITY BENEFITS

| | 11) RESOURCES | 1977/78 $ | OFFICE USE ONLY<br>1978/79 |
|---|---|---|---|
| | TOTAL ACTIVITY EXPENSE | $ | $ |
| 10) PERSONNEL REQUIRED<br>a) FULL-TIME<br>PART-TIME | SALARY EXPENSE | $ | $ |
| b) CLERICAL<br>ADMIN.<br>TECH.<br>OTHER _____<br>TOTAL (FTE) | BENEFITS<br>11.5% of SALARY | $ | $ |

| 12) COST ASSUMPTION WORKSHEET FOR NON-SALARY · | 13) % ALLOCATED | EXPENSE NO. | $ | $ |
|---|---|---|---|---|
| | | | | |
| | | | | |
| | | | | |
| | | | | |
| | | | | |
| | | | | |
| | | | | |

14) UNIQUE COSTS & EQUIPMENT

15) CONSEQUENCE IF ACTIVITY IS ELIMINATED

16)  <u>ALTERNATIVES CONSIDERED</u>

a)

_____

b)

_____

c)

_____

d)

17)                 RYERSON POLYTECHNICAL INSTITUTE RECOMMENDED ALTERNATIVE       Form

NON-TEACHING

| 1) ACTIVITY NAME | 2) DEPARTMENT | 3) BUDGET CENTRE NO. | 4) YEAR | 5) RANKING | NUMBER OF ACTIVITIES |
|---|---|---|---|---|---|
| | | | 1977/78 | 1  2  3  4<br>Dept. _____<br>Div. _____<br>Inst. _____ | _____<br>_____<br>_____ |

6) STATEMENT OF PURPOSE

7) DESCRIPTION OF ACTIVITY

8) FACTOR THAT AFFECTS CHANGE IN THE ACTIVITY

| | EST. OF % CHANGE IN 78/79 | |
|---|---|---|
| + | − | SAME AS 77/78 |
| | | |

9) ACTIVITY BENEFITS

| | 11) RESOURCES | PROJECTED COSTS 1977/78 $ | COST SAVINGS |
|---|---|---|---|
| | TOTAL ACTIVITY EXPENSE | $ | $ |
| 10) PERSONNEL REQUIRED<br>a) FULL-TIME<br>   PART-TIME | SALARY EXPENSE | $ | $ |
| b) CLERICAL<br>   ADMIN.<br>   TECH.<br>   OTHER _____<br>TOTAL (FTE) | BENEFITS<br>11.5% of SALARY | $ | $ |

| 12) COST ASSUMPTION WORKSHEET FOR NON-SALARY | 13) % ALLOCATED | EXPENSE NO. | $ | $ |
|---|---|---|---|---|
| | | | | |
| | | | | |
| | | | | |
| | | | | |
| | | | | |

14) UNIQUE COSTS & EQUIPMENT

15) CONSEQUENCE IF ALTERNATIVE ELIMINATED

RYERSON POLYTECHNICAL INSTITUTE

ZERO-BASE BUDGETTING MANUAL

4)   DECISION PACKAGE INSTRUCTIONS - FORM ZB1

P1 - (1) - (15)

Use this first page for describing the activity as it is currently being performed.

(1)  1)   ACTIVITY NAME

Describe the activity in your area.
ex. Accounts Payable, Payroll, Recruitment, etc.

2)   DEPARTMENT

Name of Department in which the activity is performed.
ex. Accounts Payable - Finance Department.

3)   BUDGET CENTRE NUMBER

Budget Office will complete.

4)   YEAR 1977/78

No action required.

5)   RANKING

Note that the rankings may not always agree.
ex. Department, Divisional and Institutional
Rank 1 - Essential, Rank 2 - Important, Rank 3 - Necessary,
Rank 4 - Marginal.

6)   STATEMENT OF PURPOSE

Brief description of what the objective is. Ex. in Accounts Payable
would be:  Process, Record and Pay Invoices.

7)   DESCRIPTION OF ACTIVITY

Ex. in Accounts Payable would be:
Receive invoice.  Check for receipt of goods.  Check arithmetical
accuracy.  Pay invoice.

8)   FACTOR THAT AFFECTS CHANGE IN THE ACTIVITY

State (a) Factor, ex. Number of invoices processed etc.
      (b) State % variation in volume that can be handled with existing
          resources, ex. 10% increase in number of invoices
      (c) State your estimate of % decrease or increase in volume of this
          factor for 1978/79 or insert a (✓) in the last column if you feel
          volume will be at same level as 1977/78.

...(2..

-2-

4)    DECISION PACKAGE INSTRUCTIONS - FORM ZB1 (cont'd)

9)    ACTIVITY BENEFITS

Ex. In Accounts Payable would be:
Accuracy.  Supplier satisfaction.

10)   PERSONNEL REQUIRED

List the number of people (FT & PT) presently required to perform
the above activity.  The PT should be expressed in FTE,
ex. if PT person employed for 1/2 year then express as 1/2 FTE.

11)   RESOURCES

The column "Office Use Only" will be completed by the Budget Office.
Total Activity Expense is the total of all costs associated with the
activity.

Salary Expense is the total salary cost of the Personnel Required
(use Salaries as at Dec. 1/77).

The Benefits are added at the rate of 11.5 % of Salary Costs.  This
is an overall Institute average.

12)   COST ASSUMPTION WORK SHEET FOR NON-SALARY

The expenses here would include things like supplies, stationery, travel,
etc.  Note, if you decide to have a separate "activity" for say travel
then do not allocate it to other activities.

If you decide to allocate or charge non-salary costs to the activity
then state clearly the cost assumption used.
ex. % Allocation, Direct Charge, Estimate based on historical experience, etc.

13)   % ALLOCATION

Ex. 10% of Total Department cost of the non-salary expense

EXPENSE NUMBER

Is the expense classification, if you don't know it then leave blank
and it will be inserted later by the Budget Office.

Show the dollar allocation, CHARGE or estimate in the 1977/78 column.

14)   UNIQUE COSTS & EQUIPMENT

State the nature of the cost.
Ex. Keypunch Equipment for the Budget Activity.  Note, if rented and a
maintenance charge paid then ensure that they are listed under Section 12
Non-Salary Costs.

...../3..

-3-

4)  DECISION PACKAGE INSTRUCTIONS - FORM ZB1 (cont'd)

   15)  CONSEQUENCE IF ACTIVITY IS ELIMINATED

          State what would happen if the above activity was eliminated.  Back-up
          sheets can be attached outlining the consequences and should be fully
          documented.  Avoid using general descriptions such as "Catastrophe" or
          "Department Will Close" etc.

   16)  ALTERNATIVES CONSIDERED (Page 2)

          This is the most important section of the Decision Package and if
          further sheets are required please attach to the package.

          After completing Page 1 the following questions should be asked:

       (i) Are there different ways of performing the same activity at less cost?
          ex. - Contract out rather than perform the activity internally.

       (ii) Can the activity be performed at a reduced level?
          ex. - Can the resources be reduced (less personnel) and/or
              - Can the output be reduced (reduce the volume,
                ex. Payroll cheques once/Month instead of Bi-Weekly) and still
                perform the activity.

          It is imperative that the advantages and disadvantages of the alternatives
          as well as the estimated costs (in 1977/78 dollar terms), be given.
          For those alternatives not chosen state the reasons briefly.  For the
          alternatives chosen proceed to Page 3 of the Form ZB1.

   17)  RECOMMENDED ALTERNATIVE

          Complete this page in the same manner as Page 1 however you must complete
          Section 11 "Cost Savings" (in 1977/78 Dollar Terms).
          The Cost Savings are arrived at as follows:-

            1977/78 Costs/Page 1 less 1977/78 Projected Costs/Page 2

          If there are intangible benefits please give details in a footnote.

FORM 2B2

RYERSON POLYTECHNICAL INSTITUTE

ZERO-BASE BUDGETTING MANUAL

4. Decision Package Ranking

| RANK | NAME OF ACTIVITY | DEPARTMENT | RESOURCES IN 1977/78 $ TERMS | | | |
|---|---|---|---|---|---|---|
| | | | PERSONNEL F.T.E. | SALARY COSTS | NON-SALARY COSTS INCL. EQUIP. | TOTAL SALARY COSTS |
| | | | | | | |
| | | | | | | |
| | | | | | | |
| | | | | | | |
| | | | | | | |
| | | | | | | |
| | | | | | | |
| | | | | | | |
| | | | | | | |
| | | | | | | |
| | | | | | | |
| | | | | | | |
| | | | | | | |

This basic form will be used for Departments, Divisional and also for the total Institution.

RYERSON POLYTECHNICAL INSTITUTE

ZERO-BASE BUDGETTING MANUAL

5.   Z.B.B. Parameters

(a)   Financial Considerations (in $ Millions)

|  | 1977/78 Latest Estimate | | 1978/79 Estimate | % Increase |  |
|---|---|---|---|---|---|
| Total Income | 35.59 | | 37.02 | 4.0 | |
| | | | | Cumulative Surplus/(Deficit) | |
| | | | | $ | % |
| Salaries/Benefits | 29.70 | | 29.70 | | |
| Supp/Exps/+ Equip of 1 Million | 7.91 | | 7.91 | | |
| Sub-Total | 37.61 | 100% | 37.61 | ( .59) | ( 1.6) |
| Special-Arch Fire/Admin Settl't | .71 | | -- | | |
| | 38.32 | | | | |
| Expenses @ 77/78 level excluding inflation | | | 37.61 | ( .59) | ( 1.6) |
| Annual'n of Sal. Apr-June '78 | | | .67 | (1.26) | ( 3.4) |
| Sal. inc. 78/79 (6%/Ann for 3/4 year) | | | 1.37 | (2.63) | ( 7.0) |
| Inflationary increase 78/79 (8%/Annum) | | | .55 | (3.18) | ( 8.5) |
| Expenses Including Inflation | | | 40.20 | (3.18) | ( 8.5) |
| Current Year Surplus/(Deficit) | (2.73) | | (3.18) | (3.18) | ( 8.5) |
| Cumulative Surplus/(Deficit) B/F | 1.77 | | ( .96) | (4.14) | (11.0) |
| Cumulative Surplus/(Deficit) C/F | ( .96) | | (4.14) | (4.14) | (11.0) |

In order to meet our overall financial objective of a cumulative
break-even by March 31, 1981 (which may result in incurring
manageable deficits in the intervening years -- example a .75
Million and .50 Million for 1978/79 and 1979/80 respectively)
we will have to find more efficient and effective ways of

(No. 5(a) continued)              - 2 -

performing the various activities in our areas.  From the above
financial data it can be seen that even if we ignore the
cumulative deficit B/F from 1977/78 of .96 Million the overall
reduction will have to be in the region of $3 Million or just
over 8% of the 1977/78 level of expenses.

It is not intended to make an 8% across the board reduction
therefore we are asking each manager to review all activities in
their area and consider the consequences of reductions in their
activities.

(b)  Operational Considerations

(i) In your review of activities ignore salary increases
and inflationary increases for supplies/expenses for
1978/79.  Use the 1977/78 volume and cost levels,
inflationary increases will be taken into account
later by the budget office.  Salaries of people should
be the salary they are earning at December 1, 1977.

(ii) If the level of your activity is affected by legal
obligations (e.g. RFA Agreement) and/or existing
Ryerson policies (e.g. Bi-monthly pay cheques), then
identify the constraining policy and suggest the
desirable change necessary to improve efficiency
and effectiveness.

...3

(No. 5(b) continued)                  - 3 -

(iii) If your activity is affected by external policies or requirements (e.g. Statistics Canada, Department of National Revenue, UIC, CPP, etc.), then identify the external agency involved and any opportunity for policy change.

(iv) If volume adversely affects "efficiency", identify alternatives which will enable you to change the "scale" of the activity.

(v) No single activity must be viewed as taken for granted because the fundamental premise of Z.B.B. is "Base Zero", therefore no activity is absolutely essential to the ongoing objective of the Institute.

(vi) No activity currently being performed should be viewed as being performed in the most cost-effective manner nor should it be assumed that they will continue at the same level of support unless full justification is given.

(vii) When reviewing the activities in your area consider alternatives that will reduce the 1977/78 level of expenses either departmental or Institutional. E.g., Centralise Activity — keypunch operators in Finance and Computing centralised; subscriptions to magazines centralised in Library, etc. E.g. reduced level of service yet maintaining functions of activity.

...4

(No. 5(b) continued)                    - 4 -

> E.g. contracting outside instead of performing internally
> -- payroll prepared by Canadian Imperial Bank of Commerce
> instead of Ryerson Payroll Clerks.
> E.g. different ways of performing activity -- Computer
> Assisted Instruction (C.A.I.) instead of conventional
> teaching methods, etc.

(viii)  On completion of review of activities ensure that you
identify the cost reductions and/or savings resulting
in re-organization of the activities in your area:
i.e. difference between (expressed in 1977/78 dollar
terms) recommended way for 1978/79 compared with the
current cost of the activity as performed in 1977/78.

(ix)  In the course of your review show separately any new or
additional income generation you expect in the 1978/79
year as a result of policy change and/or changes in
performing your activities:  e.g. increase in the charge
for student supplies, rental of facilities, change in
fees charged (non-credit courses upgraded to credit
courses), etc.  Attach separate sheet to your decision
package for that activity.

RYERSON POLYTECHNIC INSTITUTE


ZERO-BASE BUDGETTING MANUAL


6.    Process Flow for Z.B.B. and How it Fits Into the Overall 1978/79 Budget Process

   (a) Basic Process

| Z.B.B. | BUDGET |
|---|---|
| (Description & Evaluation of Activities) | (Allocation of Resources to Activities) |
| Manager of Activity | Department Manager - Budget Instructions |
| ↓ | ↓ |
| Department Review Committee | Divisional Review |
| ↓ | ↓ |
| Divisional Committee | Vice-Presidential Review |
| ↓ | ↓ |
| Deans or Directors Group | Joint Planning Committee |
| ↓ | ↓ |
| Vice-Pres - Acad. or Vice-Pres - Admin. | Planning and Budget Review Committee |
| ↓ | ↓ |
| Joint Planning Committee | Academic Council |
| ↓ | ↓ |
| Planning & Budget Review Committee | Joint Planning Committee |
| ↓ | ↓ |
| Academic Council | President |
| ↓ | ↓ |
| Joint Planning Committee | Finance Committee |
| ↓ | ↓ |
| President | Board (February 1978) |
| ↓ | |
| Finance Committee | |
| ↓ | |
| Board (January 1978) | |

RYERSON POLYTECHNICAL INSTITUTE -- ZERO-BASE BUDGETTING MANUAL

6.  Process Flow For Z.B.B. and How It Fits Into The Overall 1978/79 Budget Process (cont'd.)
    (b) Organisational Structure for
        Zero-Base Budgetting

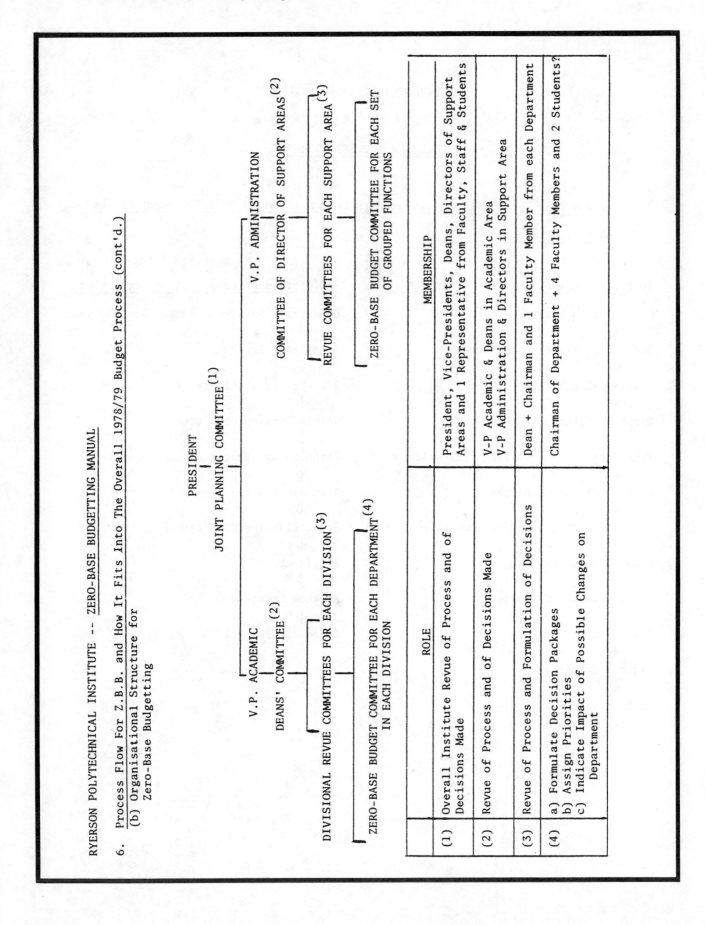

PRESIDENT

JOINT PLANNING COMMITTEE(1)

V.P. ADMINISTRATION

COMMITTEE OF DIRECTOR OF SUPPORT AREAS(2)

REVUE COMMITTEES FOR EACH SUPPORT AREA(3)

ZERO-BASE BUDGET COMMITTEE FOR EACH SET
OF GROUPED FUNCTIONS

V.P. ACADEMIC

DEANS' COMMITTEE(2)

DIVISIONAL REVUE COMMITTEES FOR EACH DIVISION(3)

ZERO-BASE BUDGET COMMITTEE FOR EACH DEPARTMENT(4)
IN EACH DIVISION

|  | ROLE | MEMBERSHIP |
|---|---|---|
| (1) | Overall Institute Revue of Process and of Decisions Made | President, Vice-Presidents, Deans, Directors of Support Areas and 1 Representative from Faculty, Staff & Students |
| (2) | Revue of Process and of Decisions Made | V-P Academic & Deans in Academic Area<br>V-P Administration & Directors in Support Area |
| (3) | Revue of Process and Formulation of Decisions | Dean + Chairman and 1 Faculty Member from each Department |
| (4) | a) Formulate Decision Packages<br>b) Assign Priorities<br>c) Indicate Impact of Possible Changes on Department | Chairman of Department + 4 Faculty Members and 2 Students? |

RYERSON POLYTECHNICAL INSTITUTE

ZERO-BASE BUDGETTING MANUAL

7.   Calendar of Events

| | NOV. | | | | DEC. | | | | JAN. | | | | FEB. | | | | MAR. | | | |
|---|---|---|---|---|---|---|---|---|---|---|---|---|---|---|---|---|---|---|---|---|
| | 1 | 2 | 3 | 4 | 1 | 2 | 3 | 4 | 1 | 2 | 3 | 4 | 1 | 2 | 3 | 4 | 1 | 2 | 3 | 4 |

STAGE 1

Issue Instructions by Exec. S. Comm.

Preparation of Initial Decision Packages

STAGE 2

Review and Ranking

Discussion/Communication with Community

STAGE 3

Summary of Results

Meeting with Community (Deans, Chairman, etc.)

STAGE 4

Proposals - Joint Planning/Other Committees
-Academic Council (special meeting)                     Jan 1-10
-Finance Committee of Board                             Jan 10-12
-Board of Governors                                     Jan 15-17
                                                        Jan 25*

Discussion/Communication with Community

Feed Back/Adjustments/etc.

STAGE 5

Preparation of Preliminary Budgets
-To Joint Planning/other Committees                     Feb 1-10
-To Acad. Council (Special Mtg.)                        Feb 11-12
-To Finance Committee                                   Feb 15-17

Discussion/Communication with Community
-To Board of Governors                                  Feb 22

*Jan. 25th critical date re possible implications
which have impact on Faculty/Staff

...2

(No. 7 continued)

- 2 -

| | NOV. | | | | DEC. | | | | JAN. | | | | FEB. | | | | MAR. | | | |
|---|---|---|---|---|---|---|---|---|---|---|---|---|---|---|---|---|---|---|---|---|
| | 1 | 2 | 3 | 4 | 1 | 2 | 3 | 4 | 1 | 2 | 3 | 4 | 1 | 2 | 3 | 4 | 1 | 2 | 3 | 4 |

## STAGE 6

Preparation of Final Proposals/Budget for 78/79

- To Joint Planning/Other Committees   Mar 1-10
- To Acad. Council (Regular Mtg.)   Mar '77
- To Finance Committee   Mar 11-12
- To Community
- To Board of Governors   Mar 29

1. Community — includes all interested parties other than Committees; e.g. RFA/RSA/CUPE/SURPI/Chairmen/Managers, etc.

2. Other Committees — includes Sub-Committee of Academic Council, Admin. and Acad. Planning Committees.

3. Stages 1-4 as listed above will be obtained by using the management tool Z.B.B. The key dates at this stage are:

 -- December 15/77 - Completion of Decision Packages & Departmental Ranking
 --- January  5/78 - Completion of Institutional Ranking
 --- January 25/78 - Board of Governors Approval

## Summary of Library Operations on ZBB Preliminary Phase—December 18, 1977

1. The activities of the Ryerson Library have been broken down into 22 "decision packages." These have been ranked at a meeting of all librarians. Each package has been numbered with its category and rank, total cost and F.T.E. staff component.

   Three rank categories have been established:

   A - activities which must continue if the library operates at any level.

   B - activities which are required to retain any reasonable level of service.

   C - activities which, although they enhance library service and the academic quality of the Institute, are not essential to library service.

2. After many years of inadequacy, the library has finally reached a level where the staff and facilities begin to approach the levels of need of our users. This has only been achieved by the patience and co-operation of the entire staff, and by constantly seeking new methods of productivity or cost reduction. Although the library does not claim to be 100% efficient, further cuts would only become a penalty for existing measures implemented before the present "crisis." Many of the ancilliary services ranked as "C" have in fact been funded by prior economies, at no additional operating cost to the Institute.

3. Although cessation of some activities in the "C" category could be made, these would be mainly cosmetic. If radical steps are to be taken, the following drastic alternative should be considered:

   Eliminate $100,000 from library acquisition budgets 4841-3617 and 3618 for the budget year 1978/79 only.

   The consequences of this would be:

   (a) the library will continue to acquire only key reference works and periodicals for one year.

   (b) the benefit of the saving would be cumulative during the three-year period towards break-even budgeting.

   (c) time saved by library staff in selection acquisition would be largely re-used to better utilize existing resources.

(d)  such a move would be conditional on guaranteed replacement
     of the sum in the 1979/80 budget and following years.

The suggestion is based on the following factors:

(a)  recent studies show that up to 40% of new library acqui-
     sitions are never borrowed.

(b)  key items published during the year may be acquired
     retrospectively.

(c)  faculty and students could be made to make more productive
     use of existing resources.

(d)  the impact of this move would affect most activities
     ranked lower than B1, and consequent savings could be
     used for material acquisition.

(e)  funding from non-government sources could be used to offset
     this area.

(f)  the impact on the library staff would be minimized.

December 14, 1977

RANKING OF LIBRARY DECISION PACKAGES
ZERO-BASED BUDGETING, PHASE I - DECEMBER 1977

| RANK | | FULL-TIME STAFF | COST |
|------|--|-----------------|------|
| A1 | Subject Depts. - Operation & Housekeeping [enclosed.] | 10.84 | $107,708 |
| A2 | Public Catalogue Production [enclosed.] | .2 | 52,001 |
| A3 | Subject Depts. - Public Reference Service [enclosed.] | 12.32 | 188,858 |
| A4 | Circulation - Book Loans [enclosed.] | 5.1 | 60,941 |
| B1 | Acquisition of Material | | 207,041 |
| B2 | Technical Services | 6.9 | 73,518 |
| B3 | Subject Depts. - Materials Selection & Faculty Liaison | 2.72 | 52,533 |
| B4 | Library Administration | 1 | 23,224 |
| B5 | Library Office | 1.2 | 16,134 |
| B6 | Circulation and Reserve - Administration | 1 | 16,244 |
| B7 | Systems | 3.9 | 46,755 |
| B8 | Media Library Services | 2.66 | 35,551 |
| B9 | Architecture Library | 1.66 | 26,410 |
| C1 | Interlibrary Loan Service | .5 | 6,936 |
| C2 | Circulation - Overdues & Fines | 1.25 | 13,487 |
| C3 | Orientation | .6 | 11,015 |
| C4 | Reserve/Short Term Loan | 4.0 | 41,842 |
| C5 | Film & Video Taping Bookings | 2.0 | 28,375 |
| C6 | Circulation - Support Services | .95 | 952 |
| C7 | Information Centre - Library Outreach Public Relations | .58 | 7,105 |
| C8 | Uncatalogued Material | .4 | 6,905 |
| C9 | Security | 1.3 | 13,000 |

Z.B.B. - PHASE I    DECEMBER 1977

MATRIX SHOWING INTER-RELATIONSHIPS BETWEEN LIBRARY DECISION PACKAGES

Library Office
Library Administration
Public Catalogue Production
Subject Depts. - Public Reference Service
Subject Depts. - Materials Selection & Faculty Liaison
Security
Film and Video Taping Bookings
Media Library Services
Architecture Library
Acquisition of Material
Technical Services
Systems
Circulation - Book Loans
Circulation and Reserve - Administration
Circulation - Overdues and Fines
Circulation - Support Services
I.L.L.
Info. Centre - Library Outreach Public Relations
Orientation
Uncatalogued Material
Reserve/Short Term Loan
Subject Depts. - Operation & Housekeeping

Library Office
Library Administraation
Public Catalogue Production
Subject Depts. - Public Ref. Service
Subject Depts. - Materials Selection
    & Faculty Liaison
Security
Film and Video Taping Bookings
Media Library Services
Architecture Library
Acquisition of Material
Technical Services
Systems
Circulation - Book Loans
Circulation and Reserve - Admin.
Circulation - Overdues and Fines
Circulation - Support Services
I.L.L.
Info. Centre - Lib. Outreach P.R.
Orientation
Uncatalogued Material
Reserve/Short Term Loan
Subject Depts. Operation & Housekeeping

| ACTIVITY AS IT IS CURRENTLY BEING PERFORMED | | | | | Package Number: A1 |
|---|---|---|---|---|---|
| 1) ACTIVITY NAME | 2) DEPARTMENT | 3) BUDGET CENTRE NO. | 4) YEAR | 5) RANKING | NUMBER OF ACTIVITY |
| Subject Depts. Operation and Housekeeping | Library | 4841 | 1977/78 | 1  2  3  4 <br> Dept._____ <br> Div._____ <br> Inst._____ | _____ <br> _____ <br> _____ |

### 6) STATEMENT OF PURPOSE

To organize and maintain the stock and facilities of the subject reference areas and information centre.

### 7) DESCRIPTION OF ACTIVITY

Shelving returned materials; clearing carrells; shelf sequence checks; preparation for binding and repair; displays and bulletin boards; staff training; general order and scheduling of department.

### 8) FACTOR THAT AFFECTS CHANGE IN THE ACTIVITY

| | EST. OF % CHANGE IN | | |
|---|---|---|---|
| Change in amount of material used and/or number of users. | + | − | SAME |
| | 10% | | |

### 9) ACTIVITY BENEFITS

| | OFFICE USE ONLY |
|---|---|
| Required materials can be located <br> Tidy work areas provided; <br> Basic staff training in library operations given; <br> Provides overall atmosphere which is tidy and efficient. | |

| | 11) RESOURCES | 1977/78  $ | 1978/79 |
|---|---|---|---|
| | TOTAL ACTIVITY EXPENSE | $107,708.80 | $ |
| 10) PERSONNEL REQUIRED | SALARY EXPENSE | $ 92,575.61 | $ |
| a) FULL-TIME          7.54 <br>    PART-TIME <br> b) CLERICAL          3.30 <br>    ADMIN.            8.42 <br>    TECH.              .75 <br>    OTHER            1.67 <br><br> TOTAL (FTE)      10.84 | BENEFITS <br> 11.5% of SALARY | $ 10,646.20 | $ |

| 12) COST ASSUMPTION WORKSHEET FOR NON-SALARY | 13) % ALLOCATED | EXPENSE NO. | 1977/78 $ $4,487.00 | O.U.O. $ |
|---|---|---|---|---|
| Employee related expenses | 60. | 3300 | 2,124.00 | |
| Op. equipment purchases | 70.3 | 3861 | 2,363.00 | |
| | | | | |
| | | | | |
| | | | | |
| | | | | |

### 14) UNIQUE COSTS & EQUIPMENT

None

### 15) CONSEQUENCE IF ACTIVITY IS ELIMINATED

Items would not be retrievable by users; this is not a disposable activity - it would have to be retained at the cost of all other services.

a) Since all material removed from shelves has to be replaced at some point, it would only be possible to reduce the level of this activity if less material was used. With the open-access collection this is impossible. A totally closed stack library might cut down the volume of this activity, but would increase costs elsewhere, and would be totally unacceptable to the library users.

REJECTED

b) Releasing part-time shelvers

Although this would show a saving of $14,400.00 the work would be done eventually by more highly-paid staff. Delays would cause aggravation, and other duties would not be performed.

REJECTED

c)

d)

| ACTIVITY AS IT IS CURRENTLY BEING PERFORMED | | | | | Package Number: A2 |
|---|---|---|---|---|---|
| 1) ACTIVITY NAME | 2) DEPARTMENT | 3) BUDGET CENTRE NO. | 4) YEAR | 5) RANKING | NUMBER OF ACTIVITY |
| Public Catalogue Production | Library | 4841 | 1977/78 | 1  2  3  4<br>Dept._____<br>Div._____<br>Inst._____ | _____<br>_____<br>_____ |

6) **STATEMENT OF PURPOSE**

To produce lists of Ryerson library's book and media holdings by author, title and subject and to produce a list of Ryerson library's periodical title holdings.

7) **DESCRIPTION OF ACTIVITY**

Record files of library holdings, produce library catalogues; monitor and correct errors on fiche; revise and update listings.

| 8)  FACTOR THAT AFFECTS CHANGE IN THE ACTIVITY | EST. OF % CHANGE IN | | |
|---|---|---|---|
| Number of books; periodicals and media items that the library acquires. | + | − | SAME |
|  |  |  | xxx |

9) **ACTIVITY BENEFITS**

| Identifies, describes and gives locations for items held by the library; provides a method of finding library materials by author, by title and by subject. | OFFICE USE ONLY |
|---|---|

|  | 11) RESOURCES | 1977/78  $ | 1978/79 |
|---|---|---|---|
|  | TOTAL ACTIVITY EXPENSE | $52,001.51 | $ |
| 10)  PERSONNEL REQUIRED | SALARY EXPENSE | $1,882.97 | $ |
| a) FULL-TIME                      .2<br>    PART-TIME<br>b) CLERICAL                     .15<br>    ADMIN.<br>    TECH.                         .05<br>    OTHER<br><br>TOTAL (FTE)              .2 | BENEFITS 11.5% of SALARY | $   216.54 | $ |

| 12) COST ASSUMPTION WORKSHEET FOR NON-SALARY | 13) % ALLOCATED | EXPENSE NO. | 1977/78 $ $49,902.00 | O.U.O. $ |
|---|---|---|---|---|
| | | | | |
| Production of microfiche catalogues | 11.26 | 3617 | 24,000.00 | |
| Printing costs of periodicals list | ---- | 5000 | --- | |
| Fees to college bibliocentre | 12.15 | 3617 | 25,902.00 | |
| | | | | |
| | | | | |
| | | | | |

14) <u>UNIQUE COSTS & EQUIPMENT</u>

15) <u>CONSEQUENCE IF ACTIVITY IS ELIMINATED</u>

There would be no adequate public records to find library materials. The users would have to browse a collection of over 200,000 items to find what they wanted.

a) Rather than update the catalogues every two months during the academic year, cut out one microfiche catalogue production allowing for only three updates each academic year. This would save $8,000.00 for the fourth update. Borrowers would have to browse to find recently acquired materials and public services staff would have to spend more time with users trying to track down library materials.

b) Produce author and title catalogues from the Master Book File (the library's brief files which are used with the Circulation system) and produce only the subject catalogues on microfiche. Cost savings $18,000.00.

The reason we don't do this now is that the Master Book File was derived from the information used to order books and is sometimes bibliographically incorrect or incomplete. It does not provide enough information to track down more complex documents like government reports. This would mean users would often not find what they were looking for even though the library possesed the item.

Although the Computer Centre does not charge us to produce such catalogues now, we will get charged next year. The costs of these printouts (min. cost $21,600.00) would more than offset the $18,000.00 saved by not producing the microfiched catalogues.

c)

d)

| ACTIVITY AS IT IS CURRENTLY BEING PERFORMED | | | | | Package Number: A3 |
|---|---|---|---|---|---|

| 1) ACTIVITY NAME | 2) DEPARTMENT | 3) BUDGET CENTRE NO. | 4) YEAR | 5) RANKING | NUMBER OF ACTIVITY |
|---|---|---|---|---|---|
| Subject Depts. Public Reference Service | Library | 4841 | 1977/78 | 1  2  3  4 <br> Dept._____ <br> Div._____ <br> Inst._____ | _____ <br> _____ |

6) STATEMENT OF PURPOSE

To assist and instruct library users in the location and use of needed information from all sources.

7) DESCRIPTION OF ACTIVITY

Answering questions; instruction for location and interpretation of data; establishing which sources are required; orientation (individuals and groups); display of new items; interpretation of assignments.

| 8) FACTOR THAT AFFECTS CHANGE IN THE ACTIVITY | EST. OF % CHANGE IN | | |
|---|---|---|---|
| Change in volume of use; change in type of use (more research papers set); level of orientation and user awareness; | + | | SAME |
| | 15% | | |

9) ACTIVITY BENEFITS

Students complete assignments and learn research techniques; enables users to broaden knowledge; users would find little data without this service; stimulation of students; contributes to academic excellence.

OFFICE USE ONLY

| | 11) RESOURCES | 1977/78  $ | 1978/79 |
|---|---|---|---|
| | TOTAL ACTIVITY EXPENSE | $188,857.99 | $ |
| 10) PERSONNEL REQUIRED | SALARY EXPENSE | $165,721.96 | $ |
| a) FULL-TIME        11.6 <br> PART-Time         .66 <br> b) CLERICAL          3.53 <br> ADMIN.            3.49 <br> TECH.             5.30 <br> OTHER <br><br> TOTAL (FTE)        12.32 | BENEFITS 11.5% of SALARY | $19,058.03 | $ |

| 12) COST ASSUMPTION WORKSHEET FOR NON-SALARY | 13) % ALLOCATED | EXPENSE NO. | 1977/78 $ | O.U.O. $ |
|---|---|---|---|---|
| Operating supplies | 15.6 | 3811 | 4078.00 | |
| | | | | |
| | | | | |
| | | | | |
| | | | | |
| | | | | |

14)   UNIQUE COSTS & EQUIPMENT

Current book stock.

15)   CONSEQUENCE IF ACTIVITY IS ELIMINATED

Academic standards drop; students fail to learn useful skills; student time would be wasted.

a)   Eliminate Part-time Librarian in Evenings

This would save $6,000.00 p/a but would cause full-time librarians to work shifts and remove them from duty during peak day-time hours, resulting in even slower service to majority of users.

REJECTED

b)   Close Library Earlier

This would save approx. $10,000.00 p/a but would penalise evening students and seriously hurt day students who need quiet study space in evenings. It is suspected that most workload would move to day-time. Pressure for longer hours is now being resisted.

NOT RECOMMENDED

c)   Convert all Full-time Technicians to Long-term Temporary (Sept.-April)

This would save $35,000.00 p/a but would cause serious problems in continuity, coverage for summer vacations, and work projects completed during summer. This alternative could be expanded to librarians and clericals, but would cause lower standards of service.

NOT RECOMMENDED

d)  <u>Merge Some Subject Departments</u>

This would enable some staff cuts and if combined with conversion of full-time to long-term temporary would minimise effect. Would probably adversely affect book selection and faculty liaison and would separate books from study space.

NOT RECOMMENDED

e)  <u>Eliminate Information Centre</u>

Some functions and services would disappear and standard of floor reference service would be diluted by more general work. Most staff would have to be relocated-savings minimal.

REJECTED

| ACTIVITY AS IT IS CURRENTLY BEING PERFORMED | | | | | Package Number: A4 |
|---|---|---|---|---|---|
| 1) ACTIVITY NAME | 2) DEPARTMENT | 3) BUDGET CENTRE NO. | 4) YEAR | 5) RANKING | NUMBER OF ACTIVITY |
| Circulation - Book Loans | Library | 4841 | 1977/78 | 1  2  3  4 Dept._____ Div._____ Inst._____ | _____ _____ _____ |

**6)   STATEMENT OF PURPOSE**

So allow users to take library books out.

**7) DESCRIPTION OF ACTIVITY**

Recording loan and return of books; inserting and stamping date due slips; tracing and holding books on requests; distributing and validating library cards; and filing manual records

| 8) FACTOR THAT AFFECTS CHANGE IN THE ACTIVITY | EST. OF % CHANGE IN | | |
|---|---|---|---|
| Number of items borrowed from the library. Figures for Sept./Oct. 1977 have shown an 8% increase over last year. | + | − | SAME |
|  | 8% |  |  |

**9) ACTIVITY BENEFITS**

Take library materials out; library finds missing books for user.

OFFICE USE ONLY

| | 11)   RESOURCES | 1977/78  $ | 1978/79 |
|---|---|---|---|
| | TOTAL ACTIVITY EXPENSE | $60,941.81 | $ |
| | SALARY EXPENSE | $40,676.96 | $ |
| | BENEFITS 11.5% of SALARY | $ 4,677.85 | $ |

**10)   PERSONNEL REQUIRED**

a)  FULL-TIME      3.8
    PART-TIME      1.3
b)  CLERICAL       5.1
    ADMIN.
    TECH.
    OTHER

    TOTAL (FTE)    5.1

| 12) COST ASSUMPTION WORKSHEET FOR NON-SALARY | 13) % ALLOCATED | EXPENSE NO. | 1977/78 $ $15,587.00 | O.U.O. $ |
|---|---|---|---|---|
| C-Deks (rent plus maintenance cont.) | 100% | 3662 | 11,457.00 | |
| Op. Equipment Rentals | 100% | 3662 | 2,130.00 | |
| Op. Supplies | 3.8% | 3811 | 1,000.00 | |
| Off. Supplies | 15% | 3611 | 1,000.00 | |
| | | | | |
| | | | | |
| | | | | |

14)  UNIQUE COSTS & EQUIPMENT

C-Dek data terminals

15)  CONSEQUENCE IF ACTIVITY IS ELIMINATED

Books would not be allowed to circulate; the library would become in effect a reference library, resulting in decreased accessibility to materials and thus many dissatisfied users. Since user needs would not be met, the theft rate of library materials would be likely to increase.

ALTERNATIVES CONSIDERED

a)  The Circulation staff could save some time and effort if library cards were not revalidated every year. This would result in a number of ineligible people borrowing books, and consequently more book loss. This would save .25 F.T.E., a saving of $2,052.

b)  The library could allow users to sign out their own materials, by turning the C-Deks around, which would save a great deal of circulation staff time. It would not, however, give very much control over what circulated or who was allowed to take out books. This would save two F.T.E., a saving of $15,090.

c)  The Circulation Department could stop taking requests and doing traces for missing books. While this would save staff time, it would result in much user dissatisfaction. Certain borrowers would monopolize library materials through continuous renewals, and many others would never locate desired books. This would save one F.T.E. or a saving of $8,540.

d)  Shorten library hours to 7:00 PM weekdays and close library on Saturdays. This would allow the circulation and reserve staff to be cut. This would save 2.5 F.T.E., a savings of $21,350.

# Example Five
# Francis Carrick Thomas Library, Transylvania University, Lexington, Kentucky

## Background Information and Librarian's Comment

Transylvania University is a small, independent liberal arts college located in Lexington, Kentucky. It was founded in 1780 and currently enrolls about 800 students. The library holds approximately 100,000 volumes and adds about 2,500 titles per year.

With the retirement of the former president approaching, other key positions were not filled on a permanent basis. So the incoming president who assumed office in September 1976 made appointments to the offices of Vice-president for Academic Affairs, Vice-president for Student Services (both September 1976 also) and Vice-president for Development (May 1977). A member of the former administration was named Vice-president and Business Manager. Other posts filled in the first 18 months of the administration included Head Librarian, Director of Admissions and Director of Financial Aid. A reorganization of the academic structure from more than 20 departments to six divisions was implemented in April 1978.

A new Controller was appointed in November 1977. That individual had had experience in zero-based budgeting in the public sector and discussions were entered as to the feasibility of attempting a similar budgeting process at an independent college. The accompanying forms indicate that a decision was made to attempt it. The library was asked to assemble an example of such a process since it exhibited characteristics of both academic and administrative units. No attempt was made to approximate reality. The example merely sought to provide an opportunity to experience the process with words and numbers rather than just directions and blanks. Accordingly, it is not a typical or model library budget. Many of the numbers are very funny.

The schedule for implementation proved to be too brief and the thoroughness of the packages submitted by program (the constituent parts of divisions) directors varied greatly. The final process was a melange of several approaches, including zero-based.

The important element of feedback was damaged by a difficult transition from a batch to an online campus computer system. The resignation of the Vice-president and Business Manager and the search for a successor made the next year's (1979/80) budgeting process considerably less systematic. At this point, it is impossible to say whether the new Vice-president for Finance will incorporate elements of the process into his budgeting plans.

## Sample Summary of Library's Overall Budget Plan

There are ten decision units (programs) and each of them has three decision packages (A, B, C) as shown in the following:

Budgeting Unit:  Library

| Programs | Level A | Level B | Level C |
|---|---|---|---|
| 1. Instruction [ Decision package enclosed. ] | 17,730 | 18,730 | 26,905 |
| 2. Staff Development [ Decision package enclosed. ] | 1,100 | 1,800 | 3,050 |
| 3. Bibliographic Control | 7,000 | 9,000 | 10,500 |
| 4. Material Preparation | 900 | 1,200 | 1,400 |
| 5. Facility | 3,000 | 6,800 | 8,500 |
| 6. Collection Development | 31,000 | 36,000 | 40,000 |
| 7. Archives and Records | 18,000 | 19,300 | 21,000 |
| 8. Information Service | 8,000 | 10,000 | 11,500 |
| 9. Planning | 3,000 | 5,500 | 6,000 |
| 10. Utilization | 6,000 | 7,800 | 8,500 |
| | 95,730 | 116,130 | 137,355 |

**The ranking of the above 30 decision packages is as follows:**

| Package Number | Cost ($) | Cumulative Cost ($) | % of $116,130 (Total of Level B) |
|---|---|---|---|
| 1A | 17,730 | | 15.3 |
| 6A | 31,000 | 48,730 | 42.0 |
| 3A | 7,000 | 55,730 | 48.0 |
| 4A | 900 | 56,630 | 48.8 |
| 8A | 8,000 | 64,630 | 55.7 |
| 10A | 6,000 | 70,630 | 60.8 |
| 9A | 3,000 | 73,630 | 63.4 |
| 7A | 18,000 | 91,630 | 78.9 |
| 3B | 2,000 | 93,630 | 80.6 |
| 6B | 5,000 | 98,630 | 84.9 |
| 2A | 1,100 | 99,730 | 85.9 |
| 5A | 3,000 | 102,730 | 88.5 |
| 8B | 2,000 | 104,730 | 90.2 |
| 10B | 1,800 | 106,530 | 91.7 |
| 1B | 1,000 | 107,530 | 92.6 |
| 4B | 300 | 107,830 | 92.9 |
| 9B | 2,500 | 110,330 | 95.0 |
| 2B | 700 | 111,030 | 95.6 |
| 10C | 700 | 111,730 | 96.2 |
| 9C | 500 | 112,230 | 96.6 |
| 5B | 3,800 | 116,030 | 99.9 |
| 6C | 4,000 | 120,030 | 103.4 |
| 8C | 1,500 | 121,530 | 104.7 |
| 7B | 1,300 | 122,830 | 105.8 |
| 1C | 8,175 | 131,005 | 112.8 |
| 3C | 1,500 | 132,505 | 114.1 |
| 2C | 1,250 | 133,755 | 115.2 |
| 4C | 200 | 133,955 | 115.4 |
| 5C | 1,700 | 135,655 | 116.8 |
| 7C | 1,700 | 137,355 | 118.3 |

Budgeting Unit:  Library

Program:  Instruction

Packages:                                                           Cost

   1.  Professional staffing at 2.3 FTE                      17,280

   2.  Supplies and printing                                   300

   3.  Student assistance at 325 hours                         150

                                              Level A      17,730

**Benefits of Level A:** Bibliographic instruction provided to all
Freshmen, electing seniors and students enrolled in 15 courses
distributed through 4 or more of the 6 divisions. Ample assistance is provided to assure an efficient program. The products
of the instruction units are made available to all other users
on a voluntary basis.

   4.  Professional travel and support of research     1,000

                                              Level B      18,730

**Benefits of Level B:** An active pursuit of an improved theory
and practice of bibliographic instruction. The possibility of
Transylvania attaining a highly visible position in the bibliographic instruction movement.

   5.  Addition of .5 FTE professional staff              5,900

   6.  Release time equivalent to one course for
      a classroom faculty member to collaborate
      on a division-wide system of bibliographic
      instruction.                                         2,500

                                              Level C      26,905

**Benefits of Level C:** The institution may not be in a position
to assimilate this much of a program at this time. It provides
instruction to an additional 10 courses. It concretely inte-
grates the classroom faculty and library instruction.

**Rejected Alternatives:**
-Assign 2 professional librarians to this program full-time
-A greater reliance on commercially available handbooks
-The utilization of library science students on a part-time basis

Budgeting Unit:  Library

Program:  Staff Development

Packages:                                                              Cost

   1.  Use of amount equal to 1% of previous year's
      salary and fringe benefit budget to be used
      for equity and/or merit.                               800

   2.  An intense two day workshop for student assis-
      tants before the school year begins.                   300

                                            Level A    1,100

Benefits of Level A: A capability of rewarding outstanding performance which is especially useful in a period of transition.
A staff of student assistants more acquainted with library
policies and procedures and interpersonal skills.

   3.  Travel to and attendance at meetings where
      institutional presence is important for
      visibility and external relations.                     700

                                          Level B    1,800

Benefits of Level B: Allows individuals on the staff to meet
and share ideas with leading librarians. Gives Transylvania
increased visibility.

   5.  Travel to conferences primarily involved
      with personally professional concerns.                 600

   6.  A series of three presentations to the staff
      on library and interpersonal skills.                   250

   7.  Attendance at conferences primarily involved
      with personal, professional concerns.                  400

                                          Level C    3,050

Benefits of Level C: Increased encouragement and support of
continuing education to improve the quality of services offered
by the staff.

Rejected Alternatives:
-Delegate all staff development responsibility  out of the
 library.
-Staff retreat
-System of financial support for formal education pursued
 outside the University.

**Additional Sample Decision Package on "Access to Uncataloged Materials"**

SUMMARY

<u>Title:</u> Access to uncataloged materials

<u>Packages:</u>   1.   Continue present system of on order-in process
                 file (2,985).

             2.   Convert files to title listing (859).

             3.   Design and implement system to make note of
                 received items available to users (1,214).

             4.   Study and make recommendations concerning
                 interface SOLINET tapes and OCLC Technical
                 Processing system (2,124).

             5.   Remove unwanted uncataloged material and re-
                 cords (1,881).

<u>Rejected Alternatives:</u>

             -    Design and implement an on-line system of mater-
                 ials control from moment of request

             -    Design and implement batch system for same

             -    Discontinue maintaining in process files

DECENTRALIZED BUDGETING FORM

1.  Package Name: Making uncataloged materials accessible
    (1 of 5).

2.  Expected Benefits: Continue present system; those familiar
    with it would continue to access it as in the past; approxi-
    mately 15 circulations per year anticipated.

3.  Plan of Action: Transfer responsibility for maintenance of
    file from professional to support level with student
    assistance has begun.

4.  Consequences of Not Approving: A system recording less
    information would be fiscally irresponsible.

5.  Resources: .3 support staff        2407
                .5 FTE student           478
                   supplies             100
                                       ‾‾‾‾‾‾
                                        2985

DECENTRALIZED BUDGETING FORM

1. <u>Package Name</u>: Making uncataloged materials available (2 of 5).

2. <u>Expected Benefits:</u> Title arrangement produces a file utilizing a more frequently unique, more easily identified element of an item. Searching time is decreased; less duplication of orders anticipated.

3. <u>Plan of Action:</u> The internal file currently utilizing main entry as the locating element will be shifted to a title-based system. This should not affect determinations on the system making uncataloged materials available through the card catalog. To be done one time, before the start of the school year.

4. <u>Consequences of Not Approving</u>: If this is not approved, searching will be more time consuming and difficult and it is less likely that students could adequately maintain the file.

5. <u>Resources:</u>  .75 support staff for 1 month    501
                    1.5  FTE student for 1 month     358
                                                     859

DECENTRALIZED BUDGETING FORM

1.  Package Name: Making uncataloged materials available
    (3 of 5).

2.  Expected Benefits: Design and implement a procedure to
    include notices of receipt in the author-title catalog;
    anticipated 100 circulations per year.

3.  Plan of Action: Study other institutions currently and/or
    previously doing similar activity; ascertain which  entry
    or entries most effective for in process material; would be
    put in place for beginning of school year; follow-up pub-
    licity campaign; record uses.

4.  Consequences of Not Approving: Failure to approve would
    leave access to uncataloged materials requiring a second
    look-up at a separate location unknown to the vast majority
    of users.

5.  Resources:      Professional supervision        minimal
               .1 support staff to implement         802
               .1 FTE student to maintain            287
                  Supplies                            75
                  Telephone, postage for study        50
                                                    1214

DECENTRALIZED BUDGETING FORM

1.  Package Names: Making uncataloged materials available
    (4 of 5).

2.  Expected Benefits: This package would produce a plan for
    this area of the library to make optimum use of machine
    readable cataloging data and of a proposed Technical Ser-
    vices subsystem.

3.  Plan of Action: Some outside assistance, correspondence and
    study would produce a report with recommendations concerning
    possible shorter term uses of cataloging archive tapes
    from OCLC and the appropriate response to the design and
    costs of a planned Technical Services subsystem from OCLC.
    To be completed in one year.

4.  Consequences of Not Approving: If this is not approved,
    the institution risks overlooking a possibly synergistic
    relationship with the archive tapes and being confronted
    with an operational and available system which has not been
    locally evaluated.

5.  Resources: .15 professional              1650
               .25 FTE student assistant      224
                   Consulting                 250
                                             ————
                                             2124

<u>DECENTRALIZED BUDGETING FORM</u>

1. <u>Package Name:</u> Making uncataloged materials available (5 of 5).

2. <u>Expected Benefits:</u> File decreased by 60%; space freed in backlog room; inventory more accurately reflects reality; conversion of unwanted materials to assets; arrearage appearing a surmountable task; less retrospective material to incorporate into a new accessing system.

3. <u>Plan of Action:</u> Recommendation to withdraw would be submitted to original requester, if still on campus. Library would make final decision for absent requester and for gifts, check value of items suspect worth, year long project.

4. <u>Consequences of Not Approving:</u> If not approved, backlog room would remain full; cost-effectiveness of making uncataloged materials available threatened.

5. <u>Resources:</u>

|     |                          |         |
|-----|--------------------------|---------|
|     | Professional supervision | minimal |
| .15 | Support staff            | 1203    |
| .5  | FTE student              | 448     |
|     | Supplies                 | 30      |
|     | Consulting on values     | 200     |
|     |                          | 1881    |

# Example Six
# Library, Arthur D. Little, Inc., Boston, Massachusetts

## Zero-Base Budgeting: A Corporate Library Experience

Arthur D. Little, Inc. is a highly diversified, profit-making professional service organization which offers consulting services on a worldwide basis. It employs over 2,000 persons, of whom more than 1,000 areprofessional staff consultants. The vast majority of these professional staff members hold advanced degrees. They include specialists in dozens of different disciplines with in-depth knowledge of several hundred industries. In addition, the company regularly draws upon the expertise of over 450 outside consultants for supplemental expertise.

The company is organized into two major components:

- Professional Operations, which consists of all the Operating Sections of the corporation. These Sections, organized along fields of activity, are the units which contain the professional staff who perform case work for the company's clients.

- Corporate Services, which is the support structure maintained by the company to assist the Operating Sections in their case work for clients. Included in Corporate Services are such functions as the libraries, report editing and production, computer services, and facilities maintenance.

Among the company's objectives are three which are of particular relevance to the operation of its libraries. These objectives are: (1) maintenance of a corporate environment which will attract and support staff members of a high caliber, and (2) encouragement of enterprise, excellence, and high ethical standards in the company's professional efforts, and (3) achievement of preeminence in the fields of activity in which the company operates.

To these ends, the company has established a library system which is intended to reflect the diversity of subject, the flexibility of case team activity, and the demand for excellence which characterize the conduct of business at a large, busy, international consulting firm.

The libraries are organized along general subject lines, and each of the Operating Sections is "assigned" to the library whose collection most closely reflects that Section's area of activity. The Sections are encouraged to make their first contact with their "local" library. Because the libraries are organized as a unit, and work very closely to coordinate their collections and staff resources, questions which cannot be best handled within the resources of one collection are referred to the proper staff member in another library.

Each Operating Section contributes to the purchase of books and subscriptions for the library to which it is "assigned"; and it is the responsibility of each library to maintain a collection which reflects the interests and activities of the staff members in the Sections for which it is responsible. In addition, the librarians operate on a fee-for-service basis when doing reference and research work for professional staff members. The librarian's time may be charged to either a specific case account, or it may be charged to a Section's general overhead account; as would be the situation when work on a prospective case was undertaken.

In addition to the support received from the Operating Sections, the libraries also receive support from the corporation itself. These funds are intended to finance acquisitions and activities which cannot properly be assigned to an Operating Section, such as expensive, multiple-use reference tools (Chemical Abstracts, e.g.) and activities of the library staff which are not case or Section related (cataloging, maintenance, administration, etc.).

There are four corporate libraries at present. They share a central processing facility which provides technical service backup. The attached chart gives an idea of the organization of the libraries relative to "assignment" of the Operating Sections [Attachment A].

In the zero-base budgeting process which was developed several years ago, a great many decision packages must be prepared. First, decision packages for each of the Operating Sections must be drawn up, offering various levels of collection and service with accompanying price tags. These levels are reviewed by the Section Head and the Chief of Operations and a level is selected which is determined by them to be appropriate within the overall business and cost structure of the Section [Attachment B].

Second, decision packages must be prepared for the corporate acquisitions budget and for each overhead expense item. These packages are reviewed by the Chief of Corporate Services and a determination is made as to which level of service or activity will be supported by the corporation. The decision packages for the Corporate Service elements of the budget are prescribed by the corporation and include such items as staffing/employment costs; acquisitions; depreciation; facilities costs; and overhead expenses, which are itemized separately [Attachments C and D]. Alternative levels of service, with an explanation of the benefits to be gained from the various levels, are developed for each of these budget categories.

Because the decision packages are so detailed, it is difficult for management to develop a comprehensive overview of the impact of the various options on the libraries as a whole. Consequently, a cost/benefit form of presentation has been developed which is used in conjunction with the ZBB format to show how a new program or funding level will work in totality. This technique enables management to assess the total impact of the various levels proposed [Attachments E1 and E2].

## Corporate Support and Library [Attachment A]

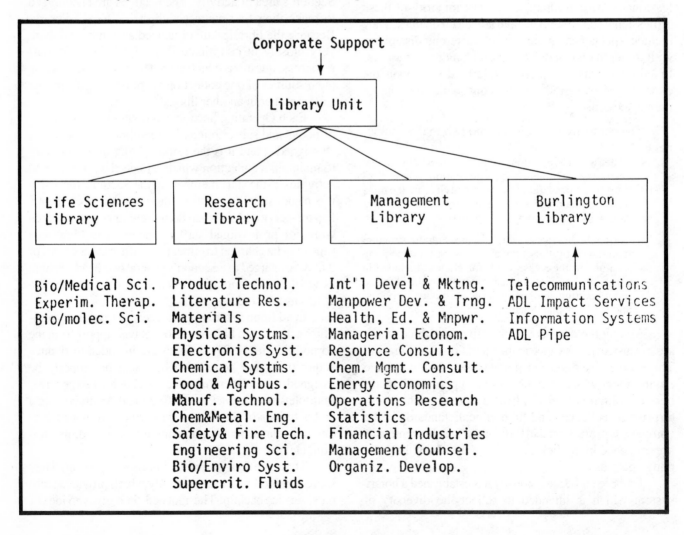

**Attachment B**

LIBRARY BUDGET - 19_____

SECTION:

Books and Subscriptions/Library collection                    $

Library Staff Charges                                          $

    Charges to cases                %
    Charges to overhead             %          _____

                                  Total     $

Were we to increase the budget for books and subscriptions by a factor of 20% ($            ), it would be possible to

If it were necessary to reduce our budget for books and subscriptions by a factor of 20%, it would affect the collection in the areas of

Comments:

Approved _____

Section Head

# Attachment C

|  | CENTRAL SERVICES | | | |
| --- | --- | --- | --- | --- |
| Unit No. | | | | |
|  | 1979 Plan | 1978 Estimate | 1978 Plan | 1977 Actual |
| **Employment costs** | | | | |
| Regular (Full-Time) | | | | |
| Overtime | | | | |
| Part-Time Regular | | | | |
| Part-Time on Call | | | | |
| Summer | | | | |
| Standard compensation | | | | |
| Standard MDT — payroll fringes | | | | |
| Total employment costs | | | | |
| **Assigned activities:** | | | | |
|  | | | | |
|  | | | | |
|  | | | | |
|  | | | | |
|  | | | | |
|  | | | | |
|  | | | | |
| Total assigned activities | | | | |
| Other expenses | | | | |
| Total costs | | | | |
| Credits: | | | | |
| Section chargebacks | | | | |
|  | | | | |
|  | | | | |
|  | | | | |
|  | | | | |
| Total credits | | | | |
| Net Cost | | | | |
| **Staffing Summary** | | | | |
| Full-Time | | | | |
| Part-Time | | | | |
| (Full-Time Equivalents) | | | | |
| — Regular (includes Co-op students) | | | | |
| — On-Call | | | | |
| — Summer | | | | |
| Total Part-Time/Summer | | | | |
| Total Staff | | | | |

## Attachment D

|  |  | DETAIL OF OVERHEAD EXPENSES | Unit No. ___ | |
| --- | --- | --- | --- | --- |
|  |  | 1979 Plan | 1978 Estimate | 1978 Plan | 1977 Actual |
| 4001 | Administration | | | | |
| 4001.01 | Computer Time Charges | | | | |
| 4002 | Personnel Hiring | | | | |
| 4003 | Books and Subscriptions | | | | |
| 4011 | Staff Relations | | | | |
| 4012 | Training | | | | |
| 4012.04/.05 | Course Assistance | | | | |
| 412X | Chemicals, Tools, Auto, Freight | | | | |
| 4130 | Communications Services | | | | |
| 4141 | Postage | | | | |
| 4151.47 | Tel. & Tel. Inst. Charges | | | | |
| 4151.48 | Tel. & Tel. Toll Calls | | | | |
| 4158 | Travel Literature | | | | |
| 4162 | Secretarial Assistance | | | | |
| 4170/4173 | Office Expense | | | | |
| 4175 | Uniforms | | | | |
| 418X | Purchased Central Services | | | | |
| 4302 | Professional Activities | | | | |
| 4306 | Professional Fees | | | | |
| 4330 | Public Relations | | | | |
| 44XX | Minor Fixtures/Instrument Repair | | | | |
| 4932 | Consultants | | | | |
| 4934 | Suppers and Lunches | | | | |
| 4939 | Miscellaneous | | | | |
|  | Total | | | | |

**Attachment E1**

PROCESSING CENTER

1979

Present staffing

|  |  | Billability | |
| Present staff | Salary | % | $ |
| Smith, A. |  | 75% | |
| Jones, B. |  | 75% | |
| Wilson, C. |  | 0 | |
| Williams, D. |  | 35% | |
| Murphy, E. |  | 25% | |
| Miller, F. |  | 0 | |
| North, G. |  | 75% | |
| | | | |
| Total |  | 47% | |

DISTRIBUTION OF FUNCTIONS

| Staffing | % of Time | Function | Billability |
|----------|-----------|----------|-------------|
| 1 | 100 | Ordering commercial pubs. | 75% |
| 1 | 100 | Ordering government pubs. | 75% |
|   | 25 | Company case file | |
| .6 | 100 | Cataloging | |
| 1 | 60 | Mail sorting & journal routing | |
|   | 35 | Individual subscriptions | 35% |
|   | 5 | Miscellaneous functions | |
| 1 | 25 | Book processing | |
|   | 30 | Miscellaneous functions | |
|   | 50 | Interlibrary loan (incl. copyright) | 25% |
| .5 | 50 | Library journals & serials | |
| 1 | 100 | Interlibrary loan | 75% |

6.1 Total

### FUNCTIONAL RESPONSIBILITIES

| Staffing | Function | Billability |
|---|---|---|
| .60 | CATALOGING (5100/year) | 0 |

    Determine if book is new acquisition
      or duplicate holding.
If in OCLC
    Check base against book,
    Adjust base to ADL requirement,
    Check recommended classification
      number against shelf list,
    Produce cards.
If not in OCLC
    Do original cataloging,
    Input into OCLC system.
When cards arrive, check cards
    against orders.
Produce acquisitions list.
Check filing of catalog cards
    and shelf list cards and drop.

| Staffing | Function | Billability |
|---|---|---|
| 1.00 | ORDERING COMMERCIAL PUBLICATIONS (3500/year) | 75% |

    Verify publisher and location.
Place order, arranging for prepay-
    ment when necessary.
Maintain files-
    Orders placed,
    Orders received,
    Orders paid.
Prepare invoices for accounting.
Distribute free/unsolicited
    publications.
Preliminary searching of OCLC
    for cataloger.
Maintain records of standards
    ordered.
Maintain deposit accounts.
Follow up on outstanding orders.

| Staffing | Function | Billability |
|---|---|---|
| 1.00 | ORDERING GOVERNMENT DOCUMENTS (3000/year) | 75% |

    Identify source of document (NTIS,
    GPO, Agency, Contractor, etc.).

Place order, arranging for prepay-
   ment when necessary.
Maintain files-
   Orders placed,
   Orders received,
   Orders paid.
Prepare invoices for accounting.
Distribute free/unsolicited publications.
Maintain deposit accounts.
Follow up on outstanding orders.
Maintain master file of NTIS and GPO
   reports ordered.

FUNCTIONAL RESPONSIBILITIES

| Staffing | Function | Billability |
|---|---|---|
| .35 | INDIVIDUAL SUBSCRIPTIONS | 71% |

All subscriptions to the Official
    Airline Guide throughout the
    company.
All personal subscriptions charged to
    group overhead or cases-
        Verify price & publisher,
        Process order,
        Prepare invoice for purchasing,
        Make copies and file for lib-
        rary records.
Answer inquiries re individual sub-
    scriptions.
Maintain group plans for appropriate
    titles.

| | | |
|---|---|---|
| .30 | MISCELLANEOUS FUNCTIONS | 0 |

Preliminary filing of catalog cards.
Delivery within the company.
Answering telephones.

| | | |
|---|---|---|
| .25 | BOOK PROCESSING | 0 |

Type books cards and labels.
Affix to book.
Cover books with plastic covers.

| | | |
|---|---|---|
| 1.50 | INTERLIBRARY LOAN (5200/year) | 75% of 1 |
| | | 50% of 1 |

Verify reference.
Locate loan source.
Arrange for loan by telephoning when
    possible, in writing when
        necessary.
Maintain files-
    Chronological,
    Orders placed by source,
    Orders placed by title (copyright
        requirement),
    Orders received,
    Orders paid.
Type interlibrary loan form.
Return borrowed materials (retrieve from
    staff when necessary).

Prepare invoices for accounting.
Follow up on orders not received.


.50        LIBRARY JOURNALS AND SERIALS                    0

Order renewals and new subscriptions.
Check cardex regularly and claim un-
    received issues.
Prepare invoices for accounting.
Maintain ADL Union List.

FUNCTIONAL RESPONSIBILITIES

| Staffing | Function | Billability |
|---|---|---|
| .6 | MAIL SORTING AND JOURNAL ROUTING | 0 |

    4 deliveries per day; mail for
       all libraries and processing
       center.
Preliminary sort by library and
       to separate journals and serials.
Journals and serials checked in on
       cardex.
Route slips attached as indicated.
Mail and journals packaged for
       delivery to individual libraries.
Route slip system maintained-
    Produce slips and file,
    Record changes in name and location,
    Make new and pull old slips as
       required,
    Maintain list for each pro-
       fessional staff member
       showing journals routed,
    Prepare annual list to staff
       members,
    Manage title changes,
    Answer inquiries re receipt
       and status of titles.

| | | |
|---|---|---|
| .25 | COMPANY CASE FILES | |

    Acquire case reports.
Arrange for microfilming.
Check out and back in.
Scan film for quality, inclu-
    siveness, and to note location
    of each case report.
Prepare material for keypunch.
Check printout when received.
Answer inquiries and provide copies
    from file.

**Attachment E2**

PROCESSING CENTER

1979

Proposed staffing

|                    |        | Billability |     |
| ------------------ | ------ | ----------- | --- |
| <u>Proposed staff</u> | <u>Salary</u> | <u>%</u>  | <u>$</u> |
| Smith, A.          |        | 75%         |     |
| Jones, B.          |        | 75%         |     |
| Wilson, C.         |        | 0           |     |
| Williams, D.       |        | 35%         |     |
| Murphy, E.         |        | 25%         |     |
| Miller, F.         |        | 65%         |     |
| North, G.          |        | 75%         |     |
| <u>Total</u>       |        | <u>57%</u>  |     |

### DISTRIBUTION OF FUNCTIONS

| Staffing | % of time | Function | Billability |
|---|---|---|---|
| 1 | 100 | Ordering commercial pubs. | 75% |
| 1 | 100 | Ordering government pubs. | 75% |
|   | 25 | Company case file |  |
| .6 | 100 | Cataloging |  |
| 1 | 60 | Mail sorting & journal routing |  |
|   | 35 | Individual subscriptions | 35% |
|   | 5 | Miscellaneous functions |  |
| 1 | 25 | Book processing |  |
|   | 30 | Miscellaneous functions |  |
|   | 50 | Interlibrary loan (incl. copyright) | 25% |
| 1 | 50 | Library journals & serials |  |
|   | 65 | D & B ordering | 65% |
| 1 | 100 | Interlibrary loan | 75% |

6.6 Total

## FUNCTIONAL RESPONSIBILITIES

| Staffing | Function | Billability |
|---|---|---|
| .60 | CATALOGING (5100/year) | 0 |

Determine if book is new acquisition
or duplicate holding.
If in OCLC
Check base against book,
Adjust base to ADL requirements,
Check recommended classification
number against shelf list,
Produce cards.
If not in OCLC
Do original cataloging,
Input into OCLC system.
When cards arrive, check cards
against orders.
Produce acquisitions list.
Check filing of catalog cards and
shelf list cards and drop.

| | | |
|---|---|---|
| 1.00 | ORDERING COMMERCIAL PUBLICATIONS (3500/year) | 75% |

Verify publisher and location.
Place order, arranging for prepay-
ment when necessary.
Maintain files-
Orders placed,
Orders received,
Orders paid.
Prepare invoices for accounting.
Distribute free/unsolicited pub-
lications.
Preliminary searching of OCLC for
cataloger.
Maintain records of standards ordered.
Maintain deposit accounts.
Follow up on outstanding orders.

| | | |
|---|---|---|
| 1.00 | ORDERING GOVERNMENT DOCUMENTS (3000/year) | 75% |

Identify source of document (NTIS,
GPO, Agency, Contractor, etc.).
Place order, arranging for prepay-
ment when necessary.

```
            Maintain files-
               Orders placed,
               Orders received,
               Orders paid.
            Prepare invoices for accounting.
            Distribute free/unsolicited pub-
               lications.
            Maintain deposit accounts.
            Follow up on outstanding orders.
            Maintain master file of NTIS and
               GPO reports ordered.
```

## FUNCTIONAL RESPONSIBILITIES

| Staffing | Function | Billability |
|---|---|---|
| .6 | MAIL SORTING AND JOURNAL ROUTING | 0 |

4 deliveries per day; mail for all
   libraries and processing center.
Preliminary sort by library and to
   separate journals and serials.
Journals and serials checked in on
   cardex.
Route slips attached as indicated.
Mail and journals packaged for delivery
   to individual libraries.
Route slip system maintained-
   Produce slips and file,
   Record changes in name and
     location,
   Make new and pull old slips as required,
   Maintain list for each profession-
     al staff member showing journals
     routed,
   Prepare annual list to staff
     members,
   Manage title changes,
   Answer inquiries re receipt and status
     of titles.

| | | |
|---|---|---|
| .25 | COMPANY CASE FILES | 0 |

Acquire case reports.
Arrange for microfilming.
Check out and back in.
Scan film for quality, inclu-
   siveness, and to note location
   of each case report.
Prepare material for keypunch.
Check printout when received.
Answer inquiries and provide copies
   from file.

| | | |
|---|---|---|
| .65 | DUN & BRADSTREET REPORTS | 100% |

Obtain or verify company name and
   street address.
Get Dun's number if possible.
Order report.
Maintain order file.
Deliver when received.
Prepare invoice for accounting.

## FUNCTIONAL RESPONSIBILITIES

| Staffing | Function | Billability |
|---|---|---|
| .35 | INDIVIDUAL SUBSCRIPTIONS | 100% |

All subscriptions to the Official
  Airline Guide throughout the
  company.
All personal subscriptions charged
  to group overhead or cases-
    Verify price & publisher,
    Process order,
    Prepare invoice for purchasing,
    Make copies and file for lib-
      rary records.
Answer inquiries re individual
  subscriptions.
Maintain group plans for
  appropriate titles.

| .30 | MISCELLANEOUS FUNCTIONS | 0 |

Preliminary filing of catalog cards.
Delivery within the company.
Answering telephones.

| .25 | BOOK PROCESSING | 0 |

Type books, cards and labels.
Affix to book.
Cover books with plastic covers.

| 1.50 | INTERLIBRARY LOAN (5200/year) | 75% of 1 |
|  |  | 50% of 1 |

Verify reference.
Locate loan source.
Arrange for loan by telephone when
  possible, in writing when
    necessary.
Maintain files-
  Chronological,
  Orders placed by source,
  Orders placed by title (copyright
    requirement),
  Orders received,
  Orders paid.
Type interlibrary loan form.

Return borrowed materials (retrieve
from staff when necessary).
Prepare invoices for accounting
Follow up on orders not received.

.50          LIBRARY JOURNALS AND SERIALS                    0

Order renewals and new subscriptions.
Check cardex regularly and claim unreceived
issues.
Prepare invoices for accounting.
Maintain ADL Union List.

# Example Seven
## Public Utilities Technical Information Center/ Corporate Library, Central Vermont Public Services Corporation, Rutland, Vermont

## Background Information

The Technical Information Center (TIC) of this public utilities organization serves the entire company, which has about 600 employees, including division offices located throughout the state. One professional librarian or manager of the TIC and one part-time assistant make up the staff of the TIC. The manager functions both as an administrator and as a professional employee. As an administrator in charge of a service department, s/he is responsible for maintaining and promoting the kinds of information, reference, and special library services each department needs, selecting the staff, formulating and executing TIC policies, and planning of the Center's budget. The manager of TIC reports to the Vice-president and General Counsel of the firm.

As the company's operations have expended and diversified, the Center's services have increased. Major professional activities include the following:

1. Selection and acquisition of materials for which the manager is responsible.

2. Organization of the collections (cataloging, indexing, etc.).

3. Reference and information services, including bibliography compilation and literature searching, and online computer retrieval.

Additional professional responsibilities include:

1. Maintenance and updating of an automated retrieval system in conjunction with the card catalog and the TIC periodical listing.

2. Development and presentation of TIC orientation programs for new corporation employees.

3. Supervision of the production and coordination of the company's annual report.

4. Development of special corporate programs, i.e., EEO projects, in-house education programs, etc.

TIC was founded in 1952. It has 2,500 books, 90 periodicals, and 40 vertical files.

**Corporation's ZBB Manual**

ZERO BASE BUDGETING MANUAL

Table of Contents

## ZERO-BASE BUDGETING OVERVIEW

The purpose of ZBB is to enhance and supplement our present budget technique and allow top management to evaluate each department's operations in order to produce an operating budget consistent with the Company's goals. Through decision packages, department heads can communicate to top management the amounts, quality and cost of the services that their department can provide to the Company. ZBB, therefore, is an appropriate tool to help department heads and top management determine, communicate, agree upon and commit their functions to the proper level of service and cost.

For the 1978 budget we will strive to achieve the purpose of ZBB stated above. In order to do this we will have to overcome the following common deficiencies that were present in the decision packages prepared last year:

1. Many costs were not properly labeled and identified with the desired level of funding.

2. Many departments did not identify all costs relating to their operations. All amounts identified in the traditional budget should be represented by decision packages.

3. In some cases documentation was scanty and hard to follow. A properly documented decision package should give a person unfamiliar with that department's operations, a perspective of what it is doing.

4. Department heads were hesitant to identify less costly levels of operating, without which management can not have a flexible budget.

We have made format changes on the decision package to help alleviate most of these common deficiencies and make it easier to prepare. (See page 4 of manual.)

## ZERO-BASE BUDGETING OVERVIEW

### GENERAL COMMENTS

The purpose of this section of the manual is to touch on areas concerning zero-base budgeting (ZBB) and, by doing so, answer some questions before they get asked. Following in other sections are general guidelines, step by step directions and examples of "Decision Packages" and "Ranking Forms" to assist the preparer in successful use of this technique.

Primarily, it should be emphasized that the function of the ZBB process is to enhance and supplement our present budget technique. All detail costing sheets and other forms used in prior years will still be completed first. After this step is done we recommend a thorough reading of the directions and review of the examples before you proceed with the development of your "Decision Packages."

The ranking shall be done by all staff and department heads who either prepare or will be reviewing more than one "Decision Package." At any point in the review process a manager can combine activities under one heading, suggest other alternatives and new ideas or consolidate all activities in his department by preparing a "Decision Package" to meet his needs.

"Decision Packages" and "Ranking Forms" are provided to be used as tools to aid the manager. We have conceived these tools to be flexible and you should also be prepared to be flexible when using them.

We anticipate further questions and a staff member will be available to help you.

## GENERAL GUIDELINES

A.  A "Decision Package" will be prepared for each level of funding for each activity.

B.  Answer questions in the "Decision Package" as they relate to the identified level of funding.

C.  The desired level of funding corresponds to the amount identified on the traditional worksheets.

D.  Complete detail expense sheets and other supplemental budget forms in the same manner as in previous years.

E.  All alternative levels should be assigned priority in order of least expensive to most expensive.

F.  At any time you find there is not enough space to properly answer a question, continue on to an additional sheet leaving directions so we can follow your trail.

G.  The ranking of "Decision Packages" is the listing in order of decreasing benefit or importance to the organization so that management can allocate its resources by determining where money can be best spent.

H.  You will again be including payroll increases in the budget year. Details will be forthcoming.

I.  In order to establish priorities (within the Z.B.B. process), it is required that the first level of funding identified on your decision package reflect at least a 10% reduction in your department's controllable costs when compared to the most recent 1977 forecast.

J.  All "Decision Packages" and "Ranking Forms" should be typed.

## DIRECTIONS FOR PREPARATION OF DECISION PACKAGES

Step No.

1. Rank - Leave Blank. This box reserved for final ranking.

2. Package Name - Short descriptive title of a specific or discrete activity.

3. Level - Assign an alternative number.

4. Desired Level - If this level of funding is your desired level, place an "X" in this block (Traditional budget).

5. # People - Identify the number of people associated with this level of funding.

6. Dollars - Identify the dollars needed to fund this function at the identified level.

7. Department/Function - The area in which the costs of your activity will be charged. Department head or other person approving this "Decision Package" should place his initials and date in this block.

8. Statement of Purpose - Describe what the activity is trying to achieve.

9. Descriptions of Actions - A description of how you are going to achieve the purpose described.

10. Consequences of Disapproval - Identify the effects of discontinuing funding at the identified level. This should point out any effects on other activities and consequences in the face of regulatory control.

11. Alternative Methods - List different ways that you feel this activity could be performed. Also list the advantages and disadvantages of the different methods.

12. Accounting Information - Identify the total cost of performing this activity, for the level identified in step #3. Relate all costs to appropriate account numbers.

13. Alternative Levels - List the levels of funding for the activity that have been/will be identified in other "Decision Packages." Identify the minimum funding required (Base Cost) and the incremental costs of adding the next levels.

EXAMPLE OF DECISION PACKAGE

| 1. Rank | 2. Package Name | 3. _Of_ Level | 4. Desired Level | 5. # People | 6. Dollars | 7. Department/ Function |
|---------|-----------------|---------------|------------------|-------------|------------|-------------------------|
|         |                 |               |                  |             |            |                         |

8. Statement of Purpose: (What are you trying to do?)

9. Description of Actions: (How are you going to do it?)

10. Consequences of Disapproval:

11. Alternative Methods: (How else might you do it?)

## DIRECTIONS FOR PREPARATION OF PRIORITY RANKING FORM

In addition to filling out this form you should approve all "Decision Packages" which come under your review. In those cases where a "Decision Package" will be reviewed and ranked by more than one person, we request all signatures (initials will do if room is a problem). Following are step by step directions for completing the ranking form.

Step No.

1. Department/Function - Identify the department or function the "Decision Packages" comprise.

2. Prepared By - Please sign your name.

3. & 4. Package Name and Alternative - Refer to the "Decision Package" and its alternative you are ranking. When ranking an activity within a department or function begin with the minimum level of funding.

5. Total Cost - Refers to the cost of performing at the identified funding level for that particular function.

6. Incremental Cost - Identifies the incremental change in cost of adding lower priority funding levels.

7. Cumulative Costs - Column #7 is for maintaining a running total of costs.

PRIORITY RANKING                                                7

1. Department/Function                    2. Prepared By:          Page ____
                                                                   Of   ____

Date

| Rank | 3.  Package Name | 4. Alternative No.  of No. | 5. Total Cost | 6. Incremental Cost | 7. Cumulative Costs |
|---|---|---|---|---|---|
| 1 | | | | | |
| 2 | | | | | |
| 3 | | | | | |
| 4 | | | | | |
| 5 | | | | | |
| 6 | | | | | |
| 7 | | | | | |
| 8 | | | | | |
| 9 | | | | | |
| 10 | | | | | |
| 11 | | | | | |
| 12 | | | | | |
| 13 | | | | | |
| 14 | | | | | |
| 15 | | | | | |
| 16 | | | | | |
| 17 | | | | | |
| 18 | | | | | |
| 19 | | | | | |
| 20 | | | | | |
| 21 | | | | | |
| 22 | | | | | |
| 23 | | | | | |
| 24 | | | | | |
| 25 | | | | | |
| 26 | | | | | |
| 27 | | | | | |
| 28 | | | | | |
| 29 | | | | | |
| 30 | | | | | |
| 31 | | | | | |
| 32 | | | | | |
| 33 | | | | | |
| 34 | | | | | |
| 35 | | | | | |
| 36 | | | | | |
| 37 | | | | | |

Following are examples of decision packages and ranking forms prepared for illustrative purposes only. The information contained in these forms have no bearing on the actual operations of these two activities.

Illustrative decision packages were prepared by the Internal Audit and the Budgeting and Forecasting activities of the Treasury Department. The completed decision packages and ranking form were included to be used as a guide to aid you in preparing your decision packages and ranking forms. If you read through these illustrations and relate the decision packages to the ranking form, the directions identified previously should be easier to follow.

[ not included. ]

## Summary of Library Decision Packages

Package 1 of 3                          $21,450*                        1 person

(1) Library will provide material and services to satisfy
    information needs of company.

(2) Library will handle purchases of books, periodicals,
    technical reports, standards, legal, and bibliographic
    services.

Package 2 of 3                          $ 1,660* (additional) 1 person

(1) $1,540 will be used to provide computer search services from
    LOCKHEED, thus library will be able to perform quick,
    detailed searches and summaries for all subject matters of
    the company's interest.

(2) $100 is the increased travel expense, and $20 is the in-
    creased office supplies budget.

Package 3 of 3#                         $ 5,000* (additional) 2 persons

The additional $5,000 will be used to hire a part-time library
clerk to perform routine clerical tasks, thus relieve the professional librarian to provide more and better services to the
user.

_____

   *Figures used here are arbitrary.
   #Represents the desired level.

| Rank | Library Package Name | 1 of 3 Level | Desired Level | 1 # People | $21,450 Dollars | 11/9/77 Library Department/ Function |
|------|----------------------|--------------|---------------|-------------|------------------|-------------------------------------|

Statement of Purpose: (What are you trying to do?)

The corporate library is a service-oriented reference and research facility, responsible for providing materials and services designed to meet the information requirements of all departments of the corporation. The corporate librarian acquires, organizes, maintains, utilizes and disseminates informational and research material pertinent to the corporation's activities. Such areas are financial (statistics and management), engineering, nuclear, environmental, economics, and legal. Management skills and a strong motivation to put knowledge to work, rather than to provide custodial care are paramount. The library handles all company purchases of books, periodicals, technical reports, standards, legal, and bibliographic services.

Description of Actions: (How are you going to do it?

The library strives to anticipate the corporation's current and future informational needs, by utilizing the existing resource material and by the implementation of other informational systems. The library can become a creative participant in research and development. By providing a service of high quality, the library can be influential in guiding the direction of the company program. The fostering of informal organizational relationships can be very beneficial in this undertaking. Resources outside the library can also be called upon to answer user's queries by utilizing inter-library loans with other libraries.

Consequences of Disapproval:
Without the library as a resource center the following would ensue:

1) Duplicate copies of books and magazines would be purchased, when fewer copies centralized would be sufficient.
2) Inadequate and poor materials would be purchased, and good ones missed as a consequence of not having anyone screening the material.
3) Free and inexpensive information would be wasted through lack of organization.
4) Decision would be delayed because of lack of information, or information that might have altered a decision turns up too late.

5)  A trip to the public library would bring scanty results.
6)  Research is less than thorough, and may, in fact, already
    have been done somewhere else.
7)  Materials stack up in unmanageable piles and are scattered
    throughout the company. Specific ones cannot be located
    when needed.

Alternative Methods: (How else might you do it?)

    Each individual in the company would be required to locate
their own resource material, and perform their own research,
including the retrieval of specific books and magazines. This
would require an enormous amount of time and effort. Management
would not have the advantages of a research facility to support
the Company's work.

## ACCOUNTING INFORMATION

| Account Number | Cost |
|---|---|
| 38-9202.5 | $12,780 |
| 38-9213.5 | 6,640 |
| 38-9212.5 | 1,090 |
| 38-9215.5 | 660 |
| 38-9216.5 | 180 |
| 38-9217.5 | 100 |
| Total Cost | $21,450 |

## ALTERNATIVE LEVELS

Alternatives Numbers

| 1 of 3 | Base Cost | $21,450 |
|---|---|---|
| 2 of 3 | Incremental Cost | $ 1,660 |
| 3 of 3 | Incremental Cost | $ 5,000 |
| of | Incremental Cost | |

| Rank | Library Package Name | 2 Of 3 Level | Desired level | 1 # People | $23,110 Dollars | Library Department? Function |
|------|----------------------|--------------|---------------|------------|-----------------|------------------------------|

Statement of Purpose: (What are you trying to do?)

The corporate library is a service-oriented reference and research facility, responsible for providing materials and services designed to meet the information requirements of all departments of the corporation. The corporate librarian acquires, organizes, maintains, utilizes and disseminates informational and research material pertinent to the corporation's activities. Such areas are financial (statistics and management), engineering, nuclear, environmental, economics, and legal. Management skills and a strong motivation to put knowledge to work, rather than to provide custodial care are paramount. The library handles all company purchases of books, periodicals, technical reports, standards, legal, and bibliographic services. Lockheed DIALOG Online Computer Service produces a mechanism for very rapid literature searches for all subject areas of benefit to the company.

Description of Actions: (How are you going to do it?)

The library strives to anticipate the corporation's current and future informational needs by utilizing the existing resource material and by the implementation of other informational systems such as the Lockheed Dialog On-line computer service. When aware of the interests of the clientele/management, the librarian can bring relevant materials and information to the attention of the users before they are requested or indirect response to the requests. Plus, utilization of the Phelps Regulatory Research Service for reference purposes. This is currently being used in our current rate case.

Consequences of Disapproval:

Without the library as a resource center the following would ensue:

1) Duplicate copies of books and magazines would be purchased, when fewer copies centralized would be sufficient.
2) Inadequate and poor materials would be purchased, and good ones missed as a consequence of not having anyone screening the material.
3) Free and inexpensive information would be wasted through lack of organization.
4) Decision would be delayed because of lack of information, or information that might have altered a decision turns up too late.

5)  A trip to the public library would bring scanty results.
6)  Research is less than thorough, and may, in fact, already
    have been done somewhere else.
7)  Materials stack up in unmanageable piles and are scattered
    throughout the company. Specific ones cannot be located
    when needed.
8)  Literature searching would have to be done manually and
    more costly in time.

Alternative Methods: (How else might you do it?)

   Each individual in the company would be required to locate
their own resource material, and perform their own research,
including the retrieval of specific books and magazines. This
would require an enormous amount of time and effort. Management
would not have the advantages of a research facility to support
the Company's work.

## ACCOUNTING INFORMATION

| Account Number | Cost |
|---|---|
| 38-9202.5 | $12,780 |
| 38-9213.5 | 8,180 |
| 38-9212.5 | 1,190 |
| 38-9215.5 | 660 |
| 38-9216.5 | 200 |
| 38-9217.5 | 100 |
| Total Cost | $23,110 |

## ALTERNATIVE LEVELS

Alternative Numbers

| __1__ of __3__ | Base Cost | $21,450 |
| __2__ of __3__ | Incremental Cost | $ 1,660 |
| __3__ of __3__ | Incremental Cost | $ 5,000 |
| _____ of _____ | Incremental Cost | $ |

| Rank | Library Package Name | 3 of 3 Level | Desired Level | 2 # People | $28,110 Dollars | 11/8/77 Library Department/ Function |
|------|---------------------|--------------|---------------|-------------|------------------|------------------------------------|

Statement of Purpose: (What are you trying to do?)

The corporate library is a service-oriented reference and research facility, responsible for providing materials and services designed to meet the information requirements of all departments of the corporation. The corporate librarian acquires, organizes, maintains, utilizes and disseminates informational and research material pertinent to the corporation's activities. Such areas are financial (statistics and management), engineering, nuclear, environmental, economics, and legal. Management skills and a strong motivation to put knowledge to work, rather than to provide custodial care are paramount. The library handles all company purchases of books, periodicals, technical reports, standards, legal, and bibliographic services. A part-time library clerk would perform the routine clerical tasks, thereby freeing the librarian to work on other projects.

Description of Actions: (How are you going to do it?)

The library strives to anticipate the corporation's current and future informational needs, by utilizing the existing resource material and by the implementation of other informational systems such as the Lockheed Dialog On-Line computer service. With the assistance of a part-time library clerk there would be sufficient time to pursue special projects, i.e., automation of existing retrieval and routing systems; conducting more in-depth research work; establish a stronger communication with the divisions; develop a CVPS employee information/library program, possibly in conjunction with Public Information; develop a plan for future needs—should we have broad subject coverage? What about priorities of services? Also organize Vermont Yankee's informational resources, and develop better informational contact with the State Energy Office.

Consequences of Disapproval:

Without the library as a resource center the following ensue:

1) Duplicate copies of books and magazines would be purchased, when fewer copies centralized would be sufficient.

2)  Inadequate and poor materials would be purchased, and good
    ones missed as a consequence of not having anyone screening
    the material.
3)  Free and inexpensive information would be wasted through
    lack of organization.
4)  Decision would be delayed because of lack of information,
    or information that might have altered a decision turns
    up too late.
5)  A trip to the public library would bring scanty results.
6)  Research is less than thorough, and may, in fact, already
    have been done somewhere else.
7)  Materials stack up in unmanageable piles and are scattered
    throughout the company. Specific ones cannot be located
    when needed.
8)  Innovative procedures in library objectives would have to
    be curtailed.

Alternative Methods: (How else might you do it?)

     Manual literature searching would have to be utilized,
which economically, from both a practical and a time-involve-
ment level would be unfeasible and unsatisfactory. The computer
takes less than a half-hour to do the work of one month—not only
in relation to comprehensive citation searching but also with
regard to the formulation of abstracts (done automatically by
Dialog).

## ACCOUNTING INFORMATION

| Account Number | Cost |
|---|---|
| 38-9202.5 | $17,780 |
| 38-9213.5 | 8,180 |
| 38-9212.5 | 1,190 |
| 38-9215.5 | 660 |
| 38-9216.5 | 200 |
| 38-9217.5 | 100 |
| Total Cost | $28,110 |

## ALTERNATIVE LEVELS

Alternative Numbers

| | | |
|---|---|---|
| 1 of 3 | Base Cost | $21,450 |
| 2 of 3 | Incremental Cost | $ 1,660 |
| 3 of 3 | Incremental Cost | $ 5,000 |
| ___ of ___ | Incremental Cost | $ _____ |

# Glossary

**A-Base Review:** A modified ZBB adopted by the Canadian federal government.

**Activity (government):** The operational functions used to carry out programs. Performance of an activity is generally evaluated by workload measures.

**Additional Levels of Effort:** Improved levels or increments of effort over and above the minimum level of effort.

**Alternative Program Levels System:** A modified ZBB adopted by the Oregon state government.

**Alternatives:** Different ways of performing the same function or activity to reach the same objective.

**APLS:** See **Alternative Program Levels Systems.**

**Base:** The level of spending adopted in preceding periods. This level would go unquestioned in traditional budgeting approaches.

**Base Package:** See **First Level Package.**

**Budget:** Statement of the financial position of an independent entity for a specified future period of time based on planned expenditures during that period and proposals for funding them.

**Budgeting:** A systematic process through which a budget is created.

**Contingency Planning:** A definitive blueprint which can be used by management to increase or decrease activity without the necessity of making a new plan.

**Control:** A disciplined effort to follow a plan or explain deviation from it.

**Cost-Benefit Analysis:** The attempt to relate the worth or benefit of a service to the cost of providing it. Ideally benefits will exceed costs.

**Cost Center:** A type of responsibility center generally associated with profit-making businesses but accepted by almost every type of organization.

**Cost-Effectiveness:** A measure of how efficiently in terms of cost a system is meeting its goals. A means of relating the cost of a project to effective performance or goal attainment.

**Cutoff Point:** The point where a line can be drawn on the ranking sheet above which all decision packages are approved and below which the packages are not approved for funding.

**Decision Package Form:** A set of forms displaying the best information available to help managers make quick and rational decisions on a funding request made by the decision unit. Types of information contained include: objectives, costs, benefits, performance measures, manpower requirements, alternatives, consequences of elimination, and service level options.

**Decision Packages:** Activities of a decision unit are divided into several alternative levels of services.

**Decision Unit:** An organizational level such as a cost center, responsibility center, or group of activities which can be meaningfully analyzed and influenced by management decisions.

**Drawing the Line:** Setting the cutoff point on the ranking sheet above which all packages are approved and below which all packages are to be phased out.

**Effectiveness:** A measure of how well a service satisfies the demands made of it by its users.

**Federal Funds:** Revenues received directly from federal agencies.

**First Level Package:** Also called base package, which establishes a minimum level of services and activities.

**Forecasting:** Making predictions.

**Formula Budget:** A budget which allocates resources according to predetermined standards or formulae.

**Funded:** Approved for funding and support.

**Increment:** An increased level of dollars or services over the previous level within each decision unit.

**Increment Package:** A package which establishes the successive incremental level(s) of services and costs beyond those of the base package.

**Incremental Budget:** See **Line-Item Budget.**

**Implementation Analysis:** A technique used to identify an organization's program and resources by function and resource requirements.

**Level-of-Effort Analysis:** (also **level-of-efficiency** and **service level**): Breaking down decision units into several discrete segments, each of which provides an incremental service level, or greater degree of efficiency than the others.

**Line Item:** Budget items divided into broad categories.

**Line-Item Budget:** A budget in which proposed expenditures are divided into broad categories. It is sometimes known as an **object of expenditure budget** or an **incremental budget.**

**Lump-Sum Budget:** A budget with a lump sum of money and no dollar limit on expenditures in any one item or category.

**Management by Objectives** (MBO): A managerial technique which involves the identification of an organization's goals, the setting of individual objectives pursuant to the organizational goals, and the accomplishment of these objectives over a stated period of time.

**Minimal Level:** The base level of service below which it is not feasible to operate the decision unit.

**Object:** Items of expenditure.

**Object of Expenditure Budget:** See **Line-Item Budget.**

**OST:** Objectives, strategies, tactics.

**Performance Budget:** A budget that concerns itself mostly with the performance of activities and services.

**Performance Measures:** A set of quantitative/qualitative measures which display changes in workload effectiveness given a change in cost. Measures may deal with productivity, benefits obtained, or services provided.

**PPBS:** Planning-Programing Budgeting System.

**Profiling:** A technique to study the behavior of an organizational unit.

**Program (government):** A set of activities which focuses upon objectives which are usually quantifiable.

**Program Analysis:** A linking technique which converts an organizational strategy into programs.

**Program Budget:** A budget emphasizing an organization's services and activities rather than individual item expenditure.

**Ranking:** The process of assigning priorities to competing increments through the weighting of costs and benefits. Crucial increments are ranked at or near the top, with remaining increments ranked in order of decreased benefit or decreasing importance.

**Ranking Sheet:** A form on which decision packages are listed in descending order of significance.

**Reduced Level Budget:** A decreased level of support (below the previous one) which can achieve the most objectives.

**Resources:** The personnel, space, and dollars required to meet an objective or to carry out a function.

**Responsibility Center:** A segment of an organization by which the unit manager is evaluated in terms of his/her effectiveness in carrying out the responsibilities delegated to him/her.

**Strategy:** A selected method of achieving an objective.

**Sunset (government):** The concept that any program or activity should be approved and funded for a fixed period of time, after which it is assumed that the program will be eliminated unless its extension can be fully justified. See the Bibliography for further relevant sources.

**System Analysis:** The organized, step-by-step study and analysis of the detailed procedure for collection, manipulation, and evaluation of information about an organization with the goal of improving control over its total operation or segments of it.

**Trade-off:** Funding a higher priority decision package by eliminating one or more of lower priority.

**Value Analysis:** A creative technique, useful in developing decision packages, aimed at determining better or less costly methods of performing a function.

**Workload and Performance Measures:** A set of quantitative indexes which reflect work done and results obtained.

# Bibliography

Allen, Louis A. *The Management Profession*. New York: McGraw-Hill, 1964.

Anderson, Donald N. "Zero-Base Budgeting: How to Get Rid of Corporate Crabgrass." *Management Review* 65 (October 1976): 4-16.

————. "Zero-Base Budgets Offer Data, Spending Control." *Industry Week* 188 (January 12, 1979): 48.

————. "Zero-based Budgeting: Weeding out Corporate Crabgrass." *AMA Managers' Forum* 3 (May 1976): 2-3, 6.

Anthony, Robert N. "Zero-Base Budgeting Is a Fraud." *Wall Street Journal* 189 (April 27, 1977): 26. [Replies by Paul Stonich and Robert J. Lipstein, in *The Wall Street Journal*, May 16, 1977, and by Peter A. Pyhrr and George Minmier in *The Wall Street Journal*, May 23, 1977.]

Austin, L. Allan. "Zero-Base Budgeting: An Integrating Concept." *Management Counselor* (January 1977).

————. *Zero-Base Budgeting: Organizational Impact and Effects*. New York: AMACOM, 1977.

Axelrod, Donald. "Post-Burkhead: The State of the Art or Science of Budgeting." *Public Administration Review* 33 (November/December 1973): 576-84.

Battle, L. C. "Carter Sets Sights on Zero-Base Budgeting," *Savings and Loan News* 98 (February 1977): 37.

Bensahel, J. G. "Zero-Based Management." *International Management* 32 (January 1977): 36-7.

Bonsack, Robert A. "Zero-Based Budgeting: A Blueprint for Better Operations?" *Chicago Tribune*, December 22, 1977.

Broadnax, W. D. "Zero-Base Budgeting—New Directions for Bureaucracy." *Bureaucrat* 6 (Spring 1977): 56-66.

Broden, Barry C. *The IFM Simplified Guide to Zero-Base Budgeting*. Institute for Management, 1977.

Broder, David S. "A Closer Look at 'Zero-base Budgeting.' " *Washington Post*, August 9, 1976), p. C7.

Brueningsen, Arthur A. "SCAT—A Process of Alternatives." *Management Accounting* 58 (November 1976): 55-60.

————; Robinson, David; and Yagielski, John. "Using Zero-Base Budgeting in Effecting Cost Reductions." *Educational Economics* 1(4) (September 1976).

*Budgeting*. Alexandria, VA: United Way of America, Systems, Planning & Allocation Div., 1975.

Canada. Treasury Board. *A Manager's Guide to Performance Measurement*. Hull, Ontario: DSS Publishing Center, October 1976.

————. "Performance Measurement: A Guide to Successful Application" 1978. Mimeographed. (Supplement to *A Manager's Guide to Performance Measurement*.)

————. Planning Branch. *A-Base Expenditure Review: A Report on Recent Experience in the Federal Government*. Ottawa: Minister of Supply and Services, 1978.

Carroll, John. "Zero-Base Budgeting Case Study in a Non-Library Setting." Paper presented at the Institute on Zero-Base Budgeting in Library Management at the School of Library Science, directed by Ching-chih Chen, Simmons College, March 31-April 1, 1978.

Carter, Jimmy E. "Jimmy Carter Tells Why He Will Use Zero-Base Budgeting." *Nation's Business* 65 (January 1977): 24-6.

———. "Planning a Budget from Zero." In National Governors' Conference. *Innovations in State Government; Messages from the Governors.* Reprinted in *Congressional Record* 122 (February 25, 1976): H314-5.

———. "Start from Zero." *Why Not the Best.* Nashville, TN: Broadman, 1975.

Carter, W.H. and Meenah, L. "Zero-Base Budgeting and Program-Evaluation." *Journal of Rehabilitation* 43 (1977): 18.

Cheek, Logan M. "Cost Effectiveness Comes to the Personnel Function." *Harvard Business Review* (May/June 1973): 96-105.

———. "Xerox Learning Systems—Zero Base Budgeting Decision Card Exercise." 1977. Mimeographed.

———. "Zero-Base Budgeting: Priorities Tool for Planners." *Newspaper Controller* 30 (January 1977): 4-5.

———. *Zero-base Budgeting Comes of Age: What It Is and What It Takes to Make It Work.* New York: AMACOM, 1977.

———. "Zero-Base Budgeting in the Federal Government: A Performance Audit of the First Year." Summary of talk to Federal ADP User's Group, Washington, DC, October 20, 1977.

——— and Austin, Allan. *ZBB Handbook.* New York: AMACOM, 1980. Chapter 5. Forthcoming. Supplied by courtesy of Logan M. Cheek.

Chen, Ching-chih, ed. *Quantitative Measurement and Dynamic Library Service.* Phoenix, AZ: Oryx, 1978.

Clark, Lindley H. "Annual Overhaul: Zero-base Budgeting, Advocated by Carter, Used by Many Firms." *Wall Street Journal* 189 (March 14, 1977): 1.

Conrad, Adam Halicki. *Zero-base Budgeting: An Annotated Bibliography.* Monticello, IL, Council of Planning Librarians, 1977. Exchange Bibliography no. 1333.

Council of State Governments. *Zero-Based Budgeting in the States.* Lexington, KY: The Council, 1976.

Davis, K. Roscoe. "Budgeting by Level of Activity." *Managerial Planning* (May/June 1975): 10-4.

Davis, Otto A.; Dempster, M. A. H.; and Wildavsky, Aaron. "A Theory of the Budgeting Process." *American Political Science Review* (September 1966): 529-47.

Delfico, Joseph F. "Proposed Sunset and Zero-Base Legislation." *GAO Review* 11 (Winter 1977): 34-40.

Dooskin, Herbert P. "Zero-base Budgeting: A Plus for Government." *National Civic Review* 66 (March 1977): 118-21.

Dudick, T.S., ed. *How to Improve Profit-Ability through More Effective Planning.* New York: Wiley, 1975.

Eccles, Mary E. "Senate Committee Reports 'Sunset' Bill." *Congressional Quarterly Weekly Report* 34 (August 14, 1976): 2238-9.

Fain, Tyrus G.; Plant, Katherine C.; and Milloy, Ross, eds. *Federal Reorganization: The Executive Branch.* New York: R.R. Bowker, 1977.

Galvin, Thomas J. "Zero-Base Budgeting in Libraries and Information Centers." *Library Acquisitions: Practice and Theory* 2 (1978): 7-14.

Garbutt, Douglas and Minmier, George S. "Incremental, Planned-Programed and Zero-Base Budgeting." *Public Finance and Accountancy* 1 (November 1974): 350-7.

Gardner, Judy. " 'Sunset' Bills: An Eye on Big Government?" *Congressional Quarterly Weekly Report* 34 (April 24, 1976): 955-6.

———. "Zero-base Budgeting Undergoes Limited Test: House Panel Studies Impact." *Congressional Quarterly Weekly Report* 35 (March 12, 1977): 441-3.

Georgia. Office of Planning and Budget. *General Budget Preparation Procedures, Fiscal Year 1978 Budget Development.* Atlanta, GA, 1976.

Granof, M. H. and Kinzel, Dale A. 'Zero-Based Budgeting: Modest Proposal for Reform." *Federal Accountant* 23 (December 1974): 50-6.

Gross, Bertram M. "The New Systems Budgeting." *Public Administration Review* (March/April 1969): 113-37.

Gross, Malvern. *Financial and Accounting Guide for Non-Profit Organizations.* 2d ed. New York: Ronald, 1974.

Halverson, Guy. "Zero-Based Budgeting." *Christian Science Monitor* 68 (October 28, 1976): 14.

Harrington, Elizabeth R. "Little Looks at Zero-Base Budgeting." *News Bulletin of the Boston Chapter—SLA* 43 (May/June 1977): 66-8

Haugh, L. J. "Carter Style Zero-Base Budget Planning Attracts Promoters," *Advertising Age* 48 (May 9, 1977): 58.

Havemann, Joel. "Congress Tries to Break Ground Zero in Evaluating Federal Programs." *National Journal* 8 (May 22, 1976): 706-13.

——— and Cohen, Richard E."Taking Up the Tools to Tame the Bureaucracy: Zero-base Budgeting and the Sunset Legislation." *National Journal* 9 (April 2, 1977): 514-20.

Hayton, Elise. "Zero-Base Budgeting in a University Library." *Special Libraries* 71 (March 1980): 169.

Hayward, John T. "Buzz Words Galore!" *Government Executive* 8 (September 1976): 19.

Herbert, Joseph L., ed. *Experiences in Zero-Base Budgeting*. New York: PBI, 1977.

Hermanson, R. and Minmier, G. "A Look at Zero-Base Budgeting—The Georgia Experience." *Government Accountant's Journal* 25 (Winter 1976/1977): 1:11.

Herzlinger, Regina E. "Zero-Base Budgeting in the Federal Government: A Case Study." *Sloan Management Review* (Winter 1979), pp. 3-14.

Hill, Walter D. *Implementing Zero-Base Budgeting—The Real World*. Oxford, OH: Planning Executives Institutes, 1977.

Hitchings, B. "Bringing Zero-Base Budgeting Back Home." *Business Week*, April 18, 1977, p. 137.

Hogan, Roy L. *Zero-Base Budgeting: A Rationalistic Attempt to Improve the Texas Budget System*. Austin, TX: University of Texas, 1975.

Horton, F. W. "Recycling Information and Zero-Base Budgeting." *Journal of Systems Management* 28 (1977): 36-7.

Korn, Don. "Industrial Advertising—Warming Up to Zero-base." *Sales and Marketing Management* 118 (June 13, 1977): 54-9.

LaFaver, John D. "Zero-Base Budgeting in New Mexico." *State Government* 47 (Spring 1974): 108-12.

Large, Arlen J. "Applying Zero-base Budgeting." *Wall Street Journal* 189 (May 24, 1977): 22.

———. "Are Sunset Laws the Answer?" *Wall Street Journal* 188 (July 9, 1976): 12.

Larson, Signe. "Bibliography on Zero-Base Budgeting (ZBB)." *ASIS SIG Newsletter*, no. MGT-3 (March 1978), pp. 2-3.

Leininger, David L. and Wong, Ronald C. "Zero-Base Budgeting in Garland, Texas." *Management Information Service* 8 (April 1976): 1-6.

Leone, Richard C. "How to Ride Herd on the Budget." *Nation* 222 (May 22, 1976): 625-7.

Levin, Merwin. "Zero-Based Budgeting." *Boardroom Reports* (December 30, 1976): 14.

Lynch, T.D. "A Context for Zero-base Budgeting." *Bureaucrat* 6 (Spring 1977): 3-11.

Macfarlane, John A. "Zero-Base Budgeting in Action." *Canadian Chartered Accountants* 109 (December 1976): 28-32.

McGinnis, James F. "Pluses and Minuses of Zero-Base Budgeting." *Administrative Management* 37 (September 1976): 22-3.

Merewitz, Leonard and Sosnick, Stephen H. *The Budget's New Clothes; A Critique of Planning-Programing-Budgeting and Benefit-Cost Analysis*. Chicago, IL: Markham Publishing, 1971.

Meskil, John. "Consumer Magazines—Jimmy Carter's 'Zero-base': An Idea Whose Time Is Ripe for Magazines." *Media Decisions* 12 (April 1977): 88, 90.

Miller, Karl A. "Zero Budgeting Works in Yonkers, N.Y." *Government Executive* 9 (January 1977): 39-40.

Minmier, George S. *An Evaluation of Zero-Base Budgeting as a Tool for Planning and Control of Discretionary Costs in Government Institutions*. Little Rock: University of Arkansas, 1974.

———. *An Evaluation of the Zero-Base Budgeting System in Governmental Institutions*. Research Monograph no. 68. Georgia State University, School of Business Administration, 1975.

——— and Hermanson, Robert H. "A Look at Zero-Base Budgeting—The Georgia Experience." *Atlantic Economic Review* 26 (July/August 1976): 5-12.

Murray, Thomas J. "The Tough Job of Zero Budgeting." *Dun's Review* 104 (October 1974): 70-2.

Muskie, Edmund S. "Effective Government: Our Next Big Challenge." *National Journal* 8 (April 3, 1976): 458-9.

Neuman, John L. "Time for Lasting Cuts in Overhead." *McKinsey Quarterly* (Summer 1975).

"One Way to Erase Needless Government Programs." *Nation's Business* 84 (November 1976): 52-6.

O'Neil, James M. and Manceri, Paul K. "Zero-Based Budgets — How They Can Work," *School Business Affairs* 43 (March 1977): 57-8.

Oregon. Executive Department. *1979-81 Biennial Budget Preparation Manual, vol. 2, Alternative Program Levels Systems (APLS)*, prepared by Laurence R. Sprecher and Robert W. Smith. Budget and Management Division, Executive Department, State of Oregon, March 1978.

"Oregon State Agency Faces 'Zero-based' Budget Demand." *Library Journal* 102 (May 15, 1977): 1092.

Parker, Diane C. and Carpenter, Eric J. "A Zero-Base Budget Approach to Staff Justification for a Combined Reference and Collection Development Department." In *New Horizons for Academic Libraries*, edited by Robert D. Stueart and Richard D. Johnson, pp. 472-82. New York: K.G. Saur, 1979.

Peterson, Walter E. "Zero-Base Management System." *Military Engineer* (September/October 1975):371-3.

Pierce, James L. "The Budget Comes of Age." *Harvard Business Review* (May-June 1954).

Pyhrr, Peter A. "The Zero-Base Approach to Government Budgeting." *Public Administration Review* 37 (January/February 1977): 1-8.

―――. "Zero-Base Budgeting." *Harvard Business Review* 48 (November/December 1970): 111-21.

―――. "Zero-base Budgeting: A Management Tool to Evaluate and Control Expense." In *Budgeting for Profit*, edited by Chandra Gyan and Swrenda Sing Hvi. Oxford, OH: Planning Executive Institute, 1975.

―――. *Zero-Base Budgeting: A Practical Tool for Evaluating Expenses* (New York: Wiley, 1973).

―――. "Zero-Base Budgeting: Where to Use It and How to Begin," *SAM Advanced Management Journal* 41 (Summer 1976): 4-14.

―――. "The Zero-Base Budgeting Process." In *How to Improve Profit-Ability through More Effective Planning*, edited by Thomas S. Dudick. New York: Wiley, 1975.

Reckers, Philip M.J. and Ritchick, Donna. "Zero-Base Budgeting — A New Home in the Federal Government." *Government Accountant's Journal* 26 (Spring 1977): 40-6.

Rehfuss, J. "Zero-Base Budgeting — Experience to Date." *Public Personnel Management* 6 (1977): 181-7.

Rider, Fremont. "Library Cost Accounting." *Library Quarterly* 6 (October 1936): 331-81.

Ridge, Warren J. *Value Analysis for Better Management*. New York: AMACOM, 1969.

Robertson, J. "Government Closeup as the Sun Sets Slowly." *Electronic News* 21 (September 20, 1976): 14.

Rusten, Alan C. and Harvey, L. James. *The ZBB Handbook for Local Governments*. Littleton, CO: Ireland Educational Corporation, 1977.

Sarndal, Anne G. "Zero Base Budgeting." *Special Libraries* 70 (December 1979): 527-32.

Sarsfield, E.William and Scheiring, Michael J. "Zero-Base Budgeting in New Jersey." *State Government* 49 (Summer 1976): 174-9.

Schick, A. "Zero-base Budgeting and Sunset: Redundancy or Symbiosis." *Bureaucrat* 6 (Spring 1977): 12-32.

Schultz, J.S. "Program Budgeting and Work Measurement for Law Libraries." *Law Library Journal* 63 (August 1970): 353-62.

Schultze, Charles L. *The Politics and Economics of Public Spending*. Washington, DC: Brookings Institution, 1968.

Shanahan, Gerald W. et al. "Budgeting Practices in Police Agencies." *Government Accountants' Journal* 25 (Winter 1976-1977): 62-8.

Sherbo, A.J. "Alternative Budget Systems." *Air Force Comptroller* 11 (January 1977): 36-7.

Singleton, David W.; Smith, Bruce A.; and Cleaveland, James R. "Zero-Based Budgeting in Wilmington, Delaware." *Governmental Finance* 5 (August 1976): 20-9.

Stein, Herbert. "How About Zero-Based Revenue?" *Wall Street Journal*, January 3, 1979.

Steiner, George A. *Top Management Planning*. New York: Macmillan, 1969.

Stonich, Paul J. "Formal Planning Pitfalls and How to Avoid Them." Part 1. *Management Review* 64 (June 1975): 4-11; Part 2. *Management Review* 64 (July 1975): 29-35.

―――. "The New Look for Budgeting: Zero Base Planning." *Today's Manager* (May-June 1976): 1-16.

―――. "Zero-Base Planning — A Management Tool." *Managerial Planning* 25 (July/August 1976): 1-4.

———— et al. *Zero-Base Planning and Budgeting: Improved Cost Control and Resource Allocation* (Homewood, IL: Dow Jones-Irwin, 1977).

———— and Steeves, William H. "Zero-Base Planning and Budgeting for Utilities." *Public Utilities Fortnightly* 98 (September 9, 1976): 24-9.

Suver, James D. and Brown, Ray L. "Where Does Zero-Base Budgeting Work?" *Harvard Business Review* 55 (November/December 1977): 76-84.

Symonds, E. "Starting from Scratch." *Accountant* 175 (December 9, 1976): 673.

Taylor, Graeme M. "Introduction to Zero-Base Budgeting." *Bureaucrat* 6 (March 1977): 33:55.

US Congress. House. Committee on Rules. *Hearings on H.R. 11734, Dealing with Zero-base Budgeting.* June 21, 1976.

US Congress. House. Committee on the Budget. Task Force on Budget Process. *Zero-Base Budget Legislation.* 94th Cong. 2d sess. June 30-July 28, 1976. Washington, DC: US, 1976.

US Congress. Senate. Committee on Government Operations. *Compendium of Materials on Zero-Base Budgeting in the States.* 95th Cong. 1st sess. Washington, DC: US, 1977.

————. *Government Economy and Spending Reform Act of 1976.* 94th Cong. 2d sess. March 17-April 7, 1976. Washington, DC: US, 1976.

U.S. Congress. Senate. Committee on Rules and Administration. *Government Economy and Spending Reform Act of 1976. Hearing on S. 2925* (to establish a procedure for zero-base review and evaluation of government programs and activities every four years and for other purposes). September 8, 1976. Washington, DC: Superintendent of Documents, 1976. 133 p.

U.S. Department of Labor. Library. *Zero-Base Budgeting: Selected References.* Washington, DC: US Government Printing Office, December 1976.

U.S. Office of Management and Budget. Library. *Zero-base Budgeting: Selected Readings.* Bibliographies, no. 5. Washington, DC: US, 1976.

Utah Foundation. "Zero-Base Budgeting and Sunset Laws." *Research Brief* (November 8, 1976).

Vancil, R. F. "Texas Instruments Incorporated." *Harvard Business School Case,* 9-172-054, September 1975.

"Ways to Make Uncle Sam Spend More Wisely." *Nation's Business* 60 (August 1972): 26-8.

Wentling, Tim L. and Lawson, Tom E. *Evaluating Occupational Education and Training Programs* Boston: Allyn and Bacon, 1975.

"What It Means to Build a Budget from Zero." *Business Week,* no. 2479 (April 18, 1977), pp. 160, 162, 164.

"What Zero-base Budgeting Is and How Carter Wants to Use It." *U.S. News and World Report* 82 (April 25, 1977): 91-3.

Wildavsky, Aaron. *Budgeting: A Comparative Theory of the Budgetary Process.* Boston: Little, Brown, 1975.

———— and Hammann, Arthur. "Comprehensive versus Incremental Budgeting in the Department of Agriculture." *Administrative Science Quarterly* (December 1965): 321-46.

Woodruff, Elaine Lindholm. "Work Measurement Applied to Libraries." *Special Libraries* 48 (April 1957): 139-44.

Wright, Norman H. "Cost Reduction Zero Base Planning and Budgeting." *Management World* 6 (April 1977): 31-4.

————. "Merging MBO with ZBB." *Management World* 6 (June 1977): 25-6.

————. "Zero-base Budgeting Decision Packages." *Management World* 5 (October 1976): 23-5

———— "Zero-Base Planning and Budgeting—The Ranking Process." *Management World* 6 (February 1977): 31-3.

Yagielski, John. *Budget Manual. Zero-Base Budgeting.* Rochester, NY: Greece Central School District, 1975. ED 136 419.

"Zero-base Budgeting—A Way to Cut Spending, or a Gimmick?" *U.S. News and World Report,* September 20, 1976.

"Zero-Base Budgeting, Advocated by Carter, Used by Many Firms." *Wall Street Journal* 14 (March 1977): 1.

"Zero-base Budgeting and the Audit Function." *Bank Auditing and Accounting Report* (February 1977): 1-2.

"Zero-base Budgeting Bares Vested Interest." *Globe and Mail Report on Business* (June 7, 1977): PB 4.

"Zero-base Budgeting Is Coming—Here's How It Works." *Bank Auditing and Accounting Report* (November 1976): 5-6.

"Zero-Base Budgeting: One Way to Ease Needless Government Programs." *Nation's Business* 64 (November 1976): 52-4.

"Zero-Base Budgeting: Peter Pyhrr Defends His Brainchild (Interview)." *MBA* 11 (April 1977): 25-6.

"Zero-base Budgeting Technique Seems Certain to Spread." *Globe and Mail Report on Business* (May 28, 1977): PB 3.

"Zero-base Budgeting Undergoes Limited Test." *Congressional Quarterly* (March 12, 1977): 441-3.

*Zero-Base Budgeting: What and How.* Self-study Cassette Program, no. 4. New York: National Association Accountants, 1977.

"Zero-based Budgeting Meets: Carter Explains Policy." *Library Journal* 102 (February 15, 1977): 437-8.

*Zero-base Planning and Budgeting Digest.* Washington, DC: Tufty Communications, Vol. 1, 1977. Monthly.

# Index

## by Susan R. Stein